May memories of West Virginia bring you laughter and happiness — and may you always consider the Mountain State your home.

Diana Lynn Duvall

Also from Populore Publishing Company:

Mountain State Stories of the People
Put It In Writing Guide For Populore Narratives

Our Mountain State Heritage

*West Virginia
Stories of the People*

Populore

Populore Publishing Company
Morgantown, West Virginia

Edited by
Pam Kasey
Rae Jean V. Sielen

Foreword by
The Honorable Senator Robert C. Byrd

Our Mountain State Heritage: West Virginia Stories of the People. Copyright © 1998 by Populore Publishing Company. Printed and bound in the United States of America. All rights reserved. No part of this publication may be reproduced, stored in a retrieval system, or transmitted in any form or by any means, electronic, mechanical, photocopying, recording, or otherwise without the prior written permission from the publisher, except by a reviewer, who may quote brief passages in a review. Published by Populore Publishing Company, PO Box 4382, Morgantown, WV 26504-4382. First edition. First printing.

ISBN 0-9652699-2-2

Library of Congress Catalog Card Number: 98-066051

Each Populore narrative in *Our Mountain State Heritage: West Virginia Stories of the People* has been assigned an identification code. The code is found at the end of the narrative with the following six components: *Narrative Number — Country — Series (General) – Series (Specific) — Volume Number — Year*. For example, the first narrative by Cheryl Ware in Chapter 1 is coded *208-001-ST-WV-002-1998*. Individual narratives will be stored in the Populore Database according to Narrative Numbers, e.g., "No. 208" for Cheryl Ware's narrative. Requests for reprints should include the author's name and the three-digit narrative number.

Reference to any narratives from *Our Mountain State Heritage: West Virginia Stories of the People* in other works should cite the author and year within the text, e.g., (Ware, 1998). Footnotes, end notes, and/or bibliographic references should include author, year, narrative title, narrative number, editors, book title, publisher, and page(s). For example: Ware, Cheryl. 1998. Growing Up in a Large Family. Narrative No. 208. In P. Kasey and R.J.V. Sielen (Eds.). *Our Mountain State Heritage: West Virginia Stories of the People.* Morgantown, WV: Populore Publishing Company, pp. 19–24.

Credits:
Cover photo courtesy of Edna Post; see story, pages 114 and 115.
Photo of Wheeling Suspension Bridge, page 27, by Zee Photo, Wheeling, WV.
Photo of Evelyn Howdershelt, page 140, courtesy of Gerson Studio, Morgantown, WV.
Photo of Julia Lucas, page 165, by Tony Alterman, Brooklyn, NY.
Appendix I photo, page 171, by Julia Lucas, Morgantown, WV.
Appendix II photo, page 175, courtesy of Julia Lucas.
Appendix III photo, page 179, courtesy of Mark Sielen.

*Dedicated to all
who call
West Virginia home*

Acknowledgments

Even a single-author book is a collaboration, but a book uniting ninety-six authors is the work of many, and we have many participants to acknowledge.

First acknowledgment is due, of course, to the authors. They shaped meaningful parts of their lives into dramatic, funny, poignant, or matter-of-fact prose; dug out treasured family photos; and sent it all out on—or near!—deadline. Less apparent to the reader are the rounds of paperwork, proofreading, and calls to clarify final details that each author stuck through. The quality of these pages is due to their patience, tenacity, and trust. Special thanks to returning Populore authors Richard Bainbridge, Judy Bennett, Sandra Bunner, Kathryn Campbell, Glenna Carroll, Charleen Evans-Thomas, Juanita Fitzsimmons, Edith Griffith, Colene Heim, Kay Hill, Evelyn Kennedy, N.J. Lewis, Richard Marks, Claris McDaniel, James Nedrow, Sylvia Parker, Ruth Phillips, W. Lilly Rodes, Polly Shepherd, Jessie Volk, Carol Warren, and Ralph Williams.

Beyond the authors, there are several whose participation has been fundamental. Our deepest appreciation goes to The Honorable Senator Robert C. Byrd for composing the foreword to this volume, and to his press secretary Ann Adler for facilitating that process. Helping us to learn about and gather stories from the West Virginia Extension Homemaker Belles were Margaret Mary Lewis, 1997–1998 Extension Homemakers president; Pat Stubbs, 1997–1998 vice-president; and Pam Godfrey of the West Virginia University Extension Service. Our gratitude goes to them, and also to Joy Gilchrist and Fred Armstrong, who put us in touch with the West Virginia History Heroes who added to this collection. Others made unique contributions that would otherwise have been unavailable to us—thanks especially to Sue Shipe, Barbara Smith, Paula Townsend, and Nick Dudley. And the timely assistance of the Morgantown Public Library and several West Virginia University libraries has been irreplaceable.

Although it is customary to list only the editors on the cover of a work of this nature, production of this collection has been wholly a team effort. We would like to recognize Paige Royse, our editorial assistant, who worked closely with the Belles and their stories; because of her friendly persistence, we were able to include so many of their stories and photos. Julia Lucas, our graphic designer, cheerfully arranged the many elements within, page by page, through various drafts. Ensuring continuity of book design and providing key miscellaneous assistance were the valuable contributions of graphic designer and Populore friend Angela Caudill. Amy Stevenson, co-editor of *Mountain State Stories of the People*, helped get this book off to a good start, as did student interns Melissa Thornhill and Shelly Maykuth. And Ken St. Louis has been behind the scenes all along, offering astute planning and general wisdom.

Finally, a personal note to all who have supported this project. One of the simple joys of publishing this type of work is the first reading of a manuscript, the moment of discovery. As we get to know each narrative, there are deeper pleasures: encountering a new word or old practice, learning a piece of history. How much fun this process has been! Creating this book with you has been a real opportunity, and we thank you all.

Preface

Personal experiences remembered, reflections on times past, anecdotes handed down—these "stories of the people" hold our common wisdom. Played over in our minds, they give our private lives continuity and meaning; shared in conversation, they deepen our relationships. But written down, collected, and published, they have the power to entertain and educate now and into the future.

Our earlier collection of West Virginia stories, *Mountain State Stories of the People* (1997), came out of our belief that such stories are well worth preserving and passing along. Our experience in compiling that book was so rewarding, and the response so encouraging, that a second collection became part of our plan. The result is *Our Mountain State Heritage: West Virginia Stories of the People.*

While the invitation to authors remained essentially the same—to submit true writings on subjects of their own choosing, ranging in length from a paragraph to several pages—we have been delighted to see this collection take shape in its own way. The stories are, in general, longer, giving us a deeper look into some aspects of West Virginia life. New topics came forth, complementing and building on what came before. And, while there is no separate young authors' section this time, we did reach out to two other special groups of West Virginians: Extension Homemaker Belles, and History Heroes.

Established by the state and federal Cooperative Extension Services in 1949, the Extension Homemaker Belle program chooses each year, county by county, an Extension Homemaker for special recognition. The Belles carry our state's important traditions in homemaking and the cultural arts and, because Belles are seventy years of age or over, their participation in this project adds a valuable depth of experience. Their contributions are delightful.

Also offering a rich perspective are the West Virginia History Heroes. A cooperative effort of the West Virginia Division of Culture and History, the West Virginia Archives and History Commission, the West Virginia Historical Society, the West Virginia Historical Association, Preservation Alliance, Inc., the West Virginia Association of Museums, the Mining Your History Foundation, and many local and community groups, this program was established in 1997 to celebrate West Virginia history. Residents who have made extraordinary personal contributions to the preservation of our state's heritage are nominated by their local historical and genealogical societies, and honored at the annual History Day celebration at the Cultural Center in Charleston. We are pleased to include stories from six awardees; see the index to locate their works.

Several aspects of this book are worthy of note. First, in the interests of preservation, we have expanded our use of authors' and editors' notes. Occasionally, practices and concepts that are mentioned in the narratives are regional in scope, or are no longer in use. Recognizing the authors as our best resources, we invited them in most cases to prepare short explanations in their own words, and have enjoyed their positive and lively responses. Where broader social or historical context was called for, we researched and wrote brief explanations ourselves. These authors' and editors' notes appear at the ends of stories throughout the book.

The index at the back of this volume includes, as before, the names of all people and places that appear throughout the book, and details the West Virginia lifestyles, traditions, and values represented by the authors and their stories as well.

Finally, we chose to organize the stories, as before, into the eight regions defined by the state's Department of Tourism. This organization emphasizes the variety that still exists in West Virginia, a state that retains much of its distinct regional character.

Personal, good-natured, and true, the narratives within memorialize the people and experiences they represent. These stories are "written tellings," satisfying to read out loud or silently. They include good front porch, fireside, and bedtime reading for natives, newcomers, and expatriates; the young and the old; the avid and the infrequent reader alike. Teachers, students, storytellers, historians, and genealogists will find these stories enjoyable and, with the inclusion of authors' and editors' notes and an extensive index, accessible to research as well.

The book has been prepared for the ages. No matter your era, we hope you enjoy this look at our state, its people, and the times.

Foreword

To those of us who call it home, there simply is no other place like West Virginia. This state holds a special appeal to us, as well as—I wager to say—to many a traveler who has only chanced to briefly linger here, among our natural treasures and in the company of good, warm-hearted folk. While thousands annually are attracted to and entranced by our lush mountains and valleys, teeming rivers, and dynamic vistas, the most enduring attraction offered by West Virginia is her people. They are what makes West Virginia unique among the fifty states, and it is their stories—not the geographic boundaries and natural resources alone—that define and comprise the rich tapestry that is West Virginia.

Throughout the ages, the telling of stories has served as much more than a form of entertainment. Stories have served as vehicles for imbuing succeeding generations with a sense of history, of values, and of the faults and failures of the past, as well as of equally important ancestral successes. *Our Mountain State Heritage: West Virginia Stories of the People* continues this time-honored tradition of passing stories down from one generation to the next.

In this book are to be found a collection of stories that will transport the reader to an array of places and times. The reader will be given a chance to see through the eyes of others, to peek into private lives, and to gain strength and insight through the words and experiences of individuals from many walks of life. The pages of this book are threaded with tales of the mighty and the diminutive, and woven with the yarns of the unusual, the outstanding, and even the commonplace.

How can we possibly appreciate the rich bounty that is ours as West Virginians if we lack an understanding of the history of our state? It is history—the challenges and sacrifices of pioneering families, the simple stories of daily events and the dramas of daring adventures, the remembrances of childhood and the wise sayings of old age—that is the bedrock upon which we build for tomorrow.

Between the covers of this unassuming publication are riches to be cherished— the stories of West Virginians. May they be read over and over again, and may future generations realize their true value and give them a place of honor in their lives.

Robert C. Byrd

The Honorable Senator Robert C. Byrd

Contents

Chapter 1: Introduction 15
A Landscape of Tales 17
Invited Narrative: Growing Up in a Large Family • *Cheryl Ware* 19

Chapter 2: Northern Panhandle 25
The Wheeling Suspension Bridge • *Beverly Fluty* 27
Mother's Stories • *Judy Globokar* 28
Blessings from the Heart • *Betty Boyd* 29
Dutch Joe • *Juanita Fitzsimmons* 30
Fall in West Virginia • *Matthew Hofeldt* 31
Too Much Fun and Not Enough Study • *David Javersak* 31
West Virginia Foods • *Ruth Phillips* 33
Mother's Visits • *Betty Boyd* 34
"Poppy's Camp" • *Diana Lynn Duvall* 35
Memories of Grandma Jones • *Alma Jean McCombs* 36

Chapter 3: Mid-Ohio Valley 37
Fox Hunting with Dad • *Mark Wayne* 39
The Year of the Pumpkins • *Polly Shepherd* 39
The Night of the Intruder • *Elizabeth Davis* 40
Quilting Tradition • *Doris Moyers* 41
My First Job • *Edith Griffith* 42
Hard Life, Good Life • *Arthelia Richard* 42
Mistaken Identity • *Edith Griffith* 43
". . . And You (Are) Part of Me" • *Kay Hill* 44
Berea, a Town with a Heart • *Mary Carneal* 45
Mike and Linda's Cabin • *Paige Royse* 46

Chapter 4: Metro Valley 49
Summer on the Porch • *Carol Warren* 51
Grade School Memories • *Richard Marks* 52
Historic Hurricane Home Refurbished • *Ralph Williams* 52
The Weekly Cleansing Ritual • *Kay Shamblin* 53
A Tribute to My Parents • *Mildred Booth* 54
A Spring Garden I Will Never Forget • *Margaret Dudley* 55
My Trip to the Folk Festival • *Eleanor Lee* 56

Interview with Thelma Thaxton • *Sue James* 57
Blind Ed Haley • *Brandon Kirk* 58
Remembering Hurricane • *Brenda Burke* 59
My Twin • *Jessica Price* 60
Williamson • *Linda Van Meter* 60
"Doc" Keadle • *Linda Van Meter* 61
Bringing Stories Back from Colorado • *Lillian Cunningham* 61
School Field Trips • *Harriette James Kirk* 62
Having Fun in Spite Of . . . • *Harriette James Kirk* 63
How I Got the Old School Bell • *Stella Rader* 64
"My Father in Me" • *Ronald Crowder and Kathryn Campbell* 65
Archie Bland, A Backward Glance • *Nancy Smith* 65
The Great Race • *Ted Elden* 66
Gaujots • *Nancy Smith* 68
Wells Goodykoontz • *Nancy Smith* 68
Two Different Worlds • *Anna M. Matney* 68
Blackberries and Chow Chow • *Richard Bainbridge* 70
Montgomery (A Smoldering Ember) • *Richard Bainbridge* 72
The Red Crayon • *Richard Bainbridge* 74
Memories of Grandma • *Kathryn Campbell* 74
E.M. Jones: Company Man and Spy Catcher • *Sam Lucas* 75
Lessons from Mom and Dad • *Diane Heim* 77

CHAPTER 5: MOUNTAIN LAKES 79
The Honeymoon • *Kay Hill* 81
Mom and Dad's Best-Kept Secret • *Jean Rigsby* 82
Thoughts of West Virginia • *Ruth Ensor* 85
West Virginia State Folk Festival, Then and Now • *Helen Garrett* 87
The Sad and the Funny • *Nellie Stephenson* 87
I Wanted to Run That Big Steam Engine • *Ralph Williams* 88
A Talented and Ingenious Man • *B.D. Decker* 89
Great-Aunt Shirley and the Cow Pies • *George Poulos* 91
Maybe the Rain Was a Good Thing • *Ken St. Louis* 92
Growing Up in the Country • *Colene Heim* 93

CHAPTER 6: NEW RIVER/GREENBRIER VALLEY 95
You Don't Miss What You Never Had • *Glenna Carroll* 97
My Country Church • *Ollie Hoover* 98
Edwin and I • *Eloise Sibold* 98
Reflections of Yesterday • *Danford Earl Bragg, Sr.* 100

Childhood Mountain Memories • *Maggie Porter* 102
Growing Up in Greenbrier County • *Vena Walthall* 103
Three Incidents in a Boy's Life • *Steven Fox* 104
My Accent • *Patty Grace* 105
My Rear Windows • *Sylvia Acord-Bragg* 106
Teaching School in Rural Appalachia • *W. Lilly Rodes* 108
An Embarrassing Moment • *Virginia Bonds* 109

CHAPTER 7: POTOMAC HIGHLANDS 111
An Ode to the One-Room Schools • *Edna Post* 113
A Real Cold Idea—How It All Came About! • *Edna Post* 114
"Cool" • *Alice Hartman* 115
Recycling by My Mother • *Betty Waller* 116
Never a Dull Moment • *Ella Bergdoll* 116
The Turkey Almost Caught • *Louise Malcolm* 118
When We Became West Virginians • *Miriam Reyburn-Steele* 118

CHAPTER 8: EASTERN PANHANDLE 123
The Court House at Midnight • *N.J. Lewis* 125
Fourth-Generation West Virginia Gal • *Dorothy Crouse* 126
I Lived Through the "Great Depression" • *Pauline Hockensmith* 127

CHAPTER 9: MOUNTAINEER COUNTRY 131
Saved from the Auction Block! • *Hazel Wysong* 133
A Tail of Black and White • *Mary Morgan* 134
Life at Home • *Dixie Thornhill* 134
Called to West Virginia • *Gail Bossart* 135
Tribute to Gail Snyder • *Gladys Eddy* 136
The Girls of '54 • *Charleen Evans-Thomas* 136
Home Is Where the Heart Is • *Judy Bennett* 138
The Wonderful Memories I Have of "Grams" • *Brian Hoxter* 139
Saved from a Terrifying Experience • *Evelyn Howdershelt* 139
Christmas as It Used to Be • *Evelyn Kennedy* 141
A Country One-Room School • *Ada Guthrie* 142
Christmases and Other Things • *Claris McDaniel* 142
The Story of a Tunnelton Landmark • *Iris Jennings* 143
A Gunner's Nightmare • *Jessie Volk* 145
Challenges in a New Country • *Jessie Volk* 146
A Club with a History • *Mary Susan Dadisman* 148
The Beauty of It All • *Sandra Bunner* 149

Changing Times for Osage and Morgantown • *Charlene Marshall* 150
No Greater Love • *Amy Shaffer* 154
Summer in a Washtub • *Amy Stevenson* 155
William D. Smith and Dick Rittenhouse • *Bill Efaw* 156
FIRE! FIRE! FIRE! • *Patricia Newhouse* 156
My Autograph Book • *Patricia Newhouse* 157
"Ol' Pancakes" • *James Nedrow* 159
Glimpses of 1924 • *Ray Pefley Hutchinson and Sylvia E. Parker* 159
A Front Porch in Halleck • *Pam Kasey* 163
Nature's Clemency • *Julia Lucas* 165
Growing Up Around Here • *Rae Jean Sielen* 167

APPENDIX I: THE PROJECT 171
APPENDIX II: IDEAS AND RESOURCES 175
APPENDIX III: WHO'S WHO—FAMILY TREE FORM 179
INDEX 183
ABOUT THE EDITORS 199
WEST VIRGINIA MAP 200

Chapter 1

Introduction

CHAPTER 1: INTRODUCTION

A Landscape of Tales

hen we take the time to hear a person's tale—when we give ourselves the luxury of being led—the teller of the tale becomes our guide. Thrills and hardships, loves and losses show up as features of the terrain, places a guide might explore. Each opportunity to walk with another guide deepens our delight in the terrain.

So it is with the stories in this book. Our terrain is simply West Virginia: her land, her people. Through the narratives of native, former, and new residents, the subtlety and richness in the terrain are revealed.

Community activity is a favorite destination of the guides in these pages. In "A Real Cold Idea" and "Growing Up in the Country," neighbors pitch in and always get something good to take home. "The Wheeling Suspension Bridge," "Saved from the Auction Block," and "The Story of a Tunnelton Landmark" are stories showing cooperation for the successful rescue of historic structures. And an entire community poses for the camera in "Mom and Dad's Best-Kept Secret"!

Meaningful life experiences make for good exploring. They're often approached with good humor—"How I Got the Old School Bell," "A Spring Garden I Will Never Forget," and "The Honeymoon," among many others—but also with seriousness when appropriate—"Having Fun in Spite Of . . . ," "A Gunner's Nightmare," and "Saved from a Terrifying Experience."

But perhaps the most prominent feature in this terrain, visited again and again by these West Virginia authors, is family. Tributes to grandparents, in-laws, and siblings still living or long missed came to us from every part of the state and from authors of all ages: "A Talented and Ingenious Man," "Memories of Grandma," "Great-Aunt Shirley and the Cow Pies." Family lineages appear in "Reflections of Yesterday" and in "Two Different Worlds"; and "Dutch Joe" is a friend who became part of the family.

Echoing these powerful ties to kin, we are especially pleased to begin this collection with "Growing Up in a Large Family," submitted at our invitation by acclaimed West Virginia author Cheryl Ware. Mrs. Ware grew up in a family of ten in Belington, West Virginia. After earning an M.A. in English from West Virginia University in 1992, she taught English at WVU, Alderson-Broaddus College, Fairmont State College, and Davis and Elkins College. Her first book, *Flea Circus Summer*, received enthusiastic reviews on its release in 1996. The book portrays a funny and articulate young girl, Venola Mae Cutright, based—*loosely*, Mrs. Ware likes to stress—on people, places, and experiences from her own childhood.

Mrs. Ware gave up teaching in 1997 to pursue writing more seriously, and has since completed *Catty-Cornered*, a sequel to her first book. As a guide to the experience of family, she makes us laugh and love large-family dynamics through richly personal examples from her own family, while appreciating each of its members individually.

As shared by many of the authors within, the lay of this land is defined broadly by community bonds, meaningful

experiences, and family. Guides who chose paths less frequently traveled—the state folk festival; regional foods; a first job or a nighttime invader; quilting, foxhunting, or riverboat races—point out the distinct features that make this landscape unique.

Take the stories at your own pace. Each alone is a walk on a particular afternoon in a particular season; together, they are several generations' experience of the terrain called West Virginia.

CHAPTER 1: INTRODUCTION

Growing Up in a Large Family

In 1950, Herbert Bender and Marlene Streets married. Two years later they started having children and continued to do so for three decades. Marlene went through childbirth ten times—the first eight surviving and the last two stillborn. The Benders have resided in Belington, in Barbour County, West Virginia, for thirty-five years.

The following essay celebrates life in a large family, something much less common nowadays. While writing, I discovered the single most shared characteristic of our family: humor. When I asked family members, "Did you ever share a room?" I was met with, "It was so crowded, I slept at the neighbors'!" And to my question, "What do you remember about car rides?" I received, "It was so crowded, I had to run along beside the car!" These quips weren't even from "the comedian" of the family.

Distinct siblings

"Brenda, Roger, Stuart, Kevin, Cheryl, Barbara, Henry, Keith!" If we really aggravated Mom, she would get so flustered that the correct name wouldn't come quick enough and she'd start down the list, from oldest to youngest, until she landed on the guilty party.

But this didn't happen often because my brothers and sisters chiseled out distinct personalities to keep from getting lost in the crowd.

Brenda admits this readily. "I was the boss. I guarded the younger ones with my life, but I expected them to follow my orders." Brenda has been watching over people ever since. She has been a nursing assistant at a convalescent home for twenty-nine years.

The second child, Roger, is the adventurous comedian. When he was younger, he came home from his jobs and repeated jokes to our mother—jokes the rest of us still wouldn't dare try to get away with. His contagious laughter can fill the whole valley. Roger said of himself, "I like a challenge and get bored if I do something too long. I like to move around." Roger has been in the army, managed a gas station, worked as a welder and a machinist, and now is a truck driver.

Stuart's personality was shaped by watching his two older siblings. He said, "I watched how Mom and Dad reacted to a low report card grade or something, and then decided I didn't want to make the same mistake." Stuart is known for helping Dad in the shed, and for his ceaseless mowing. He was also handy at comforting sick babies. Now, Stuart works long hours as a machinist, but continues to mow on a regular basis for his parents.

The fourth child, Kevin, a Methodist minister, credits middle birth order in a large family with making him the independent but group-oriented person he is today. "You didn't always get your preference," Kevin said. "There were other voices being heard. Concessions had to be made. Today, if my idea isn't picked, I'm tolerant. My early family unit tempered me not to always expect things my way."

I am also a middle child. And because of the lack of physical space, I retreated into books and my own fantasy world, visiting faraway lands and magnificent kingdoms for escape. Now I'm a writer. Ironically, one of my main characters is a twelve-year-old girl growing up within a large family in West Virginia. I return to that large family for my ideas, a comfortable sense of place, and encouragement.

The sixth child, Barbie, loves to escape into books, too. She is the traveler of the family, who has lived in such faraway places as Holland, and currently works for the government in Florida.

Herbert—"Henry"—a banker, says he always tries to be different. "I don't do things just because everyone else is. This helped me out in college, and I'm sure that my independence comes from my placement in a large family."

Keith, the youngest, talks very little. He is the one who steps back to let others go first. Early on, however, he had his own way of coping with older brothers and sisters. Stuart remembers Keith's strategy: "When Keith was a toddler, if he wasn't getting his way, he went to the kitchen, reached up into the sink, and returned

Couches were often crowded. Brenda, Cheryl, Stuart (holding Barbie), and Roger squeeze in together, leaving Kevin to sit on the floor in this 1971 photo.

with a spoon, which he then used to pop the other kids on the head," Stuart said, laughing.

Chores

As happens in many families, our parents were very strict with the first children. Brenda, Roger, and Stuart had CHORES. "Every third night we washed dishes, and we couldn't go out and play ball with the neighborhood kids until we finished," said Stuart.

Roger agreed, and added, "We learned to wash dishes, to cook, and to sew, plus mowing and all kinds of outside work."

The first children picked rocks out of the garden. "Roger and I learned to do what we were told," said Stuart. "Once we goofed off and didn't do the gardening like Dad told us, and then that night instead of going to our Little League game, we picked rocks. That was a good lesson. We listened after that."

Kevin also remembers chores and griping that it never seemed like it should be his turn already. He burned the trash every night, stared into the smoke, and daydreamed that he was a ship's captain.

By the time chores rolled around to me, number five, I don't remember *having* to do any. I ran after the occasional diaper for my mother, and sometimes rinsed dishes while Mom washed, but I had learned a trick. As long as I was doing homework, I wasn't asked to do much. Needless to say, I made pretty good grades.

Barbie, seven years later, noticed the same relaxing of rules: "By the time I came along, Mom and Dad were much less strict. No bedtime, brush your teeth if you want, comb your hair if you want, clean your room if you want, never asked about homework, and I could read whatever I wanted—whenever I wanted."

Stuart asked Dad one day about this easing up on chores, and Dad said, "Sometimes it's just easier to do it yourself than to keep after them to do it."

Grades

If the older ones had it harder with chores, the younger ones had it tougher with grades. After discussing "grades" with everyone, I found it to be the consensus that we all felt pressured to measure up, to get even better grades if possible. Teachers remembered the brother or sister who had just passed through a year or two before, and the teachers expected the same, if not a higher, degree of excellence.

Kevin was a math genius. I, three years younger, also made A's. However, I remember Mrs. Poling, eyes sparkling, telling me how glad she was to have me in her geometry class and what an Einstein my brother Kevin was. The next day, before any assignment had even been collected, I dropped geometry and signed up for business classes, and began carving out my own niche in typing, shorthand, and business math.

Roles

I mentioned earlier that Brenda's role was to watch over the others, but this was truly a shared responsibility.

In the '60s, the family briefly moved to Dallas, Texas. Because city life was unfamiliar and sometimes frightening, the older children became protective of the younger ones. Roger and Stuart left the house early to make sure their seven-year-old brother Kevin arrived safely at school. Then they sprinted the mile back past their house and two miles more in the opposite direction to make it to their own junior high on time.

On the way home, the older boys didn't have to rush as much, and they collected two-cent pop bottles, spending their profits at the "penny shelf" in the grocery store. Stuart said, "If we found four or five bottles, that meant a candy bar." They shared their treasured candy with the younger ones, who weren't allowed to go out and look for bottles.

Kevin appreciated big brothers watching out for him. "It was tough when the older kids moved away and got married. Before, if anyone started getting smart with me, I could say, 'I have a big brother.' I went from that to being the responsible big brother. The transition was hard."

Playtime

In the 1950s and '60s, Dominos, cards, board games, and checkers were staples at the Bender home. Every evening after supper we played something, and on weekends Granddad and Grandma Streets came down from Mabie to play.

Outside was the best place to be. Stuart said, "I think kids in a large family are more active. There's always someone to play ball with you. We played ball until dark and then switched to hide and seek." Most times the whole community played, and our parents and neighbors watched and visited on each other's porches.

In the late '60s, the television replaced a lot of the Dominos and board games. Our father laughed remembering Kevin's addiction to this new technology. "Mom would ask Kevie to take a bath, and he'd sit with his eyes glued to the TV, and say, 'In a minute, Mom. It's almost a commercial.' Kevie ran the water on one commercial break and had a commercial bath during the next break. That kid was fast."

Chapter 1: Introduction

Kevin remembers his early fascination with television with mixed feelings, observing that the role models we found on TV may not have been as positive as those in real life. "The American culture has witnessed remarkable changes, but unfortunately, changes in beliefs have happened too. We have skepticism we've never had before. We didn't knock the president, the preacher did no wrong, and if our dad spoke we listened because we knew he would never lie. We may have more toys and TV programs now, but we have fewer positive role models."

I, too, was weaned on television, and spent many hours watching reruns of "Gilligan's Island" and "The Brady Bunch." In fact, my parents often yelled at Kevin and me to go outside and play. However, my brother and I rarely got along well enough to play together, and there were no other children in the neighborhood close to my age.

Although the younger children loved TV too, those born in the seventies were blessed with instant playmates—each other. Barbie ('70), Henry ('71), and Keith ('73) raced and roared around the trailer on their plastic Big Wheel, Green Machine, and Red Baron, wearing the grass out from their constant circular motion—until they discovered video games.

Sharing space

In 1965, my parents and their first five children moved into a brand new three-bedroom trailer.

"Stuart and I slept on couches in the living room until the rooms were built on," said Kevin. "Privacy wasn't always possible, but I could get lost in a book. Later, it was a luxury to have my own room. I could go to my room and listen to the radio."

Stuart remembers the expansion. "Since I helped, Dad told me the big room could be mine. I loved that room, and it became a rite of passage as we grew up. The oldest kid at home got it."

Marlene sent sideways pictures to Herbert in Korea. This 1952 photo shows their first baby's—Brenda's—development.

But even with the two additional bedrooms, quarters were tight when the babies started coming in the seventies. Henry shared a crib: "Mom said she put Barbie at one end and me at the other, in their bedroom, and then Keith, the youngest, slept in their bed." Our parents kept all of the babies near them in case the furnace caught on fire.

Along the way, we all shared beds with siblings and cousins. Sometimes I'd get someone who kicked or threw an arm or leg over me, or a blanket stealer, but they were much more pleasant bedfellows than the bedwetters.

Other things had to be shared, too. Someone was always pounding at the single bathroom door, prancing on one foot and then the other.

Some had to sit on the floor when we watched TV. Barbie said, "I didn't like to sit on the floor then, and we argued for the 'best' chair, but now I prefer stretching out on the floor."

And then there was supper, with plenty of brown beans, fried potatoes, and cornbread. There was plenty of room for all to gather 'round the table, but the younger children had to sit on "The Bench," which was about six feet long. Barbie said, "For years, it was elbow to elbow and never enough butt room!"

Trips could also be trying. No one wanted to sit in the middle on the hump. Everyone wanted a window. Again, age usually prevailed. The honored child sat up front between our parents. (We usually took turns.) Babies were piled on laps; car seats or seat belts weren't around.

Barbie said, "It always felt like the clown car at the circus, trying to fit a dozen people in a five- to six-passenger car."

Kevin remembers more truck rides than cars. "We all fought to sit up front in the cab," he said. Even if the truck bed was covered with a camper top, exhaust fumes seeped in and the seat Dad bolted down for us faced backwards. We could rarely see where we were going, unless Dad was backing up.

Henry remembers the sheer number of people at mealtime. "Eating out was nonexistent. Who could afford it? When I started dating, it was a completely strange experience. I'm still uncomfortable in restaurants, especially if they mess up my order. I was taught not to complain or you fix your own next time."

Visiting grandparents

Both sets of grandparents lived in Mabie, West Virginia, about fifteen miles south of Belington. Our family visited every Sunday, and the children were expected to sit quietly while the adults talked. Roger remembers the long, torturous hours of sitting on the couch. Stuart said, "When we couldn't sit any longer, we asked if we could walk to the other grandparents'. We walked the railroad tracks and played along the way. And at Granddad and Grandma Bender's, we could catch crawdads in the creek."

I loved to visit Granddad (Harry) and Grandma (Rosa) Streets. Their houses were unique. They had one in Mabie and another at Ellamore. On Friday nights, they came to our house and played Rummy with my parents, and once when I was five or six, I begged to go home with them. When I climbed into their old truck, I never knew where we would end up. It always took forever because Granddad didn't drive over twenty miles an hour.

Their house in Mabie had all kinds of junk in the front yard, which my grandparents collected from dumps. Inside the house, everything was spotless, and I remember sleeping on a tall bed, piled so high with mattresses that only a few feet separated me from the ceiling. I felt like a princess. The house in Ellamore wasn't as nice, but was more fun. The kitchen had no floor, and we walked on loose planks tossed across the joists to get from the refrigerator to the stove. One of the things that several of us loved to do with our grandparents was visit a spring at the top of Rich Mountain. We walked across the grass by the "Historical Battleground" sign, carrying plastic milk jugs—except in late summer and early fall. During these times, Granddad and Grandma went alone, telling us to stay in the truck and out of the grass, which was infested with rattlers.

Barbie said it was neat having "MUCH" older grandparents who still lived in another era: "It was fun to spend the weekend and get to pump water, use a refrigerator that you had to pull up on the handle to open, help load a wood cooking stove, walk to the corner for a dime bottle of Coke out of a machine, and sleep under homemade, heavy quilts piled up four and five thick." Not all of Barbie's memories bask in this sweet-smelling nostalgic light. "The scary, stinky old outhouse in the middle of a cold night left something to be desired. There's nothing like holding it until morning—even if it got to the point of being painful—when you could at least SEE down the hole first to make sure nothing was going to bite your butt."

Henry doesn't remember much about Mabie. When he was very young, all of our grandparents moved right next door to us. Granddad (Jesse) and Grandma (Lillie) Bender placed a mobile home in our backyard, so that our family could help care for them, and Granddad and Grandma Streets moved into the house next door.

Henry said, "I remember getting quarters for going to the grocery store for Grandma Streets, and I remember eating home-canned blueberries with milk at the Benders'. Grandma Bender had cats everywhere, and Granddad Bender scared me because he had a cane and could hook me with it as I went past."

Part-time jobs

Dad and my older brothers mowed several people's yards, and I always assumed it was so we could afford enough milk for all the kids. Stuart said this wasn't true. "There was always enough of everything, but we mowed for the extras. Instead of one glass of milk with supper, we could have TWO glasses, and then maybe another two glasses for a snack later." When everyone was still at home, the family drank two to three gallons of milk each day.

Brenda worked as a waitress at Yeager's Restaurant. "We all helped, but I put a lot of my quarters in the jukebox. I gave Mom and Dad some of what I earned, but not like the boys. I also borrowed back what I contributed sometimes," she said, laughing. Roger and Stuart scrubbed floors and washed dishes at the restaurant.

Kevin also had part-time jobs. Kevin had paper routes and helped mow yards. Our father remembers Kevin's early mechanical aptitude: "Kevie could take apart and fix a mower when he was just a little thing."

I had a small paper route, around fifty papers, but I spent all my profits on chocolate, Dr. Peppers, and Scooter Crunch ice cream bars. So instead of gaining fresh air and exercise, as my mother had hoped, I gained quite a bit of weight.

Chapter 1: Introduction

Dating and romance

Mom and Dad often talked about their own dates. They were never alone. If Dad wanted to take out Mom, he always had to take her three little sisters—Helen, Shirley, and Sue—along, and sometimes a few cousins, too. "They kicked the seat and you always knew they were there," said Marlene.

Although my parents didn't require it, as Grandma Streets had, my brothers continued the tradition of taking the younger siblings on their dates. They often took us to the drive-in theater with them, and I'm sure we were annoying.

Barbie agrees. "It was fun to tease the older kids who had dates. I think Sandy still has a note I wrote about sitting in the tree, K-I-S-S-I-N-G. I felt important when I was allowed to go on dates with the older brothers and sisters. I felt big and trusted." Sandy stuck it out, and became Kevin's wife.

Later, when I started dating, Barbie serenaded my boyfriend Mark (who is now my husband) with a toy piano and her own rendition of the Snake-dance. It's a wonder Mark didn't run screaming. But instead he played with three children under ten, whose hobbies included sticking their tongues out at him and following us around.

Henry felt that his older brothers' and sisters' dates were coming to see him. "It was a nonstop assault on whoever dared bring someone home. More or less they were fair game! We hid behind the couch and giggled, acted like little maniacs, and got away with it, which is kind of funny because when we were out in public, we were never allowed to act up."

Age difference

Our parents have children that span three decades: three born in the '50s, two in the '60s, and three in the '70s.

Stuart said, "I married Arla when the younger ones were still in diapers. So they came to my house and played with my kids. They still do.

The younger ones agree that the relationship is different with the older children. Barbie said that it was "cool" having older siblings. "Older brothers could drive you to school if you missed the bus, which meant you weren't being dropped off by your parents and could impress the other kids. And the married ones seemed like built-in uncles who came to visit on weekends, sometimes with babies to hold and then later on kids to play with. Babies were more fun, until you got yelled at for not holding the head up—stupid babies, anyway," she said, giggling. "Big brothers were also fantastic substitute tooth fairies, and paid a lot ($1-2) for the privilege of pulling a tooth, if the darn tooth could just hold out until the weekend, that is."

More seriously, Barbie said she liked having a "family history" before she was even born. "There were family portraits that you weren't a part of, and now you are in the new ones—plus it is fun to laugh at the older sister or brother's 'style' in old photos. I remember one of Brenda in the beehive and 'cat' glasses, and another with Stuart or Roger with big swirly hair," she said.

Henry, even though he was next to the youngest, said that he always felt like the middle child. "I thought of Barbie as the oldest. She was bossy. Keith was the baby, the shy one who covered his mouth when he giggled. The three of us seemed like our own separate little family because the others were already gone. The older brothers were much more like uncles to me, or really cool friends. Our oldest brother Roger kept us busy with Jeep rides and walks in the woods. And Brenda was more like a second mother."

Barbie, Keith, and Henry (on the bottom), 1978.

Collective memories

Memories can be elusive, and when I began writing, many of my memories were vague, so I called upon the others for clarification, but to my dismay, they didn't remember the incidents that I considered earth shattering, or they remembered them completely differently (wrong). (Just kidding, guys!) So with several interviews, we've come together to paint a picture of growing up in a large family.

They've added to my trunk of memories willingly, knowing that what they handed over would probably end up in a novel someday. When I called Stuart, I said, "I need help with a project," and he said, "Okay," without even asking what he was volunteering for. That's a large-family mentality for you!

The more I write fiction, the more my true memories get mixed up with those I'm creating. However, I do have a few memories of my own left:

My father came home from work every evening carrying a not-quite empty lunchpail. He always left a melted cheese sandwich or a "bucket" cake for me.

My mother walked me to the one-room library every Friday night, and we both returned home weighed down with books.

When I was in junior high, Brenda took me shopping and let me pick out clothes for school pictures. Without even looking at the prices, she spent the money from her own minimum wage job, hoping that I would feel less awkward and geeky.

When I was five or six, Roger, then a teenage boy, rode me to dentist appointments on his shoulders, and afterwards bought me chocolate milkshakes.

Stuart, as a young man starting to date, let me sit next to him and his girlfriend at the drive-in theater.

Kevin gave his freshman kid sister rides to high school in his Z-28 Camaro, even though it would definitely not have been judged cool by the other seniors.

Barbie wrinkled up her face and stuck out her tongue every time someone told her she looked like me. Much later, she told me, "I didn't really mind. I kind of liked hearing it."

Henry was the largest baby, born nine pounds, fourteen ounces, and almost two feet long. I remember him being able to lift me when he was in third grade—I was in high school. I also remember his extensive vocabulary. Not many three year olds throw around words such as "aggravate" and "increment."

And Keith, who quit speaking at around age three—a silent little boy who walked around the yard collecting bugs and having private conversations with his dog. And now Keith, the man, who still speaks very little, but who surprises us with his vast intelligence, giving us answers to impossible Jeopardy questions, when we occasionally play.

How is a large family different from a small one? According to Stuart, not at all. He said, "But maybe that's because I modeled my own smaller family—two daughters—on the one I grew up in."

Everyone agreed that we might not have had as much in the way of material things, but we appreciated what we got more—and what we received, a large, loving support system, was much more important.

But what about our parents? Did they ever wish for more time to themselves? Not according to Marlene. "I wouldn't have liked it any other way. Sometimes people made fun of us for having so many, but we thought the children were sent to us for a reason, and we were put on Earth to take care of them." Herbert's grin, when his children come to visit, says the same.

Author: Cheryl Ware.

208-001-ST-WV-002-1998

Proud and happy parents: Marlene and Herbert Bender, circa 1980.

Chapter 2

Northern Panhandle

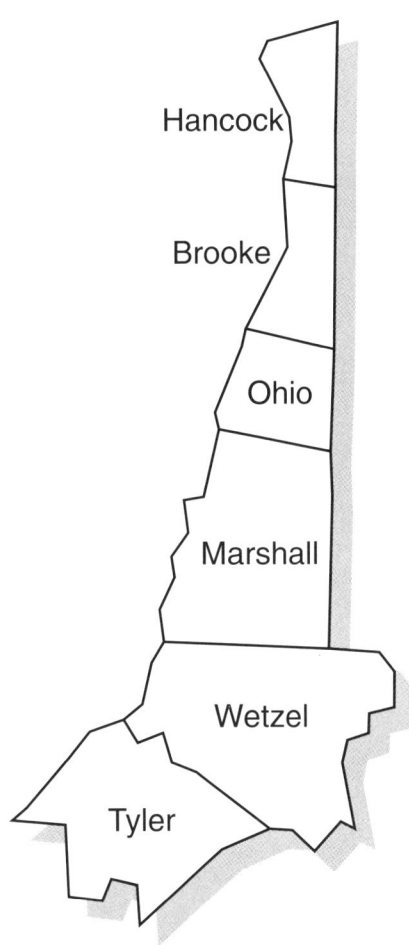

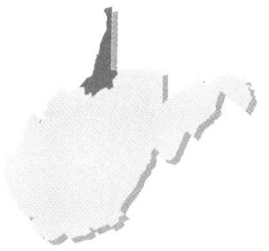

CHAPTER 2: NORTHERN PANHANDLE

The Wheeling Suspension Bridge

heeling, West Virginia has a wonderful history that is fun to research. By putting together pieces of information, you can bring a person to life for a cemetery tour, or you can discover a Wheeling patented steam tricycle for an exhibit.

Documentation of our history appears in many locations. For example, there are records in the National Archives and local newspapers that document the original construction of the 1859 Custom House, now named West Virginia Independence Hall. These papers were essential for accurately restoring the building in the 1970s. This Custom House served as the location of the "restored government of Virginia" after Virginia seceded from the Union in 1861, and served as the birthplace of West Virginia in 1863. It is a National Historic Landmark.

And then there is the internationally renowned Wheeling Suspension Bridge, a beautiful structure that connects Wheeling with Wheeling Island in the Ohio River. It is a National Historic Landmark, and a National Civil Engineering Landmark as well. There are two plaques on the eastern tower to prove it.

The bridge has intrigued me from the time my family moved to Wheeling in 1968. The following year, I was employed by the West Virginia Antiquities Commission, and one of my projects was to research the Wheeling Suspension Bridge. Through my research, it became clear that Charles Ellet, Jr., was the engineer—not John Roebling, planner of the Brooklyn Bridge, as was previously believed. It was suggested that I do further bridge research on my own time and write an article for Wheeling's Bicentennial booklet. I was fascinated by what I learned, much of which is published in *Wheeling Bicentennial: 1769–1969*.

Can you believe the suspension bridge was the longest bridge in the world when it was completed in 1849? It blew down in 1854, and had to be rebuilt. But by the 1960s, although the bridge remained open to traffic, it was badly in need of repairs; in fact, some felt that it was not worth saving. In 1970, a historic preservation organization, Friends of Wheeling, was founded, and we decided to wage a campaign to have the bridge repaired.

Wheeling Suspension Bridge repair work in progress on September 10, 1982, looking east toward 10th and Main Streets.

Little did we know that it would be extremely difficult, take years, and require an inordinate amount of work. It was, however, a tremendous help to have the assistance of the internationally acclaimed West Virginia engineer, Dr. Emory L. Kemp.

There were some difficult times. For example, it was an awful day in 1979 when it was announced that the construction of a new twelve million dollar bridge would begin in 1982—this would have been the demise of the suspension bridge. Another bad time was when it was stated that the bridge was near or at the crisis point: both the US Department of the Interior and the National Trust for Historic Preservation listed the bridge "endangered."

Finally, though, our hard work paid off, and state funds amounting to 2.4 million dollars were committed for restoration and repairs. Closed in 1982, the bridge reopened, structurally sound, in 1983. Friends of Wheeling, Dr. Kemp, the West Virginia Department of Highways, and Zee Photo received national awards. It was a pleasure to present a case study of our efforts to preserve the bridge at the fortieth National Trust for Historic Preservation annual meeting a year later.

More repair work will take place on the bridge in 1998. An exciting addition will be more decorative, dramatic lighting. The Victorian Wheeling Society, Ltd. is coordinating a fun, memorable, and fitting celebration for the 150th anniversary of the opening of the bridge, in November, 1999.

AUTHOR: *Beverly B. Fluty. Ms. Fluty has served in numerous organizations committed to the preservation of historic structures, including the Governor's Suspension Bridge Task Force, the National Trust for Historic Preservation in the United States, and the Oglebay Institute Mansion Museum Committee. She is a 1997 West Virginia History Hero, honored for bringing to light some of our state's important heritage.*

209-001-ST-WV-002-1998

Mother's Stories

Growing Up on George's Run

In the early 1920s, we were a family of seven children when, with Mom (Lula Nichols Fluharty) and Dad (J.S. "Bill" Fluharty), we left West Union in Doddridge County, West Virginia, and moved to George's Run near Shirley in Tyler County. Two more children were born here. We had a big farmhouse and lots of outbuildings, which was really great. All the girls in the dollhouse and playhouse stage could have their own playhouse. Of course, I don't remember the games my older brother and sisters played, but my younger brother, Warren, and sisters Betty Jane and Imogene and I made our own games.

We loved playing in the pasture and following the paths made by the cattle. One path in particular was a winding one that we called "55 an hour"—the fastest speed known to us at that time.

We had very few store-bought toys, but I remember a wagon that we had. It was a nice shiny red. We decided that the go-cart that some neighbor kids had built out of scraps was better, so we

Billie Fluharty Ferrell, circa 1958.

tore up the wagon and built a go-cart. Don't remember that it ran so good, but what did we care?

Another neat thing was to roll a hoop with a piece of wire. The hoops were from old barrels, and the wire was bent to an "L"-shape on one end and was used for guiding and pushing the hoops. Naturally, the big kids got the best hoops and sometimes the little ones were given a lid from a lard can to use. These didn't work, but us little kids didn't know that.

To play as if we were driving a car, we took two bolts and whatever from the workshop and drove them into the ground, and these were brakes, gas feed, and clutch. A bucket lid on a board driven into the ground was our steering wheel, and a stick in the ground was a gear shift. This was put on a slight grade and then all that was needed was something for a seat and we could travel miles at a time. This was fine until we heard company coming, and then we'd grab everything and run to hide it. Our city cousins would not have understood such playthings.

We always had the usual cats and dogs as pets, but we also made pets of chickens and a lamb named Nancy. She was so special. I believe Nancy drowned, and of course that was devastating to a bunch of farm kids.

CHAPTER 2: NORTHERN PANHANDLE

Since our Mom was just a little lady, it would have been pretty hard for her to spank four kids so that chore was given to Creel, the older brother, and did he enjoy it. He was pretty much boss over us too. I remember one time when a lamb died out in the field and, of course, he didn't want the job of burying it, so he made the four of us go bury it. From that time on, if anyone said "lamb chops," there were some kids ready to vomit. I have never tasted lamb and don't ever intend to.

Uncle Boyd and Aunt Doris (Seckman) Nichols lived just over the hill from us. We would climb the hill behind our house, cross the ridge, and go down the other side to Uncle Boyd's house. They always had lots of jelly and apple butter, and we made many trips over that hill for a jar of apple butter in the spring when we had eaten all that our mom had made the fall before.

Living on a dirt road meant that the dust was inches thick. We would take a wide board, put it on a rock, and pile dust on one end and then jump on the other end, throwing dust in the air and, of course, all over ourselves. I don't remember Mom saying so much about that—I guess she was just glad to have us out of her way for a while.

Were we happy? You bet we were.

These are just a few of the many stories that our mother, Billie Fluharty Ferrell, used to share with my brother, Charles, and me, and with her nieces and nephews, and finally, with her grandchildren.

She and our father, Stanley Ferrell from Davis Run in Tyler County, were married in 1940, and although they never lived on a farm during their married life, her years growing up in the country were always held in a very special place in her heart.

We are so glad that she took the time to put some of her stories down on paper knowing that, over time, details and some of the humor would be lost by us.

AUTHOR: *Judy Ferrell Globokar submitted these recollections recorded by her mother, Billie Fluharty Ferrell. Billie was a life-long West Virginia resident, retiring from the Clarksburg-Philippi and Shinnston offices of the Pittston Coal Company after thirty years as a purchasing agent. She passed away in 1988.*

210-001-ST-WV-002-1998

Blessings from the Heart

I was born about two miles from Claysville, Pennsylvania, but I lived most of my life in West Virginia, in Marshall and Ohio Counties. I was fifteen years old when I was married in 1938, to Russell Elmer Terrill. I have ten children: six sons and four daughters. Our first three children were daughters. I loved them dearly, but longed for a son. I remember my mother wrote to me and said if it was God's will we would have a son. I will always remember the letter she wrote me. It was very comforting.

When our fourth child was born, it was a son. Oh the love and joy we felt! I thanked God that he had heard our prayers. Our next child was a son also. I was a very busy mom. We lived on a farm and those were busy times, with a lot of household work and outside chores. The cows had to be milked and cared for, and the chickens and sheep had to be cared for too. I helped with all of this besides my household chores. But I loved it all.

Our next child was a daughter. My children were all so sweet. I remember getting the boys off to Sunday school. They had to be dressed in their best white shirts and ties, and their shirts had to be starched. I sewed many things for my daughters and many were made from the flowered feed sacks we got the cow and horse feed in.

Betty Boyd, 1996 Ohio County Belle, at the West Virginia Folk Festival in Glenville, West Virginia.

We raised a huge truck patch and I canned everything I could get my hands on. It was nothing to can three or four jute sacks full of sweet corn in a day. And the beans, oh my, it was work, but I was proud of caring for my family. We picked wild raspberries, blackberries, and black heart cherries in the summer for jams and jellies.

The peach trees were always full and we canned them. We also made apple butter. We were a busy family. Hugs and kisses were quick, but they knew it was real.

We had three more sons. I always thanked God that my children were healthy. Isn't that a lot to be thankful for?

I was two months pregnant with my ninth child when my husband was killed in an accident. I was devastated, but I had to think of my family. When my ninth child, a son, was born, we had to leave the farm. We had a sale and I felt as though my whole world was falling apart.

Four years later, I met my second husband, Earl Woodrow Boyd. He was a bachelor and he fell in love immediately with me and my children. They all loved him too. I was very cautious for quite a while but love has a way of overcoming obstacles. We were finally married and had one son.

My second husband passed away a few years ago, but I feel like I have been blessed. My health is very good and I miss my second husband. There is an empty place in my heart. God has been good to me.

Author: Betty Beatrice Chedester Boyd. Betty's children are Helen, Dorothy, Phyllis, Harold, Charles, Martha, Roy, Norman, and Russell Terrill, and Earl Robert Boyd. They are scattered everywhere, except the youngest, who is still with her. She lives in Valley Grove, West Virginia. Her hobbies are quilting, fishing, and caring for her yard. See index for additional work by Ms. Boyd.

Dutch Joe

The old house is gone now, and nothing much remains to remind one that there ever was a house there, but I remember. In my mind's eye I can see that old house yet. It was more of a shack than a house . . . but therein my story lies.

He was old, his face weathered and brown. But those eyes! They were as blue as an October sky. He was small of stature and moved about quietly.

His name was Joe Horter, and he lived alone, except for Jimmy, a small brown dog that followed at his heels. Folks called him "Dutch Joe," but Joe was a Frenchman, born in the Alsace-Lorraine area, on the border between France and Germany. He had come to America as a small boy, a stowaway on a ship. Those early years were hard, and he often knew how it felt to be cold and hungry. I never knew why Joe came to settle in our rural area. He worked sometimes as a stonemason and he sometimes helped the farmers with the harvest.

We lived in a very rural area of Marshall County. Our family consisted of my father, Archie Stewart; my mother, Theo Holmes Stewart; and myself. Joe was a frequent visitor at our home. Often we would see him coming across the barnyard early in the morning, just in time for breakfast with us. We were always glad to see him coming, and were happy to share our meal with him. Just a slice of homemade bread and jam was fine with Joe.

Some folks were afraid of Joe, and when they walked past his house they walked quickly, with their eyes toward the ground. There was no reason for anyone to fear, for Joe would not harm a soul. To them he was "different."

He would do little things to help my mother. He called her "Ceel," and in his book she was the finest cook anywhere.

It was two miles from the school bus stop to my home, and that walk took me past Joe's house. My short little legs got very tired walking through the mud and snow. Often I was wet and cold, and Joe always had a fire crackling in his fireplace, and insisted that I come in and get warm before I continued my journey homeward. He often bought little treats for me, crackers and cookies. His meager pension left little for "extras."

Joe called me "The Kit" (the Kid), and he would have laid down his life for me. I was too young to fully understand the horrors of war, but I have seen tears roll down his cheeks as he would listen to the radio news broadcast during World War II, and hear of fighting in and around his hometown. "Ach" (Arch), he would say to my Dad, "just think of it . . . little ones like the Kit there . . . being blown to pieces . . . I just don't understand."

I have often wondered if somehow our family might not remind him of someone he had left behind when he left France. Perhaps he could see a resemblance and found comfort in being with us. Whatever it was, I hope we were able to fill the void.

Joe died January 21, 1947, and was buried at the Beeler Station Church Cemetery. I don't think he knew his exact age. Joe did not leave a big mark in this world. He wasn't rich or famous, or any of those things that people write about in the history books. He was just plain Joe. A kind and tenderhearted little alien who came to live among strangers, and taught a little girl a lesson in loving and caring.

Author: Juanita Stewart Fitzsimmons. Mrs. Fitzsimmons was born and raised near historic Fort Beeler in rural Marshall County, West Virginia. She still owns acreage from her family's "homeplace."

CHAPTER 2: NORTHERN PANHANDLE

Fall in West Virginia

One of my fondest West Virginia memories occurred before I even came to the state in fall, 1995, as a student at West Virginia University. It was a Saturday in mid-October of my senior year in high school, and I was visiting Wheeling, where many of my relatives live. One of my cousins was getting married that day.

The morning of the wedding, my grandparents drove me and my mother up to Oglebay Park to look around. We parked and walked to an overlook area. What I saw then was one of the most beautiful sights I have ever seen.

Sprawling out before me were the brilliantly decorated rolling hills. Each tree in its different shade of yellow, orange, and red blended together to form an extravagant fall landscape. The valleys still had their morning mist, making the scene even more enchanting. In the calm autumn breeze, the trees were rustling slightly. At that moment, everything seemed to stand still, and I felt like I was in perfect harmony with nature. All I could hear was the breeze through the trees and the occasional bird singing its morning song. Even though other sounds of people walking and talking were present, I tuned them out. I was in my own world. I enjoyed this serenity for a good fifteen minutes as I scanned the whole landscape. I thought to myself, "What a great way to start a morning!!"

Having lived in Colorado and Utah, I have seen a lot of beautiful sights. However, no fall scenery from either of those states, or any other for that matter, could match the beauty of that October morning in West Virginia. I have seen many other fall sights since I have lived in this wonderful state. The first one will always remain most special to me.

AUTHOR: *Matthew Hofeldt is a student of biology at West Virginia University. His family has lived in Colorado, South Carolina, Utah, and Georgia, but he traces his roots to West Virginia.*

213-001-ST-WV-002-1998

Too Much Fun and Not Enough Study

Roberta Kimmins Gray wanted to be a teacher, so she enrolled at West Liberty Normal School (WLNS), a teacher-preparatory institution in Ohio County, in West Virginia's northern panhandle, a short distance from her family's farm near West Alexander, Pennsylvania.

Her father drove her in a wagon over the dirt roads to the small hilltop village of West Liberty. Theodore Roosevelt was in the White House, the American flag contained only forty-five stars, and the year was 1903.

West Liberty Normal's annual catalogues for the years 1903 to 1906 list her as an "unclassified" student. She did not come to the school to complete the teacher training program, called the Normal Course, but only to earn enough credits to enable

Bowman's boardinghouse, circa 1905.

her to teach in the elementary grades. Arithmetic was her favorite subject, but she also enjoyed algebra and Latin. Other studies included grammar, writing, history, and geography.

What made the school attractive? "Those things which are opposed to study," stated the 1905 catalogue, "are largely wanting at the West Liberty State Normal School. A more quiet and yet attractive place could not be found for a school." A life-long member of the Women's Christian Temperance Union, Mrs. Gray—then Miss

Kimmins—found West Liberty's social atmosphere attractive. "West Liberty," boasted school officials and townspeople, "[was] free from saloons and other haunts of vice . . . This, with the culture and refinement of the people, and the retirement of the situation, makes West Liberty a most advantageous place for successful student life." Moreover, "The town [was] free from malaria and typhoid influences and [had] pure, sparkling mountain water."

The town, however, was not "free" of smallpox, which Mrs. Gray contracted in her final academic year. While she was quarantined in her room at Bowman's boardinghouse, her teachers and Principal Lorain Fortney appeared outside the building to give lessons, but they refused to enter or to permit Roberta and other infected students from returning to classes.

There were no dormitories on the West Liberty campus until 1920. Students secured lodgings in private homes or in boarding hotels. To reduce her expenses, Mrs. Gray and her roommate prepared their own meals; their rent amounted to $8 a month. Her boardinghouse, owned by a Mrs. Bowman, housed young women on one side and young men on the other. A 1906 rule stated: "No lady student shall be allowed to occupy rooms where a family does not reside permanently."

Tuition and fees were minimal by modern standards. State residents paid no tuition, but did pay an incidental fee of $1.50 per term; out-of-state students paid the incidental fee plus a tuition of $2 a month. Mrs. Gray's expenses came to about $30 per term.

WLNS was a state-run, non-sectarian institution, but students were expected to attend chapel exercises in Academy Hall's auditorium, where, according to Mrs. Gray, students sang sacred songs, read Bible selections, and prayed.

Discipline, Mrs. Gray emphasized, was the watchword for Normal's students. Like most schools of that period, WLNS followed the Latin dictum, "in loco parentis," that is, it acted in the role of its students' parents. There was strict regimentation, with rules governing male-female relationships and use of language, tobacco, and alcohol. Students were not permitted "to go riding or driving with the opposite sex without permission of the faculty."

Mrs. Gray recalled with a grin the young man who was admonished by Principal Fortney for his promenade with a young woman along the boardwalk that paralleled WV Route 88 north of the campus. She also remembered the social events, which were "permitted only on Friday and Saturday evenings so as not to interfere with preparation of school work." Although all social activities were chaperoned, Mrs. Gray's mother frowned upon her attending dances. Mostly, she and her friends "sat out on the porch," stayed up late and drank tea, and visited local stores like Uncle Tuck's and Waddle's. A 1903 regulation, however, forbade "loafing in the stores or loitering at the post office."

West Liberty Normal School field trip, circa 1905.

No student activity, in the years from 1885 to 1925, matched West Liberty's literary societies for student participation and student excitement. Mrs. Gray belonged to the Irving Literary Society; its rival was the Bryant Literary Society. Both societies held regular meetings at which members developed their skills in declamation, debate, oration, and parliamentary procedures. Her forte was oratory.

The highlight of the year came during commencement week in June, when the two societies competed for the Harmar Silver Wreath. The coveted award, won first by the Bryants, was won most often by Mrs. Gray's Irvings. The intensity and spirit of the competition equaled that now found in modern-day collegiate athletics. Indeed, the intellectual warfare during Mrs. Gray's last year at West Liberty became so intense that Principal Fortney discontinued the contest for the Harmar and hid the wreath after the 1906 competition. It was not found until 1922, and even then, neither society was allowed to claim it.

Mrs. Gray left West Liberty in 1906, when she passed a test by which Ohio County, West Virginia educational officials allowed her to teach elementary school. She taught in the Morrison School near Valley Grove, and at Triadelphia Grade School. Her first contract paid the salary of $20 per month; her last contract, for the 1910–11 school year, $50 a month. She traveled to school on horseback or in horse-drawn wagon.

She married Elmer Gray in 1911, retired from teaching, and moved to a farm near Valley Grove, where she lived until Mr. Gray died.

From 1972 until her death in the summer of 1989, Mrs. Gray resided at the Altenheim Home for the Aged in Wheeling. This writer interviewed her shortly before her 102nd birthday. She spent only a small part of her long life at West Liberty Normal, but her memories of the school remained rich and vivid: the friendships, the long hours of study, and her teachers. "We had too much fun," she recalled, "and not enough study."

AUTHOR: *David T. Javersak, a 1967 graduate of West Liberty State College, teaches history at his alma mater, and serves as Dean of the School of Liberal Arts. He is one of forty-six honored as History Heroes in 1997 by the state of West Virginia for their contributions to the preservation of our state's heritage.*

214-001-ST-WV-002-1998

Roberta Kimmins Gray, taken at Altenheim, March, 1989.

West Virginia Foods

Each season in West Virginia comes with its own special food. I grew up in the 1930s and early '40s in Hastings, a small Wetzel County community in northwest West Virginia, and I especially remember spring and summer foods.

In the early spring, usually between snows, my mother, Ruth Gaynell Morgan George, and I would pick "squaw cabbage"—a plant that resembles a violet plant—and fix it like wilted lettuce. A little later, other edible plants would spring up, such as meadow lettuce, dandelion, and white top. These would be cooked the same way as spinach. In May, after the other greens had become bitter, we picked the tender shoots of poke and milkweed. Cooked together, they're delicious!

My mother would order 100 biddies, or chicks, through the mail. By the Fourth of July, the roosters in the flock were big enough to fry, while the hens were spared for laying. The Fourth was celebrated with everyone—my brother Pete (Cecil Arnold) George, and sisters Mary Simon and Audrey Crawford and families—coming home for a feast of fried chicken (we also ate the feet, which were cleaned by dipping in scalding water and removing the outer layer of skin), green beans, slaw from cabbage from the garden, noodles and mashed potatoes, wilted lettuce, and fresh-baked light bread. Freezers of ice cream were made using blocks of ice purchased from the Hope Natural Gas Company, for a small price.

We also made schmiercase from our own milk. The cows were milked morning and night, and the milk was strained into crocks that were set in the cellar. Nice, thick cream would rise to the top, and was skimmed off and put in a crock to spare for churning. The remainder was clabber, from which the schmiercase was made. This was done by heating the clabber slowly to separate the curds from the whey, then straining it through muslin. Sweet cream and salt were added to the curds, and we had schmiercase, or cottage cheese. You can't imagine how different it tasted from the store-bought cottage cheese we get these days. The whey was put in the hog slop; we never wasted anything!

Late in the summer, pickle beans were made. A bushel of half-runner beans was cooked in a large tub, being careful not to cook them too done, and without salt. The beans were then drained and left to cool. Then a layer was put in a ten-gallon crock, about six quarts at a time, and sprinkled with a handful of coarse salt, and

the layers repeated. A dinner plate was placed on the beans and covered with a piece of muslin. A clean, heavy rock from a creek bed was placed on the plate, and cool water was added to bring the brine up as high as the plate. Another cloth, usually a feed sack, was placed over the crock and tied securely with a string. The beans were left to set about a week, then tasted to see if they were just right. These cannot be made during the hot Dog Days—they will spoil instead of pickling. Trust me!

Green tomato ketchup was made by chopping cabbage, green tomatoes, and hot banana peppers together, and preparing as you do sauerkraut.

You can tell people are from West Virginia if they talk about "roas'eneers" (I don't know how to spell it but I can talk it!)—what other people call "corn on the cob"—or pickle beans (not "pickled"). One time, my husband and I were in a grocery store in El Segundo, California, and I heard this man tell his wife to get some roas'eneers. I just had to ask them if they were from West Virginia. Sure enough, they were.

AUTHOR: *Ruth Phillips. Mrs. Phillips is a retired executive secretary, wife of an Air Force retiree, and mother of three daughters, Patricia, Debra, and Sharon. The family has lived in Florida, California, Ohio, and Okinawa, Japan.*

215-001-ST-WV-002-1998

Mother's Visits

I was born about two miles from Claysville, Pennsylvania. My parents, William and Ola Lindley Chedester, named me Betty Beatrice. I came from a large family of fourteen. I have spent most of my life in Ohio and Marshall Counties in West Virginia; most of my life was also spent on a farm, and I miss that life very much.

I married Russell Elmer Terrill at the age of fifteen. We had nine children—five sons: Harold, Charles, Roy, Norman, and Russell Elmer; and four daughters: Helen, Dorothy, Phyllis, and Martha "Sue." When I was two months pregnant with our last child, Russell Elmer, my husband was killed in an accident. Four years later, I met my second husband, Earl Woodrow Boyd, and we had one son, Earl Robert.

While she was alive, my mother would come to visit during the summer and the holidays. I have fond memories of these visits.

Betty Boyd with her mother, Ola Lindley Chedester, during one of "Mother's Visits."

These visits all took place in rural Ohio County, West Virginia, near West Alexander, Pennsylvania, in the 1960s, '70s, and '80s.

One summer while mother was visiting, our youngest son, five-year-old Earl, was playing in the yard with a ten-gallon milk can. We were in the kitchen when we heard him crying. Here he was in the milk can, all but his head. We were scared to death. How were we going to get him out? Finally, my mother said to try greasing him with butter. So we did, and he just slid right out of that milk can—thanks to Mother.

We had another visit from Mother for Thanksgiving one year. It was a few days before Thanksgiving, and we were all sitting at the dinner table; I had baked bread and we had fresh rolls for dinner. After dinner, Martha and Roy were real curious if anything was wrong with the rolls, because no one had said a word. Finally, Mother said she had found a button in her roll. Roy and Martha had stuck a button in one of the rolls before they were baked. Mother said she was taught to always mind her manners, so she hadn't mentioned it. Some gal she was!

Sometimes Mother's visits became very interesting and amusing. We had the little outhouse out back, and two plum trees between the house and the outhouse. I kept telling Mother she had better quit stopping at the

plum trees every time she went to the outhouse. She didn't take my advice and all of a sudden one day she was making tracks back and forth pretty steady from the house to the outhouse. She did stop eating the plums, and we had a lot of laughs over that.

I recall another occasion for some laughter. It was Mother's ninety-sixth birthday, November 8, 1986. Mr. Chet Carroll of Balloons 'N Tunes dressed up like a gorilla and came and sang her a song. She kept joking and laughing and talking with Chet, and we really had a ball with her. It was fun and I will never forget these times.

My mom lived to be ninety-six years old, healthy all her life. Mother and my second husband Earl are both gone and I miss them. Mother was a fine lady and my story is a tribute to her.

AUTHOR: *Betty Boyd. See index for additional work by Ms. Boyd.*

216-001-ST-WV-002-1998

"Poppy's Camp"

assing through the gate, I saw corn fields—green stalks next to green stalks next to green stalks, seeming ten feet high—which I had never seen before. They led down a gravel road to the camp. Over to the left was the farm, and often I would see someone on horseback there.

I remember riding to Poppy's camp in the late '70s on dirt roads and over three or four one-lane bridges. I never realized until years later that we only went out through Elm Grove—a section of Wheeling—down past the Convenient Mart, and on back roads to what is known as Big Wheeling Creek. We were still in West Virginia.

There at Poppy's camp, in the shed, was our swingset that my dad and Poppy, his father, Harry Norwood Duvall, would set up. Out came the hornets, little yellow specks all through the grass. "Be careful when you step," they said, even after making sure I stayed inside long enough to avoid getting stung.

We always had picnics, usually on the Fourth of July. My Nana, Ada Catherine "Betty" McDonald Duvall, always prepared food, including her homemade potato salad.

One time Nana was in the kitchen, and all we heard from outside was her screaming, "Alan . . . Alan . . . Alan!" My dad came rushing in as we followed. There Nana was, standing on the sink counter—or rather, cowering, since she is about six feet tall and it seemed a low ceiling. Below was a garden snake. "Kill it," she shrieked, and my dad took a hoe and split it in two. He wiped up the blood with a paper towel.

Nana's half-sisters, my Aunt Alma and Aunt Eleanor Allen, usually did the yard work. When it came to fireworks, Aunt Alma always warned me not to play with them; she had lost her hearing in one ear when a firework went off too close to it, she told me.

My mom, Sandra Klein Duvall, my dad, and Poppy and I often went fishing. Once I caught a twelve-inch carp. Mostly though, we caught catfish that we later grilled.

Scot, my brother, who is seven years older, and I, if not playing outside, would play the bowling machine, which I loved most. We also listened to old records on the player. One song reminded me of a circus, and sometimes I'd dance around.

After sundown, we sat on the screened-in porch, drinking our drinks and listening to the crickets. If it was a near-winter visit, Poppy built a fire in the living room. First he crumpled up newspapers, then he put on the logs. He took tall matches and lit the ends of the paper until the logs caught fire. Sometimes it took a while, but Poppy would prevail. He always asked me how you start a fire without matches. "By rubbing two sticks together," I said.

What I remember most is never wanting to go to bed. At night, the adults played penny-ante poker. There I lay in the bunk bed, holding my tattered doggy stuffed animal, wondering what was all the fun. I'd hear my family laugh, and I'd pop out of bed and mosey into the kitchen. I'd sit on someone's lap and learn the wild-card games spread across the green tablecloth: twosies and threesies; fives and tens; queens, fours, and one-eyed jacks, the man with the ax, a pair of natural sevens takes all. Not your usual draw poker.

Then finally to bed; but before I could feel rested, I heard chirps of every type of bird imaginable. I looked up at the window, wondering, "Still dark? What time is it?" Slowly the sunlight came in.

AUTHOR: *Diana Lynn Duvall, born in Wheeling, West Virginia on February 8, 1973. "Dee" is a 1995 graduate of Waynesburg College in Waynesburg, Pennsylvania, with a bachelor's degree in English Communication Art Media Studies, emphasis in professional writing. She has been a newspaper journalist with the* Dominion Post *in Morgantown, West Virginia since October, 1997. She was a reporter for* The Times Leader *newspaper in Martins Ferry, Ohio from June, 1995 to October, 1997.*

217-001-ST-WV-002-1998

Memories of Grandma Jones

I shall always remember my grandmother, Nellie Hartley Jones, born October 21, 1879, on Wayman's Ridge, Marshall County, West Virginia. Grandmother lived with my mom and dad, John and Alma Webb, from the time they were married. Over the years, the family grew to seven children, plus five adults: Mom, Dad, Grandma, Grandpap, and Uncle Bud.

We lived in McMechen, which is in Marshall County. This was during the Depression years, and Dad worked as a railroader. He worked twelve-hour shifts—mostly at night—and he spent most of his daylight hours sleeping.

Grandma was a big help to Mom. She was always there for everybody, every day. I can not remember her ever being sick a day, until the year before she died, at the age of eighty-five years. This was in January, 1964.

She was an excellent seamstress, but I remember her best working in the kitchen. She baked all of our bread. We very rarely had store-bought "bakers bread." Of course, we kids thought it was a real treat to go to the store to buy bread. Not only was Grandma an excellent bread baker, she also baked delicious pies, cakes, and cookies. Most of the time, she didn't use a recipe or measuring utensils—it was just a pinch of this and a handful of that.

Our house always had the mouth-watering aroma of good food. What a thrill it was when we came home from school and the smell of lemon greeted us before we reached the door. We knew that Grandma had baked her lemon crackers. What a treat awaited us: a glass of cold milk and a lemon cracker. As we headed toward the kitchen she would warn us, "Do not peek into the oven! It will make your eyes cry."

It is difficult to get all the ingredients for the crackers today. The recipe calls for bakers' ammonia, and we would buy it at the drug store. Back then the druggists mixed their own pills and medicine from items they had right there in the store. They also mixed up certain ingredients for bakers. I will share my recipe for Grandma Jones' Lemon Crackers. Maybe your favorite pharmacist will be able to secure the bakers' ammonia for you. I spent a lot of time with her figuring out the amounts she used:

Grandma Jones' Lemon Crackers

2 1/2 cups sugar
1 cup lard
1 pint sweet milk
1 tsp. baking powder
2 eggs
1 tsp. lemon oil
2 oz. bakers' ammonia

Dissolve ammonia in the milk. Mix all the ingredients using enough flour for medium stiff dough (approximately 12 cups). Roll as for cookies and cut in squares. Put on lightly greased cookie sheets. Bake 375° for 8–10 minutes. Be careful when opening the oven—IT WILL MAKE YOUR EYES CRY!

AUTHOR: Alma Jean Webb McCombs. Alma Jean is a dairy farm wife who lives with Ivan W. McCombs, husband of fifty-one years. They have four children, eleven grandchildren, and two great-grandchildren.

218-001-ST-WV-002-1998

Nellie Hartley Jones standing on the back porch of her McMechen home. The photo was taken in 1920.

Chapter 3
Mid-Ohio Valley

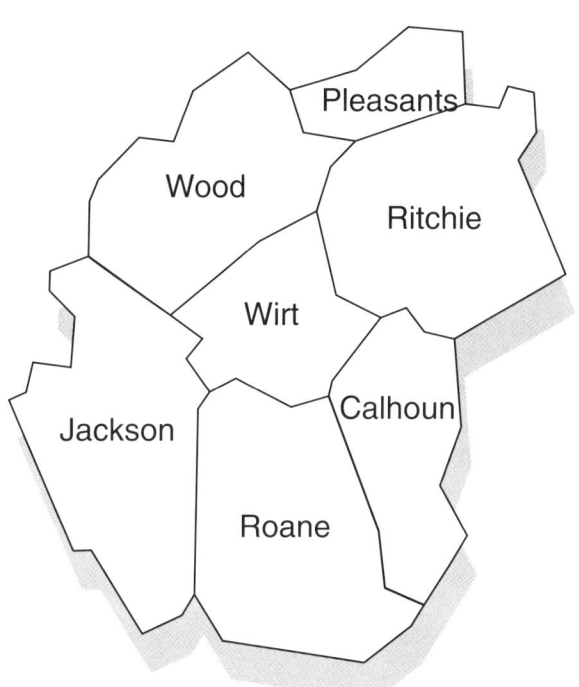

Fox Hunting with Dad

My dad, Dennis Wayne, has fox hunted all his life. Fox "chased" is a better term, for the object is not to kill a fox. Houndsmen have long been advocates of the noble red fox which, far from being reviled as an adversary, is respected as a partner in the "sport of kings." Indeed, the fox often seems to enjoy his role in the ancient drama.

Dad took me fox hunting for the first time when I was three years old. We went from our home at Cottageville in Jackson County to a place called Evans Ridge near Ripley, and camped in a new tent on top of the hill. Before us was the majesty so common in West Virginia, rolling ridges of meadow and pastureland, and wooded hollows down below.

Dad had "given" me a hound. We called her "Juicy," as I had trouble saying "Lucy." I'm sure I was unable to stay awake very late that night, gazing at the stars as hunters do, and listening to the music of the hounds. The excitement of being with Dad on a fox hunt probably wore me out at an early hour.

At exactly eight o'clock the next morning, I was awakened. "Hurry," Dad whispered. "We are going to see the fox!" I tumbled out of the tent, suddenly aware of the cry of foxhounds driving their quarry. They were coming up the "holler" below.

"Be still," Dad said, motioning toward the ridge on our right. "The fox is going to cross right out there." My heart pounded with anticipation. My eyes scoured the timber for movement. The hounds grew closer. I wondered if they could see what they coveted so desperately.

Up across the ridge he suddenly came, not one hundred yards away. Sunlight glistened on his scarlet coat. He seemed not to be in a hurry. He stopped to look back, then went on, apparently unconcerned that he was being pursued so closely.

The hounds entered the meadow as the fox disappeared beyond the ridge. Ol' Juicy led the way. In chorus, the hounds sang to us as they crossed. They faded into the hollow, circling almost out of hearing. Their voices again grew louder. Three times the fox and the hounds passed by us that morning. Each time I tingled with excitement.

I fox hunted with Dad for over ten years. We ran some outstanding hounds, made a lot of friends, and savored God's creation on many a starlit night. We also competed at the field trials and bench shows held by local hunt clubs. I enjoyed the camaraderie of the older hunters. I was just a boy, but I was treated like a man.

"Mark and I kind of grew up together," Dad has often said. We made a lot of memories fox hunting. We would stop at Wheeler's store on Route 87 in Mason County and pick up a ration of bread, Colby cheese, fresh bologna, a couple of ripe tomatoes, and some chocolate milk. Usually we were joined by other hunters, and laughter was plentiful while we waited for the hounds to "strike." All grew

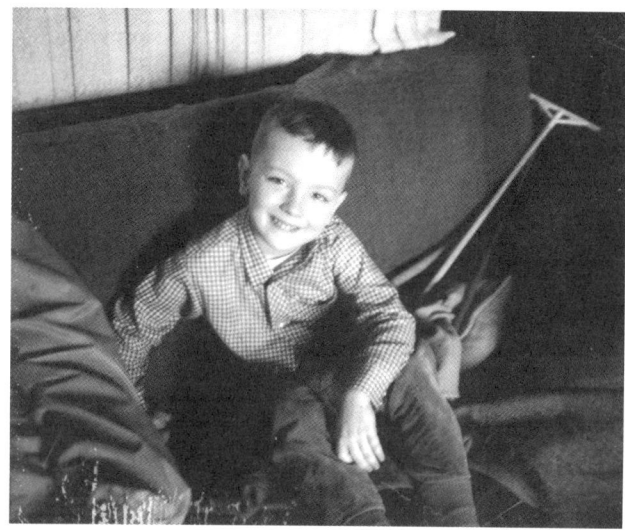

Mark Wayne at age five, in 1969 or 1970. Photo taken at home in Cottageville, West Virginia.

quiet, however, once the chase began. The thrill of the race and the music of the hounds combined for an experience that was at once peaceful and exhilarating. The business of life has pulled me far from those days, but I will always cherish memories of fox hunting with Dad.

AUTHOR: *Mark Hampton Wayne is a high school government teacher and basketball coach in Fairfax, Virginia. His father, Dennis Wayne, still fox hunts in West Virginia.*

219-001-ST-WV-002-1998

The Year of the Pumpkins

My mother was Stella G. Eneix Nutter Moore. She was born at Tariff, in Roane County, West Virginia in 1917. She was the daughter of John Pearl and Marietta Twyman Eneix. She had four sisters and two brothers. In Mother's teens, the early 1930s, they lived beside the Hughes River at Greencastle in Wirt County. Today people travel close by on Route 47 at the Newark Road turn-off.

Mother told me and my children many stories of her childhood. This story we called "The Year of the Pumpkins."

One summer, a big rain came and the lower grounds along the river became flooded. As mother watched the water flowing very swiftly by, she noticed pumpkins beginning to float downstream. She tied one end of a rope to a post, and the other onto my grandfather's john boat. Mother then rowed out far enough to gather pumpkins into the boat, and took them to shore to unload. After many trips, she carried home all that my grandmother thought they could use. She then carried the rest to the side of the road for the neighbors and passers-by to take. A lot of families had pumpkin to eat that winter.

Mother said she and my grandmother baked several pies, and the rest of the pumpkin they canned or dried. She said they got tired of eating pumpkin, but it was a hard winter and food was scarce.

My mother passed away in 1995. I have made notes of everything I can remember Mother telling me. I want to make several booklets and give them to my family so these stories won't be forgotten.

The Davis house, in Williamstown, West Virginia. The balcony porch and the front porch roof that take part in the intruder's retreat are visible.

AUTHOR: *Polly Shepherd has been married for forty-four years to Franklin D. Shepherd. They have five children and nine grandchildren. She enjoys writing, reading, gardening, and crafts.*

220-001-ST-WV-002-1998

The Night of the Intruder

We live in Williamstown, in Wood County, West Virginia, in a large, three-story house that is one hundred years old. The Davis families have lived in this house for fifty years. Pappy and Norma Davis brought up seven children, and we have brought up five, plus a few others—we were foster parents for eleven years. After all those fifty years, there are many stories that could be told. One of the most exciting is about the night of the intruder.

It was the fall of 1993, and all was quiet. Our teenage son was out of town, camping at the New River Gorge, and our older children were grown up and on their own. An old house has many noises of its own, and you get used to them, but this night I heard a noise that I did not recognize. I got up to investigate, and heard noises coming from upstairs, on the third floor. I asked my husband Jerry if he had locked the back door, and when he said yes, I just went back to bed. But at 1 AM, I woke up and saw an animal in our bedroom! It was big! A raccoon or something.

The animal stands up and slowly turns and goes upstairs. I wake Jerry up and tell him there is a big animal in the house, and he tells me I am hallucinating. I tell him if I am, it just went upstairs. He gets up to go see about it, but he can't find it and tells me again that I am hallucinating. Well, I can hear this animal scratching and rustling around in the upstairs. The intruder is trying to find a way out.

I tell my husband to turn off the ceiling fan so he will be able to hear it, too. He does, and finally hears it. So he grabs his housecoat, a flashlight, and an 84 Lumber yardstick! He goes back upstairs to the third floor and chases something all around the room. By this time, we know it is not a skunk. I hear a crash-bang, and Jerry chases the creature behind the couch. Finally, it goes out the third floor window and is hanging on for dear life, with Jerry swatting at it with the yardstick.

The animal drops to the front porch roof. My Hero runs down the stairs to the balcony porch, with me right behind him, and he steps out onto the porch roof to see where the midnight intruder went.

I am telling him to be careful, because I don't want him to fall off the roof. Cars are going by, and I think they are wondering, "What is going on at the Davis house tonight?" Jerry sees the raccoon run to a tree that is by the porch. Then the raccoon climbs down the tree and lumbers off into the neighbor's yard.

Our neighborhood had been harassed by this raccoon for some time. It was very bold about getting into things. It would parade down the alley every morning about 5:30 AM, not in the least bit worried about being seen. This raccoon had even had a confrontation with our neighbor Tonie on her back porch one morning as she left for work. So I could not wait to tell June, another neighbor, about our visitor. I asked him if he had any trouble with the raccoon last night. He said, "No, and we won't either anymore, unless he has a road map." Don, another neighbor, had caught the animal in a trap later that night. They took the raccoon and a skunk that he had also caught the night before out into the country to a farm, and released them both.

We did a little detective work and figured out how the raccoon got in the house. The raccoon had climbed up the house using the rain drain. It had climbed to the third floor roof and gone in the skylight, which we had left open, and taken the stairs from the skylight to the floor. Then, we figured out, the raccoon went down to the kitchen and got into some cat food that was by the back porch door—the bag was out in the middle of the room, and there was a hole in it. On its way back up, the raccoon made the wrong turn and went into our bedroom. That's when I saw him, and the chase began.

AUTHOR: Elizabeth Davis. Mrs. Davis enjoys warm water exercise and writing. She loves art books and gardening.

221-001-ST-WV-002-1998

Quilting Tradition

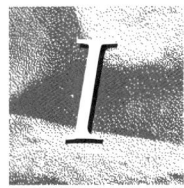

In 1945, I was living with my husband's parents, Lewis L. and Rhea L. Moyers, in Morrtown, West Virginia, in Wood County. My husband, Lewis V. Moyers, was serving in the South Pacific. I had my first child after he was drafted. I named her Rhea.

Mary Prichard, a woman in the area, had organized a Farm Women's Club in our neighborhood. It was a really good thing for my mother-in-law and her friends, so I joined early on. Most of those charter members are gone now.

I lived next door to my in-laws after my husband came home. My mother-in-law helped me with my children each time I went to get another baby, five in all. Soon my children were having children and my mother-in-law started making quilts for her great-grandchildren. I had never made a quilt in my life. I was just too busy helping raise my family and helping with their babies. I was involved in Homemakers Club, 4-H, and scouts. Later I joined the YMCA and swam and worked out.

Doris Moyers and great-granddaughter Becky Louise Boker, who was five years old when this picture was taken, in August, 1997. The quilt pattern is a "flower-garden diamond."

After my father-in-law died, my mother-in-law took turns staying with her three children. While she was with me, she pieced her last quilt and my first. It was a simple four patch. My last grandchild, the twelfth, came just four months before my great-grandchildren started arriving. I made two baby quilts alike, one for my mother-in-law's last great-grandchild and one for her first great-great-grandchild.

My mother-in-law had given me a much-used little quilt that her mother-in-law, Emma Moyers, had made in 1919 for her grandson, my husband. One day I looked at it closely for the first time and realized it was a nine patch set on the bias with border stripes. This is a pattern I have used three times.

I just finished squares for my ninth baby quilt. I am waiting to learn if I should set them in pink or blue. Maybe one day, the baby or a descendant of our family will look at this baby quilt, when the baby has long since outgrown it. I hope they think of me as I think of my mother-in-law. Maybe the quilting tradition will even continue!

Author: Doris Moyers. Doris was born the seventh of ten children of Elbert and Myrtle Hale. They were raised on a farm in Bellsville, West Virginia. To date, all ten are living, and their ages range from sixty-nine to eighty-eight. Doris bowls on two senior leagues. Her vacation this year will be bowling in the women's WIBC National Tournament in Davenport, Iowa.

222-001-ST-WV-002-1998

My First Job

It was the morning after I graduated from Parkersburg High School, in Wood County, West Virginia, May 29, 1949, and I was on my way to "seek my fortune."

I grew up with the understanding that, when one graduated from high school, one was obligated to find gainful employment and not only support oneself, but also contribute to the rest of the family.

In keeping with this belief, the morning after graduation I donned my best dress (which also happened to be my graduation dress), put on my high-heeled shoes, and was off to town to find a job. My first stop, picked at random, was a lending institution. I was in luck, they were looking for an employee! After filling out an application and taking several exams, I was ushered into the manager's office for an interview. While going over my paperwork he noted that I was only sixteen years old. He said, "We have never hired anyone under eighteen, but your application looks good and you have passed all your tests, so call me when you are seventeen." He planned to check with his home office in the meantime as to whether or not he might be permitted to hire me.

On June 17, my seventeenth birthday, I again dressed in my very best (same dress), talked my feet into accepting those high heels again, and set off for town. I had to make the trip into town, even though he had asked me to call him, because we had no phones where we lived in Mudlick, a very rural section of Wood County. When I made that phone call from the real estate office of a family friend, it was the first time I used a phone. I was just simply amazed that I could hear the other person so well. I wonder, now, if I shouted into the phone!

I did not get the job, but I was referred to another company that needed someone with my qualifications. Peerless Mills, Inc. hired me and I went to work immediately.

My first few days at Peerless Mills were traumatic. I was assigned to figure inventory, standing—remember, I still have on my high heels—for four hours at a time. I was given a manual adding machine, which operated by entering the figures, then pulling a handle that caused the figures to register in the machine. Although I was exhausted and my feet were killing me, I would never have asked for a seat to work from or for a rest break. My starting salary was $22.50 a week for five days. When I left this job in 1956, I was making $45.00 a week.

I lived on this income, paying my "room and board" and all my other living expenses. On what would seem today to be a meager income, I not only supported myself but bought my mother her first gas range and myself a bedroom suite, and even managed a small savings.

Author: Edith Griffith. Ms. Griffith is a retired Internal Revenue Service officer. She is the mother of two daughters, Susan Morris and Linda Roberts. See index for additional work by Ms. Griffith.

223-001-ST-WV-002-1998

Hard Life, Good Life

My name is Arthelia Christina Shimer Richard. I was born on March 24, 1920, and grew up in Freed, West Virginia, in Calhoun County. I am the daughter of Okey Shimer and Annie Cunningham Shimer of Freed. I have seven sisters, who are all living except one. I have one brother, who is deceased. He was only an infant when he died.

When we were small my father would take us upon his lap and tell us bedtime stories that he had made up. Or, he would sing to us. We would all really look forward to this time with him. My mother would even join in and listen to the stories with us. It was a very good life, even if we did work hard helping our mother, or working in the fields with Dad hoeing corn all day long. After we were finished with our work we would go to the creek and bathe.

Chapter 3: Mid-Ohio Valley

Arthelia's mother, Annie Cunningham Shimer.

We all enjoyed church. We attended Hoy Chapel. Sometimes we would walk miles and miles but every Sunday we would go. When we girls were growing up we would get together every evening on our porch and sing hymns. It made us feel good because our neighbors would sit and listen to us sing. We really enjoyed singing.

I went to a one-room school called Leatherbark School, in Ritchie County near the town of Smithville, West Virginia. When we girls were school age we moved from Freed to Leatherbark. After a few years we moved back to Freed. I had many great teachers at Leatherbark School, but my favorite teacher was a man. His name was Rooland Dye. All of us students liked him so well that we made him a quilt with our names on each square. He was very pleased with it.

One time, Mom and I made apple butter in a big brass kettle over an open fire in the yard. We cooked it all for a long time and when it was done we put it in jars and set it beside the door to cool. After that we went to the garden to work. When that work was done we went back inside the house to clean up, and to our surprise someone had taken all of our apple butter. That was really a blow for us. But, we just made some more.

When I was seventeen I got married. The wonderful man was Linza H. Richard of Munday, West Virginia, in Wirt County. We have six daughters and one son. From our children we have thirty grandchildren, forty great-grandchildren, and two great-great grandsons. I enjoy every one of them.

Arthelia's father, Okey Shimer.

I'm a faithful Christian and I enjoy worshipping my "Lord" and Savior. I belong to the Extension Homemakers Club and Senior Citizens of Elizabeth, West Virginia. I also love to cook and bake. One of my mother's favorite recipes was Raisin Pie. I don't even have it written down. This is just from memory. All my children love these pies.

Raisin Pie

1 box raisins
1 1/2 cups sugar
1/2 cup all-purpose flour
3/4 cup butter or margarine
2 tsp. vanilla

Cook raisins in water till softened. Mix flour, sugar, and margarine together. Add flour mixture to raisins while they are still cooking. Cook till they are a little thick. Cool. Then add vanilla. (It's better if they are cooled overnight.) Put in a two-crust pie. Bake at 400° till brown.

Makes two pies.

Author: Arthelia Richard. Arthelia is seventy-seven years old now and in good health. She enjoys being a Belle, and had a great time on her trip to Glenville, West Virginia, for the annual West Virginia State Folk Festival.

224-001-ST-WV-002-1998

Mistaken Identity

I was employed as a revenue officer (R.O.) with the Internal Revenue Service from 1976 to 1990. Revenue officers were required to carry a pocket commission to be used as identification. The pocket commission contained the revenue officer's name, post of duty, and the revenue officer's picture. It was mandatory that the R.O. present this identification to any taxpayer he/she contacted, or to any third party.

While working with the Internal Revenue Service, I came across the following true story: An R.O. was in the southern part of West Virginia trying to locate a taxpayer in a small coal town. He walked up to a coal miner sitting on his front porch, presented his ID, and asked if the coal miner could give him any information as to the whereabouts of the taxpayer, also stating the taxpayer's name. The coal miner, after carefully studying the ID, drawled, "No, I don't believe I know him, but he sure is an ugly cuss, ain't he?"

Author: Edith Griffith. See index for additional work by Ms. Griffith.

225-001-ST-WV-002-1998

Our Mountain State Heritage

"... And You (Are) Part of Me"

"I was all of you, and you were part of me," sings Greek vocalist Nana Mouskari, in "Only Love." We are all a part of everyone who has touched our lives. The "me" that I am is combined of every person whom I have known. There are, however, several women who have had particular influence in creating the "me" that I am. Some are yet alive, others deceased for many years; some are relatives, others neighbors and friends; some are in West Virginia, others are not. To describe their influences requires borrowing from the 4-H's Head, Heart, Hands, and Health emphasis. Together these create a complete person when another equally important area is added, namely, the spiritual influence.

Miss Hannah C. Reynolds, maiden schoolmarm and "Mistress of Prim and Proper," embodies the Head. My Aunt Hannah was so dignified that it was difficult to be disrespectful. It is said that she called school to order simply by holding one finger in the air—students came immediately, quietly. She is the one to whom I credit the common sense aspect of "me." Yet she inadvertently also assisted in giving me a sense of humor. Some of her prudish ideas left others laughing, particularly the time in 1930 when she asked a recent high school graduate about career plans. When the young lady stated her intention to become a nurse, Aunt Hannah went into her infamous "cultured voice" tizzy and vowed that this "just would not do," because *everyone* knew that the first job given to greenhorn nurses was (pause and whisper) "to shave a man's privates."

The Heart of "me" comes from Lena Mae Reynolds Young, my mother. She believed in education and family. She watched out the window each morning as we six children left for school. Upon our return in the afternoon, she was waiting, either in her armchair or in her huge mission-style rocker on the front porch, to share our recently-passed hours. Mama loved unreservedly, accepted unconditionally, disapproved privately.

She also strongly believed in helping the underdogs of her world. No hungry person left her presence still hungering. No naked person left her presence still unclad. No unloved person left her presence still longing for a touch of warmth. Sam Walter Foss wrote of this woman, decades before her birth, "Let me live in a house by the side of the road and be a friend to man."

Many years ago, following my mother's death, I still needed a mother. Mary Bielecki became my prosthetic Heart when she said, "Yes," as I asked if she would allow me to adopt her, a reverse of the usual procedure. "Me dearest udder mudder" was the greeting when I wrote to her in a personal care home in Florida. "Guv," she called me. She died in late 1997.

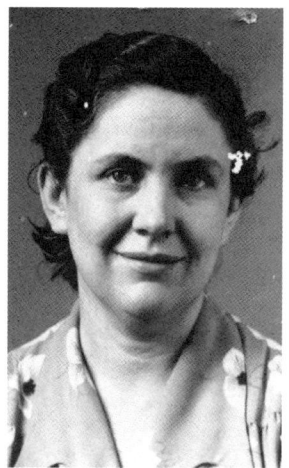

Lena Mae Reynolds Young, mother of the author, circa 1935. As a young woman, she and her sisters, Kate and Alberta, sang across West Virginia. They were known as "The Reynolds Sisters," and as "The Three Shades of Blue," for their blue eyes.

Hands. Busy Hands. Miss Hazel Thaxton was an unmarried mother in the 1940s, considered quite scandalous by some. She raised her son alone, with no income to speak of. Constantly, neighbors saw her walking up and down the "holler" looking for creasy greens or ripe berries. Hands dirty. Hands scratched. The greens were for her table. The berries were invariably picked into a gallon can and taken to various neighbors, repayment for groceries shared. Hazel's accolade to a hard-working, honest, departed acquaintance was that he or she "was a good berry picker."

Three women, Gail Saugstad-McNew, Esther Carroll, and Lois Montoya, represent Health, mental Health specifically. Without that, the physical Health suffers. These three women have given me reasons to go on at times when I might have chosen otherwise. "Miss Gail" was the first to use my college education for volunteerism, when I assisted her second-graders with their math. Mrs. Carroll needed help in the local school library. For fifteen years I have given her countless hours of service as clerk, out-loud reader, listener, and landscape designer for New Era Living Heritage Museum. She is my friend.

Through the connections of Wood County Extension Homemakers and my church, I found my friend Lois Montoya. Lois resided at the Cedar Grove Personal Care Facility, outside Parkersburg, West Virginia. In her mid-nineties, Lois slowly declined as I read to her almost weekly. She passed away in early 1998. My need for reading aloud began with my father's final illness. As a lad he had memorized classical works of prose and poetry, and later read them aloud to school children and recited them to his own six children. When, near death, he had forgotten how to

read, I read his favorites aloud to him, returning the joy in reversing the procedure.

The Head, Heart, Hands, and Health have been complemented in my life by two strong spiritual influences. Hattie Alkire, who reared three fine children within the 4-H lifestyle, was one of the most serene Christians I have ever known. Her spiritual self was evident. When Hattie knew death was near, she remained steadfast in her faith, eager to rejoin husband Claude, certain of where her Lord would lead her. Such an example!!

Granmaw Elpha Rosetta Young, another spiritual influence, was constantly singing hymns or whispering prayer. Not one to upbraid another for lack of faith, she simply lived her own. I've been told an amusing incident demonstrating this, that happened in the early 1940s. For years, Granmaw had saved scraps of clothing far beyond their original use, and finally had sufficient for a runner rug to be braided. It was rolled onto the floor at last, declared "too pretty to use," re-rolled, and placed onto a kitchen chair for storage. Grandpaw cursed every time he came in, not having a place to sit. Due to her pride in such a lovely rug and due also to Grandpaw's cursing, both being sins in her home caused by the rug's presence, Granmaw eventually burnt it. In her words, "It was full of evil spirits."

Kay Young Hill, circa 1955. Before I became what I am today.

So who am I? I grew up in the 1950s and '60s north of Charleston, West Virginia, and was educated at Marshall University in Huntington, to be a science teacher. Several years were spent in the classroom as a full-time or a substitute teacher and as a home-bound teacher. During that time, I married and had three children, who all make their mother pleased with their efforts and hers. One is a good mother herself, repeating much of what I watched my mother do. The second has found his impetus for completing college. The third is in grade school, doing well at what she should be doing right now—learning, playing, becoming a caring person. I watch the school bus until it's out of sight. I, too, am at home when that girl returns at three-thirty, just like Mama was always there.

I am fortunate to be able to offer much of my time as a volunteer. During another period in which I earned no money from my efforts at home or elsewhere, Daddy declared my education was being wasted. I disagreed then, as now. I have spent thousands of hours volunteering at school, reading to Lois, listening to first-graders practice their reading, gathering litter for Adopt-a-Highway, sewing for 4-H camp dorms and for foster youth, making apple butter for New Era. I would be a less useful volunteer without that degree.

The self-proclaimed "Trashy Woman" of Butcher Bend Road, with her plastic bags and litter grabbing tool, probably would not be out there walking that road without the influence of the women who shaped me into the "me" that I am. Their embodiment of the 4-H themes of Head, Heart, Hands, and Health, plus the spiritual completion, have helped to create a whole person.

AUTHOR: Kay Young Hill was raised in a 100-plus-year-old house on Tuppers Creek, in Kanawha County, West Virginia. While in college at Marshall University, she met James Bernard Hill of Huntington. They married in 1968 and, after short moves to Ohio, Florida, and Virginia, settled with their three children in Wood County. See index for additional work by Mrs. Hill.

226-001-ST-WV-002-1998

Berea, a Town with a Heart

Our ancestors came here in the early 1800s, cleared land, and built log cabins on hills and in the valley. I say "our" because we are all related. The community was built on the banks of the Hughes River, where the grist mill, stores, church, and blacksmith were built. Later the machine shop came to accommodate the oil field needs. This became the town of Berea, in Ritchie County.

Preston Randolph loaned his barn for the first school. His daughters were the teachers. Later, as the valley filled further out, two small schools were added. Distance from town, mud roads, and bitter weather made this necessary.

Farmers found working together on the larger jobs got it done faster. They traded labor for labor when cutting corn, hay, or wheat or shearing sheep, and they even traded labor for building purposes. When the threshing machine came to the valley and farmers brought their crops, the bill would be paid with grain or straw. I sat under the chute and bagged grain. An itchy job. The women came to prepare food for workers.

My parents were Guy Toy Sutton and Bertha Davis Sutton. Mother and horse kept garden and potatoes plowed; I hoed. Dad did day work for Aunt Calphurnia (Callie) Maxson Meathrell and Uncle John Meathrell, a prominent family, leaders of the church and in community affairs. The Meathrells had four children. Conza and Draxie were both teachers and both lived over 100 years. Rupert was also a teacher, and Julia stayed home and worked the farm. They were all active in church, and Julia was loved by young people.

Women went to aid others in times of sickness, childbirth, and death. Folks came to be with the family until the deceased was laid to rest, usually in Pine Grove Cemetery, a very peaceful place. The tradition of veterans placing flags on the graves was practiced for many years. Memorial Day is still very important in our town. We still honor our war dead from the Spanish-American War to the Vietnam War. Besides being a day to honor war veterans, it is also the day for our Homecoming Picnic. Folks travel great distances to respect their deceased and renew friendships and family ties. Our generation made lasting changes by going to war, or by following wartime jobs to other places. Not all returned.

And, we are making progress in old and new ways. Churches and organizations continue to pull together to help older people in many ways. We have aid for working mothers with small children, a bus for doctor appointments, and food delivery to shut-ins. There's a center for recreation and a good meal, and more. Yes, this town with a heart is still here.

Conza Meathrell. Berea, West Virginia, circa 1924.

AUTHOR: Mary Genieve Sutton Carneal. Mary was born April 20, 1925, in Berea, West Virginia, and still owns her uncle's 100-year-old home there. She has four children: Adrian Francis, Paul Edwin, Darrell Dewain, and Linda Louise. She has been a "jack-of-all-trades," working as various kinds of clerks and secretaries, and now she cares for her invalid husband. She feeds birds, guinea pigs, cows, deer, dogs, and cats. She enjoys working on her family's genealogies.

227-001-ST-WV-002-1998

Mary Carneal with her granddaughter, Carrie, after a school play, Oliver, 1994.

The 1950 flood took most of Berea away, leaving only a few houses, lots of broken debris, and five dead. Our hearts mourned. With hometown spirit and hard work, the town stands, though much smaller. Our stores and school are gone, our church is closed, though the building is now used by SDB Youth Camp and rented out for other use, and Camp Joy. The post office and Bonnell's repair shop are closed. But, we are here!

Mike and Linda's Cabin

Mike and Linda Smith are old family friends. My father went to high school with them—Mike and Linda were dating then and have been together ever since. They lived in a cabin for several years, about fifteen miles from Spencer, West Virginia, in Roane County, near the center of the state. An old man had lived in the cabin before them and it wasn't much more than a shack when they found it. They put up newspaper and burlap so you could no longer see through cracks in the walls. They had a wood-burning stove, and later electricity, but no running water. They had a well, but the well water wasn't suitable to drink, so they carried their drinking water from town for a couple years, until their landlord put in a new well. This rustic place became the setting for one of my most vivid childhood memories and formative experiences.

It was 1975, and I was five years old the night I first saw the cabin. There was a raging thunderstorm that night. My parents, Donald Royse and Joyce Reed Royse, and I had driven from our home in Morgantown, West Virginia, to Spencer, in the downpour, only to get the car stuck in mud at the bottom of a mountain. I remember that my father worked long and hard with rocks and branches, trying to get the car out, but it wouldn't budge. Since we were in the middle of nowhere with no way to telephone Mike and Linda, he decided we should get out and walk! He thought we were close. My mother and I were not convinced. I was wet and cold, and the loud thunder scared me, so my father carried me on his back. Sure enough, about a mile or two straight up the side of that mountain, we spotted a little cabin. My dad let out a yell—he knew it was the place because there on the porch were his old army boots. Mike must have borrowed them at some point in the past.

Mike and Linda had gone into town for some reason. We let ourselves in, got dry, and started a fire. I was so relieved to be safe inside! The place was a warm, dry haven. Handmade quilts were hung on walls and piled on bunks. When Mike and Linda returned, we had dark, heavy whole-grain bread, fresh grape juice, and vegetables from their garden. There was laughter and conversation as old friends reunited. I watched the firelight and listened until I fell asleep, exhausted.

We spent a week with them there, getting a glimpse of their way of life. After an adult chopped wood, I gathered wood chips, and I helped in the garden a bit. But being only five, I was free to enjoy myself most of the time. The adults worked hard, but there were also long walks in the woods and picnics by a river. I remember my dad carrying me piggyback again, and jumping from rock to rock in that riverbed. From my five-year-old perspective, there appeared to be vast chasms between those rocks, and I wouldn't have been more impressed if he had announced he could fly! Sometimes we bathed in that river with homemade soap.

We took a couple of trips into town, to Spencer. At that time the roads were dirt roads, and the storefronts looked like something from "Little House on the Prairie." There was a post office, a lumberyard, and a general store where Mike and Linda bought staples like flour and sugar. Linda had one of those storefronts with her loom set up inside, and she did weaving there.

Mike and Linda lived in that little cabin like homesteaders for several years, nearly self-sufficient, hard-working, and earth-friendly. An especially severe winter nearly had them snowed in without firewood one year, and after that they opted to leave the cabin behind. Although Mike and Linda's lives are quite different now, I know the experience must have had a positive and profound influence on them. I was only there for a week, and it certainly worked its way into my ideals and dreams. I'm grateful to them both for a wonderful childhood experience.

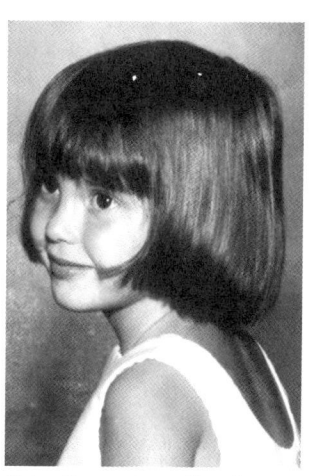

Paige Royse at age five, in 1975, the time of her visit to Mike and Linda Smith's cabin.

AUTHOR: *Paige Elizabeth Royse. Paige lives in Morgantown, West Virginia. She enjoys hiking and other outdoor sports, reading, and painting. She likes to travel, and lived in Japan for two years, where she developed an interest in the language. She hopes to someday own a small, simple, rustic home.*

228-001-ST-WV-002-1998

Chapter 4

Metro Valley

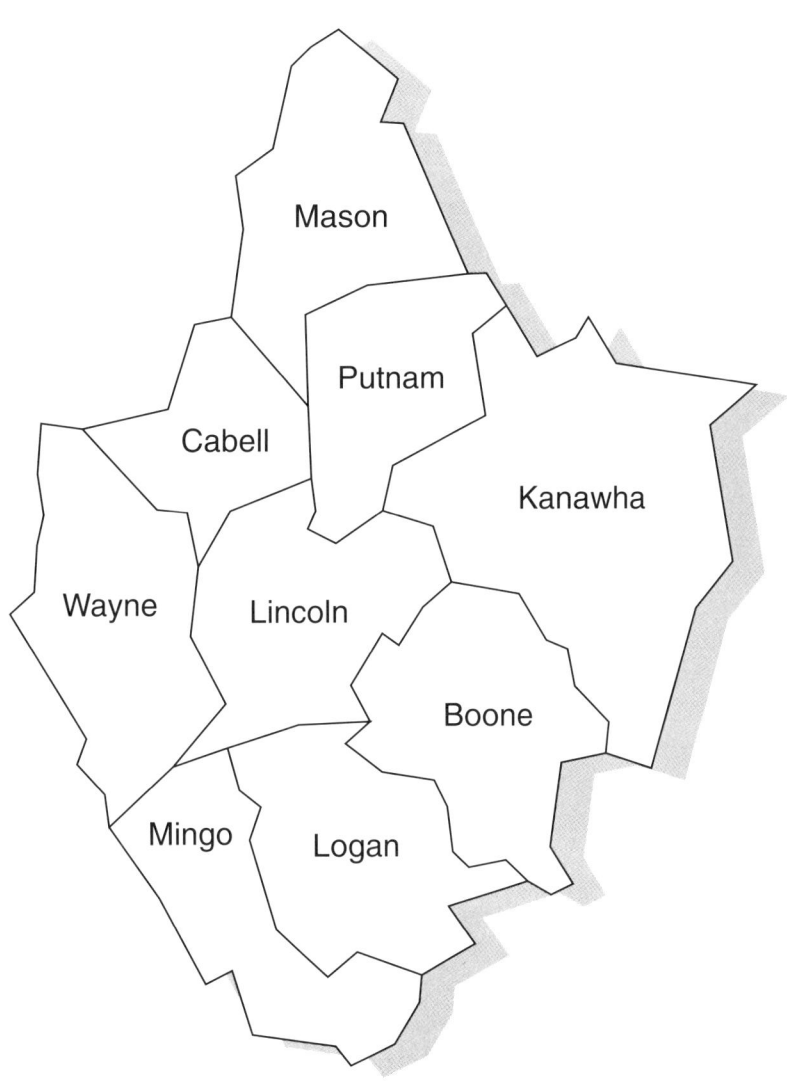

Summer on the Porch

When the weather turns warm, there's only one place I want to be: my grandparents' front porch in Kanawha City. Realistically, that's a problem. My grandparents, Isabelle Hanna and J.T. Warren, are gone now. The house is gone, too—it burned down about thirty years ago—so I can't even walk by it and remember. Thank goodness for the clarity of imagination. It could take me places that never existed, so re-visiting a real place isn't such a leap.

That porch was the center of all kinds of activity, and a good deal of laziness, too. Somehow, there was always a breeze, making the porch the most tolerable place on a hot summer day. We hadn't yet heard of air conditioners! My brother Joe and I would stretch out flat against the cool tile floor, until we were caught and instructed in the purpose of chairs.

We'd wait impatiently for the wind to stir the small, fan-shaped leaves of the stately ginkgo tree in the front yard. It was a wonderful tree. Its branches spread wide to provide a large pool of shade. My greatest regret was that it had no branches low enough for me to reach, which discouraged attempts at climbing.

I do remember hearing that my father, Robert K. Warren, was more successful as a little boy. He apparently got quite close to the top—and couldn't get down. My grandmother Izzy was reportedly in her bedroom upstairs when she heard a shout: "Help, Mother, help! I'm stuck!" Moving the curtain aside, she peered out and saw her son there, wedged in the ginkgo tree. In the true manner of a mother, she is said to have called out, "Bobby! Come down from there at once!"

Our grandmother's approach with my brother and me was more subtle. She occasionally invited us to play a game called "Dead Dog." It sounded rather gruesome, which was possibly the attraction, but it was a very mild game. As my grandmother explained it, the object was to see who could sit perfectly still, without speaking, for the longest period of time.

We'd each pick a chair (no chance of being allowed to sit on the floor) from which we could survey the traffic on Virginia Avenue and watch whatever was going on in the neighborhood. Rocking in the chairs was permitted, but no other fidgeting. I have no idea how long the games actually lasted. I do know it seemed like an eternity of silence and calm on those summer evenings. Still, this was a game we played with our grandmother, so I suppose for that reason

The author on the porch of her grandparents' house at 5320 Virginia Avenue, S.E., in Charleston, during the summer of 1954.

alone we would have enjoyed it. I hate to confess how many years passed before I figured out the real object of "Dead Dog." Izzy was not the sort of grandmother to tell the kids to "stifle it."

One summer, my grandfather Scoop bought me a pair of red sneakers. They made my feet look like a couple of skinny tomatoes, but were a whole size larger than the ones I'd had the previous summer, which was extremely significant at the time. We'd play running games all evening, starting in front of the house and racing around it. I ran to the left and my father ran to the right—an early indication of our future political arguments. I suspect the intent was that he could walk part of the way without being seen, thus allowing me to win.

As a result, my red sneakers were grass stained and muddy by the time it grew dark. I crept onto the porch and into Scoop's lap, mumbling how sorry I was to have messed up the great shoes he'd gotten me. "Why that's all right, baby," he cooed in his soft Alabama accent. "That just shows you've been havin' a good time in 'em." Reassured, I leaned back against my grandfather and let the sound of the cicadas in the ginkgo tree lull me to sleep.

AUTHOR: Carol Warren. Carol is a religious educator and writer, living in Webster County with her husband, Todd Garland, and their daughter Joy. She is a native of Charleston, West Virginia.

Grade School Memories

It was sixty years ago when I started grade school in Kanawha County, West Virginia. I still have many memories of those years. I recall them as some of the best of my life, and a different world, maybe a better one.

I attended grade school at the former Grandview in North Charleston and Sugar Creek in Sissonville, and the Second Ward (now Mound) in Dunbar. None of the schools had sports teams, ballfields, auditoriums, clubs, or a cafeteria, yet the biggest crime was an occasional late student. During my entire time in grade school, I never heard of drugs.

My teachers were "Gods"—my parents would never think of questioning the teachers when it came to my grades or behavior. I could never imagine being disrespectful.

Most textbooks came in continuing series for grades one through six. Each book would be marked "Book One," "Book Two," and so forth to indicate the grade level for its use. Unlike today, the same books were used for years. Though you could buy new books for less than two dollars at the dime store, most students bought used books or rented them from the school.

Grade levels were divided into an "A" and "B" semester. We were promoted at the end of the first semester to the "B" semester, which started in January. Some subjects were just for one semester. Many of the textbooks would probably fail today's "politically correct" criteria. My school textbooks are now destined for the archives.

Our curriculum included Reading and Literature, Writing, Spelling, English, Arithmetic, Physical Health, US History, Geography, Science, Civics, Music, and Art. In the sixth grade, we had a West Virginia history course for which we received a West Virginia Explorer's Club Certificate.

Grading was by the conventional "A" through "F," which was never questioned. Rote memory was in, and learning your multiplication tables to twelve times twelve was mandatory. Spelling was learned by phonetics, a system that is now coming back in favor. Our report card not only reported our grades but also rated us for "learning attitudes" and "social habits," probably to a different standard than that of today. A check mark meant a "good record" and a minus mark indicated "needed improvement."

In the first grade we were given a Reading Circle Certificate, which we were to keep through grade six. Each school year, numerical seals were affixed indicating the number of books read that year. My certificate indicates I was a big reader—I only remember *The Wizard of Oz*. In addition to this certificate, and that of the Explorer's Club, I still have my awards for School Safety Patrol, Wartime Scrap Paper Drive, and Perfect Attendance.

A typical school day was from 8:30 AM to 3:15 PM, with a half hour lunch and morning and afternoon short schoolyard recesses. I don't recall any "snow days." Most students went home for lunch and were encouraged to do so. Those who couldn't "brown bagged" it at their desk. I can recall teachers often "brown bagged" in their classrooms.

Author's Note: During World War II, paper, scrap metal, and rubber collections, which were called "drives," were popular collection efforts in my home town. My elementary school had a continuous program whereby we could bring paper to school daily, while scrap metal and rubber drives were frequent events requiring special efforts. Posters encouraging one to save scrap were common—one poster reminded us that "Junk Makes Fighting Weapons." Awards were often given to students and citizens who made unusual contributions, usually to those who collected the most.

AUTHOR: Richard Marks went on to graduate from the University of Charleston, Marshall University, and George Washington University. He is now retired as an education and training officer and staff officer from thirty-five years with the US government. Currently, he is the author of more than 135 articles of genealogical and historic interest and five short books. Residing in Gambrills, Maryland, he teaches an occasional course for local colleges.

230-001-ST-WV-002-1998

Historic Hurricane Home Refurbished

Known for many years as the Rappold House, the house at 2707 Main Street in Hurricane, West Virginia, stands on land that was owned by railroad magnate Collis P. Huntington in the early 1870s, while he was building the railroad from Huntington, West Virginia, to Richmond, Virginia. It is believed that he may have built the house for his workers.

The property was sold to the Central Land Company around 1888 and purchased by M.L. Dunfee in 1903. John L. Henderson purchased the property in 1910 and resold it to Virginia and Robert Roberts. A Leonard

CHAPTER 4: METRO VALLEY

Historic home of Joseph and Sarah Jarvis, in Hurricane, West Virginia, has ties to nineteenth-century railroad magnate Collis P. Huntington.

Oxley purchased the property in 1912. Mr. E.F. Rappold bought the house in 1925 and for a time used the front porch for a barber shop. The house is listed as a historic property in the *Putnam Year Book*.

Later, my son-in-law and daughter Luther and Phyllis Jarvis bought the house and made inside repairs and added a new roof. Their son Joseph and his wife Sarah Jarvis purchased the house from them in 1991, and have added new windows, vinyl siding, a new air-conditioning and heating system, banisters all around the front porch, and new steps to the front walk. The house has been preserved as near as possible to the original style with the old fireplace, high ceilings, and chandeliers still in place, and the cinder block garage once added in the back has been removed. The back yard serves as a playground for the Jarvis' girls, Regan and Rachel.

AUTHOR: Ralph Williams. See index for additional work by Mr. Williams.

231-001-ST-WV-002-1998

The Weekly Cleansing Ritual

My mother is Luella (Conner) Arthur of Charleston. Mother was born in 1911 and was the second born of seven Conner children. Her mother and father were Hubert and Ida (Page) Conner. As a child, I loved to visit the family home with the big front porch on Bigley Avenue every Sunday after church and listen to the stories about the way things were when my mother was a little girl.

One of my favorite stories was the one that was told about the weekly cleansing ritual. To set the stage, you must first understand that, even though my grandparents lived in the heart of the biggest city in West Virginia, they had no indoor "facilities" at this time. However, there was running cold water in the kitchen and on the back porch.

As it was told, every Friday night after dinner, all seven children would report to the back porch to begin the customary weekend ritual. The first activity was the hair washing. Each child's hair was scrubbed with grandmother's homemade soap. After the scrubbing, my grandfather would break a raw egg on each child's head and rub it in, for conditioning. (He had heard this was good for your hair.) Every head was then held under the cold water spigot at the end of the porch for a thorough rinsing.

Once all heads were squeaky clean, everyone filed into the dining room. In the center of the dining room table was a large punch bowl filled with tea that had been brewed from leaves and roots in the family soup pot while everyone's hair was being washed. This medicinal tea was called "seiny tea," and was known to have strong laxative properties. Everyone had a cup, whether they needed it or not. My mother does not drink tea to this day because of the memory of the taste and the association with the results!

On Saturday, a large galvanized tub was placed on a table in the kitchen and hot water was boiled in anticipation of "the bath." The youngest were always allowed to go first. They had the advantage of getting in the water while it was warm and clean. The older children never felt quite as clean as their younger siblings.

All of this cleansing was in preparation for Sunday. Every Sunday the family walked to Central Methodist Church on the west side of Charleston. I can see them, all together in a row, with the sun coming through the stained glass window shining off their clean hair and not a speck of dirt on any one of them.

AUTHOR: Kay Smith Shamblin is a registered nurse. She lives in Charleston, West Virginia, with her husband, Dr. Jack F. Shamblin. Kay is the mother of three sons: Geoffrey, Rodney, and Christopher Smith.

232-001-ST-WV-002-1998

A Tribute to My Parents

Having been born in 1913, I look back on all those years in wonder at how I bounced through the social and economic crises of the times, healthy in body, mind, and spirit. I know now it was due to the wisdom, foresight, and generosity of my parents, James Jared Dawson and Mary Helen Lannen Dawson.

They were educators, not in the strict academic sense, but in the way they prepared me, my sister, and my brother for life. My sister's name was Marian Dawson Ireland. She died in 1972. My brother's name was Robert Harold Dawson. He died shortly after his service in the Korean War.

My father grew up on a farm near Keyser, West Virginia, one of thirteen children. He completed business school, and became a member of a wholesale produce firm in Johnstown, Pennslyvania. He married my mother when she was thirty-four and he was thirty-eight. Neither had been married.

My mother taught me at an early age, and gradually, all the intricacies of housekeeping. Between ages six and ten I participated actively in most forms of housekeeping, except the washing. Although in summer I was permitted daily to go swimming in the morning, I was expected to be home by 11:00 to set the table, pare potatoes, shell peas, or help in any other way with the preparation for the big meal at noon. After dinner and duties, my sister and I (and any friends who came to play) spent a quiet hour making doll clothes or embroidering quilt patches.

At four years of age, under my father's instruction, I learned to read, as my brother had done before and as my sister did later. My first book was about famous paintings for children in rotogravure. I can still see *The Age of Innocence*, by Reynolds; *Girl With Cherries*, by Russell; *The Gleaners*, by Millet; and *Madonna of the Chair*, by Raphael.

When I was studying in college later, I realized my father had used the technique of behavior modification in setting goals and rewarding us in accomplishing them. He always gave us a piece of candy at the end of each "lesson." He made learning fun as we vied to be the first to read.

My piano lessons began at age six, with dancing as a part. It was also the time I began keeping a diary. Each evening I was to write one sentence telling of an experience that day, for example: "Freddie C. hit me with a mud ball today."

During the week we rode bikes with our friends, acted out plays, and had fights with neighborhood kids, but on Sundays, after church and Sunday school, our family played board and card games together. After work in the summer evenings my father took us to carnivals and circuses. He made stilts to our size and taught us to walk with them. We all made a production of buying bathing suits and learning to swim. And when we were older, before we could get a driver's license, we each went through the experience of changing a tire. Thus we were encouraged in freedom and independence as soon as we could handle it, always with guidance.

Two slogans I remember my father repeating: "Moderation in all things," and "If someone thinks you can do something, don't say 'no' until you try it."

James Jared Dawson and Mary Helen Lannen Dawson, 1939, the only photo Mildred has of her parents taken together.

AUTHOR: *Mildred Dawson Booth. Mildred and her husband, Ashley Booth, had two sons and a daughter. After her children were well into school, she became an elementary school teacher and went to college to earn a BS and an MA degree. When her husband died in 1977, she moved to the Booth family home in Huntington, which they had inherited. Mildred has three grandchildren and two stepgrandchildren. She makes her own clothes, exercises, plays bridge, reads, and travels. Since 1978, she has been a docent at the Huntington Museum of Art, guiding school children in appreciation of art—a most favorite thing. She is also active in her church and at the YWCA, and has done several years of literacy tutoring.*

233-001-ST-WV-002-1998

A Spring Garden I Will Never Forget

I was raised in Kanawha County, West Virginia. The area is now the South Hills neighborhood of Charleston. I was born in 1919 and had five brothers and sisters. My mother was from nearby Dunbar, and my father was born and raised on the same land he raised his family on.

Dad was one of thirteen children, six boys and seven girls. His father was a farmer, and the entire family worked raising food and crafting handiwork until they were old enough to work away from home. All six of the boys went to work for the telephone company. When they were older, the old home place was divided between the thirteen children. My father bought out four brothers' and one sister's shares. This land then became my family's farm.

Dad also was a farmer, and he eventually left the telephone company to work the farm and raise hogs. We also had horses, cattle, and chickens. Mother made our shirts and dresses from colorful fabrics that were used to hold the horse and cattle feed. I can remember my mother going to the feed store to pick out the prettiest colors for our clothes. Sometimes it would take two feed sacks to make one dress. My mother also used the feed sacks to make quilts with other ladies at the Oakwood Baptist Church. There was always lots of work and chores on the farm, but mostly I remember lots of love in our family.

My family is of stout Irish ancestry, and Dad and his brothers possessed the fabled fiery Irish temper and love of life. Temperance was not part of their nature. In particular, two of Dad's brothers were always fighting over the homestead and the property lines. Mainly, I think, my two uncles just liked to fight and cause problems. When I was about eleven years old, they really got into a big fight, and I'll never forget it.

With Dad's permission, one of the brothers had planted a garden on our property, just across the hollow from our home. One evening my cousin was helping my uncle work the garden, and when I heard them I went over to help. Soon after I got there, the other uncle arrived and started an argument, demanding that we come out of the garden. He had obviously been drinking. His wife got out of the car and went up on the hill to get away from the brothers, because she knew what could happen when they started fighting. She, too, could be mean, and was rumored to carry a gun. Needless to say, I was scared to death and ran home to tell my dad what was going on, saying that someone was going to get killed.

Dad took off alone over the hill to see if he could stop the fight. It wasn't too long before I heard a gun shot. I loved my dad so much, and I was afraid he had been shot. Mom and all of us were looking for Dad all over the hillside. It had gotten dark, and we'd had no luck and gone home. Shortly thereafter, he returned. He said that his brother had been "hunting for trouble for years and now he had found it." We didn't understand what had happened. A few hours later, the sheriff came to the house to ask Dad a few questions, then they took him to the courthouse to ask him some more. They also took his gun, and he spent the night at the courthouse.

My dad was indicted for shooting his brother, who was not badly hurt but had some buckshot in his lower legs and spent several days in the hospital. Dad said he didn't do it. During the trial, Dad's lawyer asked that the jurors go to the scene of the shooting. There were no reliable witnesses, as it turned out that everyone had been drinking heavily. Also, Dad's gun had been found clean and in pieces, stored in the closet as usual. When the jurors were at the scene, the defense put pieces of straw in the holes of the fence post where some of the pellets from the shot had hit. The straws pointed up the hill, where it was said my uncle's wife had been standing. Arriving at the scene from our house as he did, Dad would have come from the bottom of the hill, the opposite direction. My dad was cleared, but there was a lot of confusion and no one else was charged.

Who really shot my uncle is still a mystery. One rumor is that Dad really did do it. It is said in farming lore that, if you remove a fence post while the moon is sinking, you can remove and replace it cleanly, leaving no evidence that it has been moved. Dad believed and followed such lore. In any case, I guess my uncle learned his lesson, because he didn't come around anymore.

AUTHOR: Margaret Lewis Dudley. Mrs. Dudley lives in the house and orchard where she was born, once outside of and now part of Charleston, West Virginia. She loves riding her horse; growing vegetables, fruits, and flowers; and cooking and canning. She turned seventy-eight in September, 1997.

234-001-ST-WV-002-1998

My Trip to the Folk Festival

Andrew Dunlap, in his article in the West Virginia State Folk Festival newspaper, entitled, "A Living Heritage," revealed that the first West Virginia State Folk Festival at Glenville was held in 1950, and was dedicated to "preserving the remnants" of West Virginia culture.

On a bright and sunny morning in June, 1997, I accompanied three former Mason County Belles, Annis Blessing, Rae Mitchell, and Sibyl MacKnight, on a three-hour ride from Point Pleasant to Glenville, to attend the Forty-Eighth Annual West Virginia State Folk Festival.

Upon arriving at Glenville State College (GSC), our headquarters for the weekend, the Belles representing twenty-seven counties, registered, were assigned rooms and were told to meet in Pickens Hall. We dressed in our old-fashioned costumes.

During orientation, it being a very warm day, Mrs. Helen R. James, the 1997 Belle representing Gilmer County, gave each Belle a fold-up fan, which was very much appreciated. Mrs. James, an elegant, stately lady, became a very special friend. It impressed me when she said that the beautiful rose gown she was wearing had been worn by her mother thirty years earlier when she represented the same county as their Folk Festival Belle.

The town of Glenville, in Gilmer County, is a quaint old-fashioned town built on the hillsides. The only flat street is in the center of town, so no matter where we were to meet it meant walking up or down steep hills.

Our first official meeting was in the GSC Ballroom, Heflin Center. This was the Belles' Luncheon, a fantastic affair, one which I shall never forget. Former Belles were introduced, and then, one by one, each 1997 Belle was announced. To be a Belle, a lady had to be at least seventy years of age, be in good health, and be able to take care of herself. The application also required that she tell something interesting about herself, like her hobbies, accomplishments, and interests. On my application I stated that I was a member of the Mason County Extension Homemakers, who sponsored me. Among my interests, I wrote that I am a philatelist. Well, the announcer said she had to go to the dictionary to find that a philatelist is one who collects and studies commemorative postage stamps.

Patty Looman, an expert on the hammer dulcimer, played three numbers. One was my grandmother's favorite tune, "Red Wing."

After the delicious luncheon, we posed for pictures, individually and collectively. From this point on, we Belles were known by county names and always arranged alphabetically. In the evening we met for dinner in the GSC cafeteria. Because of the heat, the ladies were instructed to go upstairs where it was cooler. I decided I would just wait in the lobby adjacent to the cafeteria. My roommate, Evelyn C. Straub, the Belle from Monongalia County, and Carlene Amelia McCray Jarvis, Belle of Marion County, decided to stay with me. Kris P. Snyder, our wonderful leader, came rushing down the stairs, shaking her finger at me and saying, "You're in big trouble. When I called county names, you didn't respond to your county, nor did Marion or Monongalia Counties." From then on, we three Belles were known as the three Ms, and stuck together most of the time. Then it was down the hill and up another to the Fine Arts Auditorium for the evening concert of folk music played with fiddles, banjos, and guitars. Ground rules of the festival intrigued me: must be traditional West Virginia music, no electrical amplification, no three-fingered banjo style, and no ASCAP or BMI music permitted.

Eleanor E. Lee, 1997 Belle in the Point Pleasant "Always a River" Festival and Parade.

I believe every church and organization in Glenville had some part in the weekend activities. They provided receptions, breakfasts, luncheons, dinners, and entertainment. On Saturday morning we visited the Country Store and Museum, which had crafts and demonstrations. Dwight Diller presented a Hammons Family Slide Show, which depicted the rugged life of this family living in the back woods of that area.

CHAPTER 4: METRO VALLEY

Twenty-seven Belles at the 1997 West Virginia State Folk Festival, at Glenville State College.

The Lions Club Parade of marching bands and antique autos was the highlight of the day. We Belles walked single file the three short blocks. As we passed the bank at 1:30 PM, I noticed the temperature was ninety-four degrees. Whew! The names and counties we represented were announced as we passed the reviewing stand. What a thrill!

The afternoon was free to pursue the many interesting events. I enjoyed taking part in the old-fashioned spelling bee. The words given were taken from an old McGuffy Reader. Both the spelling bee and the shape-note singing class were held in Trinity Methodist Church. Another good folk music concert on Saturday evening was followed by a reception hosted by the Gilmer County Extension Homemakers.

Sunday morning they bussed us out Route 5 to Job's Temple, an old historic log cabin church, where we had a closing ceremony. The church has three small windows, and board planks for seats; one oil lamp provided a little light for the speaker. After regular services were discontinued about 1912, singing schools were conducted in that building. What a wonderful way and place to end our stay at the West Virginia State Folk Festival.

AUTHOR: *Eleanor E. Lee. Mrs. Lee retired from Linwood, New Jersey US Postal Service, December 31, 1977. Mrs. Lee lives in Point Pleasant, West Virginia, and is an eighty-two year old great-grandmother. She would like to acknowledge and thank the Mason County Homemakers for giving her the privilege of experiencing the sights and sounds of West Virginia's past during the West Virginia State Folk Festival.*

235-001-ST-WV-002-1998

Interview with Thelma Thaxton

It was 1939 and I had a diploma in a frame at my boarding house. I was trudging along the dusty road to my first assignment: Trace Fork School, a one-room school in the opposite end of my home town of Sissonville, in Kanawha County, West Virginia.

As I was sitting at my desk going over my lesson plans that I had made a week before, I heard something. I heard a high soprano voice singing and yodeling. When

Our Mountain State Heritage

I looked out the window I saw the children coming. They were following a slightly built girl that looked to be ten or eleven years old.

When the children entered the school, I introduced myself and I had name tags to pin on them. I found that my singer of songs was Betty Barnhart.

After assigning seats to the children, I asked them to be seated. We discussed some of the things we must do and must not do. Everyone was very polite and almost shy.

I asked them to stand and we would pray the Lord's Prayer and then we would salute the flag. After doing this, I removed my pitch pipe from the desk drawer and asked that we all sing "America the Beautiful" together. I blew on my pitch pipe and started directing the music just as I learned in Music 301. After all, I was a music major. These children would love my singing. Not so! They were giggling, even the little ones, and the boys in the back seats were howling. Nevertheless, I finished my song.

We had classes until recess. During recess, little Betty Barnhart came running to my side. She asked me to come inside the school with her. She had big unshed tears in her eyes. She said, "Teacher, you are singing wrong for us, you are singing proper and we just sing from the heart." She went on to say that she was sorry that the kids all laughed at me.

I never learned to yodel, but I learned to sing from my heart from Betty B. and the other children. I learned ballads, hymns, and real West Virginian Mountain Music. I also taught the children some of my music, but it couldn't compare with what Betty B. taught me about music from the heart.

AUTHOR: *Sue James, a sixth-grade English teacher at Sissonville Middle School, lives in Cottageville, West Virginia. Her neighbor Thelma Thaxton told her this story about her first day as a school teacher.*

236-001-ST-WV-002-1998

James Edward "Blind Ed" Haley (photo courtesy of Lawrence and Pat Haley).

Blind Ed Haley

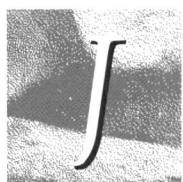

James Edward Haley was born in 1885 to Milton and Emma Mullins Haley, and was raised on the Trace Fork of Big Harts Creek in Logan County, West Virginia. When he was three years old, he fell victim to the measles and, despite efforts by his father to cool his fever by immersing him in ice water, the affliction worsened and little Ed went blind. This setback in Ed's early life was followed by the deaths of siblings at young ages, and then by the tragic loss of his parents. In October of 1889, Ed's father, Milton, along with a friend named Green McCoy, was brutally murdered by a mob at the mouth of Green Shoal in Lincoln County, West Virginia, after being accused of ambushing a local wealthy couple on Harts Creek. About three years after this tragedy, Ed's mother died.

When Ed was a small boy, one of his uncles gave him a cornstalk fiddle and he became so good at playing it that he eventually outgrew the local musical talent. A friend and fellow musician, Johnny Hager, persuaded him to travel with his talent and agreed to accompany him on his journeys. From the Guyandotte Valley in southwestern West Virginia, Ed made his way over into Twelve Pole country and into the Tug Valley. He went up north as far as Parkersburg and as far east as Greenbrier County. Haley spent a great deal of time in central West Virginia—sometimes staying for months at the home of Dr. Laury Hicks in Calhoun County, where his legendary status has taken on mythical proportions today.

After marrying Martha Ella Trumbo, a blind musician and teacher from Morehead,

in western Kentucky, Ed settled with his wife and growing family in Ashland, Kentucky. The two of them traveled with their music throughout West Virginia, southeastern Ohio, eastern Kentucky, and southwestern Virginia, and made a comfortable living playing on street corners, in contests, at schools, at fairs, and on courthouse lawns.

Ed Haley died in 1951, after directly inspiring such writers and musicians as Jesse Stuart, Jean Thomas, Clark Kessinger, Georgia Slim Rutland, Fiddlin' Cowan Powers, Molly O'Day, Curly Wellman, Wilson Douglas, and Slim Clere.

AUTHOR: *Brandon Kirk. Mr. Kirk is co-authoring a book on Ed Haley's life story with John C. Hartford, a Nashville musician most noted for composing "Gentle on My Mind" and for his appearances on the Glen Campbell Show.*

237-001-ST-WV-002-1998

Remembering Hurricane

ront porch swings . . .

*Lives of great men remind us
We can make our lives sublime,
And, departing, leave behind us
Footprints on the sands of time . . .*
—*from* Longfellow, "The Tide Rises, the Tide Falls"

Longfellow could have had my mother in mind when he wrote these lines. I suppose most of us hope that we will leave something good behind. My mother, Faye Coyner Coiner Estes, does not live in Hurricane—she died in 1992. She is permanently gone from Virginia Avenue. Let me add that her body is gone—her spirit lives in me and my children forever. She left something great behind, and we will never forget her. I can still see her sitting in the swing on her front porch, waiting for us to arrive. (Whatever happened to front porches, rockers, and swings?) Mother lived all of her sixty years in Hurricane, and I don't believe that she ever wanted to leave. She was content. You know, I believe that most people were. Why leave a place where one is happy?

For the most part, I do not remember people complaining. Ever. It could have been that I did not pay attention. It could have been because of the convenience—one could get to Huntington or Charleston quickly. It could have been that people were happy with their lives. I like to believe the latter.

Almost heaven . . .

*Sunset and evening star,
    And one clear call for me,
And may there be no moaning of the bar,
    when I put out to sea.
But such a tide as moving seems asleep,
    Too full for sound and foam,
When that which drew from out the boundless deep
    Turns again home . . .*
—*from* Tennyson, "Crossing the Bar"

Home . . . Home to me is West Virginia. I remember hearing a joke in church (when we were living in Ohio) in the 1970s. "There were rooms in heaven. One room was full of people chained to chairs. St. Peter said, 'Those are the West Virginians. They always want to go home on weekends.'" I feel that way. I am sure that there are many who do. I wonder if those graduates (Hurricane High School Class of 1965) who still live in Hurricane realize how fortunate they are?

Of course, when Tennyson wrote this poem, he was not thinking of returning to his birthplace to live. I think he was writing about his death. That is one thing that is so wonderful about poetry; we can interpret it the way we choose. One day, I will turn again home.

Adopted moms . . .

*Wasn't it pleasant, O brother mine,
In those old days of the lost sunshine
Of youth—when the Saturday's chores were through,
And the Sunday's wood in the kitchen, too
And we went visiting, me and you . . .*
        —*from* Riley, "Out to Old Aunt Mary's"

What a wonderful way of life it was according to the words of James Whitcomb Riley. I remember those Sundays. We went to church and then visiting. No one hurried to get anywhere. It was a slower pace. We enjoyed that day just resting and seeing people. Today, few people still do that.

In Hurricane, Mrs. Annie Searls still lives in the home where she and her husband raised ten children. Every Sunday, not most Sundays, every Sunday, will find family and friends at the Searls' home. Her children, grandchildren, greats, nieces, nephews, friends, and adopted children (me, for one) are found at her home. She does not expect them to come. She does not make them feel guilty. They want to come. She is eighty-eight years old—they come because they love her and each other. I am sure there are other families

59

like hers, but I don't know any. She is an icon of society—a little, wonderful woman who has mothered me for years; I love her—all of her family loves her.

When one pulls into Annie's yard, there are many cars there or a few. It does not matter. When one goes into the house, it is full of love. She is as happy to see one person as she is to see twenty or more. I love standing at her kitchen sink, thinking, washing dishes (something I usually hate doing—dishes), looking out at those West Virginia hills. It is a time for reflection. Time that few of us have anymore.

When I am not fortunate enough to be at Annie's, I might call and talk to the ones who are. I envy them because I want to be with them. I know that they are happiest when they are with their mom, and she is happiest when they are with her. She looks forward to those days, but what makes her so very special is that, if none of them could come, she would not fret. She would accept it.

An American icon—do you wonder if such a thing exists? Yes—visit this family and you will see that, in fact, it does.

AUTHOR: *Brenda Coiner Burke was born on Virginia Avenue in Hurricane, West Virginia. She graduated from Hurricane High School in 1965, and left in 1968, when she married Michael Burke. They lived in Huntington, West Virginia; Circleville, Ohio; and Summersville, West Virginia, and owned Burke's Hallmark in Summersville from 1987 to 1997. Her son Nathan D. Burke is an attorney in Texas; her daughter Katheryne K. Taylor is a teacher in Indiana. Mrs. Burke graduated from Glenville State College in 1994; she currently teaches high school English in South Carolina, and plans to buy a house and move back to West Virginia in 1998.*

238-001-ST-WV-002-1998

Jessica Price, age eleven, September 14, 1996, with her "twin," Bunny, and her grandmother Debbie Escue.

When I first got Bunny she was a very light gray, fluffy, and soft, and now she's brown. Her white cotton tail is now gray and she's matted and raggedy all over. She's had an eye replaced by a button and her right arm has been sewn back on. At one point I hated my dog Beethoven because he was the one that chewed off the eye and the right arm of Bunny.

I got her when I was born, from my Aunty Cara. Maybe Aunty Cara gave me my rabbit because I was so big that the doctor said I might be twins, and when I wasn't, she wanted me to have a playmate. And what a wonderful playmate Bunny has been! I have lots and lots of stuffed animals and I really like collecting them, but Bunny is and always will be my favorite.

AUTHOR: *Jessica Dawn Price. Jessica and Bunny are thirteen years old and live with Jessica's mother, Linda, and brother, Matthew, in South Charleston, in Kanawha County, West Virginia.*

239-001-ST-WV-002-1998

My Twin

he's my pride and joy!

Bunny and I have really been through a lot in our thirteen years together. She's stayed by my side most of the time. She always sleeps with me.

Bunny has nursed me through many illnesses. She didn't even mind when I had a stomach virus and threw up all over her. She still loved me.

Bunny even moved to Florida with me. I wanted to take her to pre-school with me, but Mommy wouldn't let me, which made me and Bunny very sad.

Williamson

ow the bustling seat of Mingo County, the city of Williamson lies where once there was only a cornfield. Wallace J. Williamson, a pioneer settler of the Tug Valley region and founder of Williamson, named the city in honor of his father, Benjamin R. Williamson. Soon after the city was incorporated in 1905, John B. Williamson, brother of Wallace J., became its first mayor.

Enjoying prosperity as a coal metropolis and a stop on the Norfolk and Western

Chapter 4: Metro Valley

railway, Williamson has long had city improvements that many small communities would like to have: a fire department, police department, city council, radio station, and daily newspaper. It has its share of wild stories, too, like having two police chiefs at the same time (that's another story); being close to the scene of the Hatfield-McCoy feud; and serving as home to Wells Goodykoontz, who became a congressman after having been a state senator.

Williamson once had a coal mine within its city limits, and still boasts one of the largest railyards in the east. This yard is no longer the Norfolk and Western, having become the Norfolk Southern in recent years due to mergers. Coal and rail are still the leading industries in the area.

Williamson has experienced many floods in its short existence. Disastrous floods occurred in 1977 and 1984. Many businesses and people were forced to relocate during these times. A floodwall has now been constructed under the supervision of the US Army Corps of Engineers and with the support of the Honorable Robert C. Byrd. Hopefully, there will be no more disasters of that kind, and Williamson will have a peaceful future.

Author: Linda Van Meter. Ms. Van Meter is a 1997 West Virginia History Hero, honored for her work with the Williamson Area Heritage Book Committee. See index for additional work by Ms. Van Meter.

240-001-ST-WV-002-1998

"Doc" Keadle

Present at Mingo County's birth in 1895, Newton Jasper Keadle was appointed sheriff by then-Governor McCorkle. Upon assuming his duties, Keadle moved his wife and three children into the upstairs apartment at the jail in what would, in 1905, become the town of Williamson. A son was born while they were residing there. This son, aptly named Mingo, delighted in telling people that he was born in jail. The family produced more children after moving from the jail and eventually building a home on Fourth Avenue. This home is still standing, and is currently the home of the youngest child of ten, Virginia.

The new sheriff brought law and order to the bustling new community of Williamson. He was instrumental in helping to control the violence, which ranged from feuds to union organizing. He also was very helpful during a smallpox epidemic, carrying food and water to those in quarantine.

This family played a formative role in Williamson's and Mingo County's history. "Doc" Keadle served as sheriff, assessor, postmaster, even prohibition officer, finishing his public service as a justice of the peace. Some of these positions were elected; some appointed.

When "Doc" Keadle died, the *Mingo Republican* newspaper read, "It was not so much as a public official but as a man of sterling qualities that Mr. Keadle became enshrined in the hearts of the people. He gave of his time, of his money and himself, and it can be truly said of him that he loved his neighbor and his fellowman."

Author: Linda Van Meter. See index for additional work by Ms. Van Meter.

241-001-ST-WV-002-1998

Bringing Stories Back from Colorado

One day, my granddaughter said, "Granny, what is a one-room school?" I replied, "Listen, my dear, and I will tell you about the one I attended a long time ago."

It was a small white building set on a slope just below my grandparents' house in Yuma County, Colorado. My grandparents, Charles and Lillian Morris, with eight of their nine children, went from West Virginia to Colorado to homestead in 1907. They gave a portion of that land for a school and "Bunker Hill School" was built. My brother and I moved to Colorado in June, 1920. Bunker Hill School looked so small to my brother, George, and me. Our school back in West Virginia was *big*. It was two rooms up, two rooms down, outhouses on the creek bank and a well with a big iron pump in the front yard.

Bunker Hill had rows of desks bolted to the floor. The large ones were at the back, and the smaller in front. A large coal stove took a lot of space, and off to the side was a table with a bucket of water with a dipper in it. The water was carried from Granddad's well, and the big boys begged for the privilege of going to get it. The girls kept the blackboards clean and the erasers dusted.

There were three smaller buildings at the back with the two at the side labeled *Boys* and *Girls*. The building between was the coal house with a place to tie our horses. Our fathers took turns bringing bales of hay to feed the horses that stood saddled all day.

The code about toilet trips was rigidly enforced. No boy and girl were to go out at the same time. Somehow the teacher knew who was out and woe to the kid who ambled close to the building labeled the sex he wasn't.

In 1923 we moved back to Saint Albans, West Virginia, in Kanawha County, and renewed friendships we had left in 1920. We really had tales to tell—being snowed in, prairie dogs, and coyotes.

The first Christmas that we spent in Colorado, it snowed so much that we couldn't go the five miles to the post office to pick up the Christmas gifts sent to us from family in West Virginia. It was so exciting to my brother and me that we didn't mind! We never, never missed school because of snow, though. Our uncle lived about a half a mile from us, and he'd pass our house on the way to the school, and pick us up in a big sled made from a wagon, with runners. We'd pile on and slide off to school—no excuses!

Lillian Miller, ten years, and George Miller, seven years, circa 1921, in Wray, Colorado.

In the fields behind our house, there were whole prairie dog towns. We'd see them out there in the summer, sending signals to each other. There would be a prairie dog on lookout duty, and if you got too close, he'd stand up and bark at another one, and that one would stand up and bark at the next, and so on, passing the message along.

At night, we could hear coyotes howling. Those coyotes were smart. Sometimes our father would go out in his wagon to work in the fields, and while he was at work, the coyotes would chase his dogs up under his wagon. So Daddy bought a gun. As long as he took that gun with him, the coyotes would stay away, but if he forgot it, the coyotes would be right back at his dogs. Farmers used to say, "Coyotes can *smell* a gun." Sometimes when they would get overpopulated and start causing mischief, the men would go out to do a "coyote roundup." Our parents would never let us around when they did this, because it was so violent and cruel. They'd form a big circle and drive the coyotes toward the center, closing in until the circle got smaller and smaller, and then they'd kill the coyotes. But my brother and I still heard those coyotes howling and howling, all night. It wasn't a scary sound; it was lonely. I will never forget their mournful howls.

My mother, grandmother, and great-grandmother were one-room teachers, and I became a teacher in West Virginia, but not in a one-room. I taught primary grades, and they loved the Colorado stories I told. They especially liked the idea of riding horseback to school. I let them know it wasn't fun in a blizzard in below-zero weather. I think they thought I lived in Daniel Boone's time.

We've kept in touch with many of our prairie friends, and now I tell my stories to my granddaughter. As I write this, I think, "If I don't give my memories a good home, who will?"

AUTHOR: Lillian Miller Cunningham, a native West Virginian, is eighty-seven years old. She's a widow after fifty-three years of marriage. She and her husband, Marshall Cunningham, had three children: Charles, who was a lawyer and died at forty two; Alice, who died at twelve; and Sally, who lives with her. She has good health, keeps busy, and has five grandchildren and five great-grandkids. Lillian has been a church member for seventy-three years, and has served as a Sunday school teacher at First Baptist Church in Saint Albans, West Virginia, and in other areas. She graduated from Marshall University and was Kanawha County Belle in 1974.

242-001-ST-WV-002-1998

School Field Trips

don't remember how many field trips we took when I was in elementary school during the thirties. I can remember only two. Chances are there were very few others, because of the difficulties of transportation. To my knowledge, we had no school buses available for our use. Nor was public transportation convenient. I don't remember how we were transported for these two trips, but we did get there.

One of the trips was to Charleston, to visit the state capitol. I was in about fourth or fifth grade. The most memorable part of the tour was viewing the dome. From the inside, it was so high, I thought it must reach to the stars! And then,

CHAPTER 4: METRO VALLEY

looking at the dome from the outside, we were told it was covered with gold. Unimaginable! It certainly did (and does) glisten in the sunlight!

The most exciting field trip was right there in Institute when I was in the fifth or sixth grade. At that time, 1938 or 1939, the Charleston airport was located in Institute because it had one of the very few areas of flat land in the Kanawha Valley. We went to the airport for a very special reason—to see Eleanor Roosevelt arrive. What a momentous event! To have the opportunity to see the First Lady in our own hometown was unbelievable! She was on her way to a small town about sixteen to seventeen miles west, on behalf of the coal miners there. The town was later renamed Eleanor, West Virginia.

I can remember us craning our necks to be able to see her as well as possible. That worked pretty good! The most fascinating incident, however, was hearing her speak. Movie newsreels and the radio had made me aware she had a rather high-pitched, distinctive voice. So when she emerged from the terminal to go to her waiting limousine and turned to call to someone, "My bags! Where are my bags?" all I could think was, "She really does sound like that!"

AUTHOR: *Harriette James Kirk. Born in Charleston and reared in Institute, Mrs. Kirk, a retired elementary teacher, lives in California. Her parents were Edward L. and Stella G. James. See index for additional work by Mrs. Kirk.*

243-001-ST-WV-002-1998

Harriette James Kirk, 1996.

public pool within walking distance, we could not swim there. As for the Kanawha County Public Library, we had no branch in Institute, and we were excluded from the main branch in Charleston.

You see, the time was the late thirties and very early forties, long before the Civil Rights era. Segregation was king. We all were very aware that this was not right, but no one, like a Thurgood Marshall or a Martin Luther King, Jr., had yet been able to do much about it. Consequently, we had to dream up things to do to keep ourselves occupied on those long, hot, and sometimes rainy afternoons.

It never occurred to any of us to do anything stupid such as steal or vandalize someone's property. The police would never have done anything about it, because our parents would have stepped in first and there would have been nothing left of us for the police to even chastise!

The wide expanse of the college campus provided us with sidewalks to ride our bikes, scooters, and skates. This was okay as long as we didn't get in the way of the students as they moved about the campus. A favorite place for skating was "The Grove." The grove was a beautiful, idyllic area that separated the main part of the campus from the faculty housing area. It was a low piece of grassy land with many trees and a wonderful little creek that meandered through on its way to the nearby Kanawha River. On one side of the creek, there was a long flight of widely spaced stairs. These stairs ended in a sidewalk to a bridge over the creek, and across that to a steep flight of stairs on the other side. It was the widely spaced stairs that attracted us as skaters. It was really an accomplishment when any one of us finally dared "hop the stairs," because by the time we reached the bottom, we had gained enough speed to carry ourselves over the bridge to the foot of the steps on the other side. That is, if we didn't land on our bottoms first. What a ride!

Having Fun in Spite Of . . .

rowing up in the small town (village?) of Institute, home of West Virginia State College, had its advantages and disadvantages. My friends and I did not realize the fantastic advantages of growing up in a college community with all its educational activities. We were much more concerned with the disadvantages of that period.

For my group of friends, ages ten to thirteen, finding something to do on a summer afternoon was often difficult. Although there was a movie theater only two miles away, the closest one we were allowed to attend was in Charleston, ten miles away. Even if there had been public transportation then, we would not have been allowed to go "uptown" alone. The college did not have a swimming pool, and though there was a

Something else I remember with fondness is 25¢ picnics! Two or three of my closest girlfriends, especially Jennie Mae Jones—now Buckner—and her sister, Gertrude—"Snooks"—and I would often get together in one of our yards, sitting under a tree, to talk about whatever it was that little girls liked to talk about. When

we were able, we would pool our money to have at least 25¢ with which we would have a "picnic." We would buy a nickel's worth of sliced bologna (a stack more than an inch high), a nickel loaf of bread (the bread with no holes cost a dime), a half-pint jar of Hellmann's mayonnaise for 10¢, and a 5¢ package of Kool-Aid. We took turns "snitching" the sugar for our drink from home. What a wonderful time we had eating and talking and giggling—giggling and talking and eating.

Rainy afternoons often found me at an enjoyable pastime—reading. I was lucky enough to have many books of my own. As I recall, *The Bobbsey Twins* series was a definite favorite.

In 1942, in time for the summer session, the college completed construction of a new gymnasium, Fleming Hall. We finally had a swimming pool we could use! There was open swimming for the public every afternoon and evening. Whenever Mother wondered where I was, she could always find me at the pool.

The old Pine Grove School bell, 1998.

AUTHOR: *Harriette James Kirk. See index for additional work by Ms. Kirk.*

244-001-ST-WV-002-1998

How I Got the Old School Bell

So many memorable things happened when I was growing up in the early 1930s on our family farm in Charleston. I fondly look back on the days I spent in my first school, Pine Grove School on Oakwood Road in Charleston. The faces of the kids now seem long lost, but we had such a good time. Our families were all poor, but that did not matter; we learned at an early age to make what we had last. For the most part, our manner was one of respect for other people's property, and nobody went around messin' or destroyin' something that was not theirs. I remember one exception, however.

Back then, in the early '30s, when I was around nine or ten, the old schoolhouse had become just that—old, and too small for the number of children. It was only two rooms, sometimes with fifty students in each room. It had no running water, but it did have a nice big bell. In the fall and winter, when the leaves were off the trees, that bell echoed crisply through the valley. The old Pine Grove School bell was a part of all our early years.

It came to pass that the schoolhouse was to be torn down within the year. All the kids would be separated and bussed to different schools. We would miss the school, and I would miss my friends.

The school was just up the hill from our house. One night I could not sleep and, looking out my window, I noticed flashlights in the schoolhouse. I ran up the hill, and when I got close I crept slower till I got even closer. There were two boys climbing on top of the school where the bell hung. They had tools to take it down, and I could hear them whispering, "You got it, you got it?" The bell crashed to the ground with a loud "Dong!" It was way too heavy to be carried by the two boys alone, so they dragged it into a hollow below the school and covered their tracks. Apparently, they wanted a memento to remember the school by. I did too.

The next morning I got up real early and went to where I knew the boys had hidden the bell. Using a work horse from our farm, I hauled it away and hid it from them. A couple of nights later I saw the flicker of their carbide lights as they searched for the bell. Each night I could hear and see the boys searching. I really enjoyed this, and it went on for a week or so. Soon I dragged the bell to my daddy's shed for safe keeping. Today that bell sits in my front yard, and no one ever believes how it got there.

AUTHOR: *Stella Louise Rader. Mrs. Rader is seventy-five years old. She retired from E.I. DuPont eight years ago, and loves to can and raise a garden.*

245-001-ST-WV-002-1998

Chapter 4: Metro Valley

"My Father in Me"

In a hollow of Campbell's Creek, a few miles up the Kanawha River from Charleston, West Virginia, the Crowder family lived on a small four-room farm. Poppy, my grandfather, worked in a blue jean factory. Granny Lou, my grandmother, tended the farm, canned fruits and vegetables, churned butter, and raised four boys during the Depression. Then they moved to the west side of Charleston.

William Crowder, Jr., my father, met Mom, Ruth Long, and they married September 29, 1941. Soon after, Dad was drafted and went to Europe as a paratrooper, while Mom worked at Libby Owens in Kanawha City. While in Europe, Dad was at the Battle of the Bulge. His thoughts were with his black-haired angel, whom he wrote a final letter to, yet he lived to see it delivered back home to his beloved wife. They had three sons and came to settle in Dunbar. He worked for forty years as a truck driver. He raised his family with God, love, a stern hand, and a good ear. He taught responsibility and independence.

William Crowder, Jr., and Ruth Long Crowder, in the 1970s.

Dad retired early to spend time with Mom. They traveled, collected, and sold antiques and Fenton Glass, but as time passed Mom's health declined. Dad slowly withdrew from the world and loved ones. No one knew of the demands and responsibilities he faced with his loved one suffering from Alzheimer's disease. It slowly kills one piece at a time, robs you of your dignity, and takes a toll on the ones who care.

I have memories of Dad sitting beside Mom, his arm around her, holding her hand tenderly and kissing her passive face telling her it was alright, he was there. Though she was far away in her mind, there were times of clarity, the words "I love you," and a smile. The look on my father's face said it all, and still brings tears to my eyes.

For the longest time, Dad refused help and it took its toll. Dad had a stroke and came home a different man in many ways. My fiancée and I moved in to take care of them both twenty-four hours a day. God bless the nurses who did come and help. During this time I saw a humble man in my father, who made his peace with all.

Our last day with him was the day after Christmas. Dear friends came to visit, and he showed his antiques to them. That evening he went into a coma, and we lost him on January 11, 1996. Mom seemed to know he was gone. Her last words ever spoken were "He's gone and I'll see him soon." She lived on until May 31, 1996.

My granddaughter, Kahtrena (age five), told me last March that her great Pops and great Granny each had a new heart and body and that we will see them in heaven. Of course I had to leave the room but I believe what she said in my heart.

Dad left me something I will cherish forever: loving memories like the song Paul Overstreet sings, "My Father in Me." I am more like him as each day goes by.

AUTHORS: Ronald Crowder and Kathryn Campbell reside in Dunbar, Kanawha County. This story is a tribute to Ron's parents, who were devoted to each other.

246-001-ST-WV-002-1998

Archie Bland, a Backward Glance

In 1918, when I was twelve years old, my father, Ned Bland, took my brother William and me by train from Louisville, Kentucky, to live near Williamson, West Virginia, because he had gotten a job in the mines at nearby McVeigh, Kentucky. There my father remarried and made a home for us in the coal camps.

Our time in the coal camp as a family was short-lived; my father was killed in a mine accident. I took William, who was four years younger than I, and went to Williamson to get a job. I had never had a job or been on my own, but I knew I was going to take care of us. William went to school and I got a job at the Day and Night Restaurant. Later I worked at the Cinderella Cafe on Third Avenue. I found us a place to live upstairs in a rooming house next door.

I had to get up early for work and would leave William in bed. One morning, while working, I learned that a fire had broken out upstairs. I rushed out to get to

William. I carried him out of the burning building across the street to a doctor. William was taken to Huntington Hospital due to his serious burns. He died two days later. This was a very low point in my young life.

My father had always insisted we go to church, so I had been attending St. James A.M.E. Church on Sixth Avenue. The church members and my stepmother were there for me at this sad time. My stepmother then returned to her home in Alabama.

About 1930, I got a job at the new Mountaineer Hotel and worked there until Pearl Harbor, when I was drafted. While stationed at Fort McClellan in Alabama, I married Ruby Lynch of Williamson. We had two girls, Kay and Vivian. I was later sent to Europe.

After the war I returned to my job at the Mountaineer and later started working at the Tug Valley Country Club with Chef Leon Anderson. I stayed there until I retired in my 80s. I served all the famous and the not-so-famous people of the area and enjoyed every minute of it.

AUTHOR: *Nancy P. Smith wrote this story from an interview with Archie Bland of Williamson, West Virginia. Ms. Smith is a 1997 West Virginia History Hero, honored for her work with the Williamson Area Heritage Book Committee. See index for additional work by Ms. Smith.*

247-001-ST-WV-002-1998

The Great Race

Nelson Jones, at age fourteen, initiated Charleston's Great Annual Regatta Festival, which has grown since 1971 to its current ten days of September festivities and hundred thousand visitors and participants. Nelson and his father, Captain Charley Jones, operate the *Laura J.* sternwheeler on the Kanawha River, carrying West Virginia's precious coal to distant ports. A sternwheeler is a steam-powered boat with a large paddle wheel in the rear. Charley and his wife, Mary Ellen, invite friends aboard their large sternwheeler during the festivals to enjoy the view from the river.

The highlight of the Sternwheel Regatta Festival is the great sternwheeler race down the Kanawha from the Kanawha City bridge, near the state capitol, to the downtown bridge near the heart of town and the crowds on the Haddad Riverfront Park. The excitement of the race is felt by the crews and the thousands of spectators who line the shores to watch this heated match.

Sternwheeler Races—Down the Kanawha

The last of summer's Hot Salty Days . . .
   Here sit I on the *Laura J,*
In Coal Town, Charleston, this fall festivity
   centers on banks of our Capital City!

Soon cast away, break free of our ties,
   paddle from where our final dock lies.
We pause upriver—at Capitol Dome
   patiently we drift, we float, we roam.

The riversides render classic façade,
   formal forms, spacious promenades.
Banks are peppered with pleasure boats,
   skiers, cruisers, at anchor, afloat.

Waiting, watching, bets grow keener.
   Who'll be winner, the fastest steamer?
Soon the paddlers align our heat.
   Aboard we're restless, shift our seat.

Tensions mount for Pilots, Captains,
   crews, friends, and family happenings.
Spectators strung along the shore,
   line their chairs, out they pour.

Ashore, a cannon volleys and thunders,
   waters churn, incite our wonder.
In motion now, we leave our mark,
   away we'll steam to Riverfront Park.

Our paddles churn waters to froth,
   viewers watch, we've started, we're off!
Adjacent racers turn waters to foam,
   outriggers bubble, the river they comb!

Waters gargle over running boards,
   destiny now—to River Lords!
Renowned Cap'n Jones, our Captain Competitive,
   this day, this race—he's sought—elected.

He "invites" his guests afore on the ship.
   "Better Viewing," he jests and quietly quips.
Later, I learn—It's speed for the ship!
   Ah, clever Captain—your guile is hip!

With weight of patrons balanced at bow,
   the ship takes shape, a distinctive prow,
  Underwater, streamlined, its hidden profile
   gives an edge, all-important, in the distant mile.

CHAPTER 4: METRO VALLEY

The sternwheeler Virginia *edges by a competitor as they pass Charleston, West Virginia's capitol building, as seen from the finally victorious* Laura J. *during the 1997 Regatta Festival.*

Pass we now our Capitol Dome,
   down the river, the engines hone!
Banks burgeon with boaters, bathers,
   at water edge—waving waders!

Fathom by Fathom, a lead we take,
   churning the water, cutting a wake!
Neck and neck, we pace our heat,
   this Lady's legend, can't be beat!

At river's bend, the sight we seek,
   the bridge in distance, that ends our heat!
We squint at sun, sighting the edge,
   the spectators dot the arc of bridge.

With power and pull, speed to spare,
   soon comes the end, we're almost there.
Contenders beside, we outreach a length,
   all along, we've held this strength.

Our Captain, stealthy, slips back his throttle.
   Our engine quiets, slips to idle.
An eerie danger—uncanny gamble,
   beside us now, abreast they ramble.

Finally, explosive—triumphantly,
   our Captain blinks and pulls us free!
A valiant victory, we're out front,
   Showman, Vicar—oh, what a stunt.

We glide beneath the bridge's edge.
   Renowned Victor, his heart's pledge.
His strategy, feign, this fractional knot,
   without which A Win, we'd had not!

Ah, the victory, feel the glory!
   Here we bask in his story.
Tied at the dock, we talk and dazzle,
   of our Captain's Victory and all this razzle.

Thanks Capt. Jones, First Mate Nelson!
   Thanks Mary Ellen, the mostest of Hostess,
For showing us this nautical lesson!

AUTHOR: Ted Elden. Mr. Elden is an architect and photographer, and describes himself additionally as a computer guru. He and his spaniel Lady Grace live in a self-built, inspirational home / office / studio overlooking Charleston, West Virginia.

248-001-ST-WV-002-1998

Gaujots

In the Williamson, West Virginia home of Wallace Graham and Nancy P. Smith hangs a painting of Napoleon, emperor of France. The picture has been in the family since it was given to Graham's great-grandfather, Ernest Rene Claude Gaujot, by John Wanamaker, founder of the Wanamaker department stores of Philadelphia, in the early l900s.

General—a title that the Japanese emperor bestowed on him after he opened coalfields in Japan—Gaujot brought his five sons and two daughters to Williamson about a century ago. He was born in 1840 in Alsace, France, and had married Ellen "Nellie" McGuigan of Tamaqua, Pennsylvania. He was a civil and mining engineer. Two of his sons are the only American-born brothers to win the Congressional Medal of Honor: Captain Julien E. Gaujot and Corporal Antoine Gaujot. The Gaujot National Guard Armory in Williamson is named in their honor.

Daughter Clothilde married Randolph Bias, a prominent Williamson attorney, and Marguerite "Daisy" was a private tutor and governess here and abroad for many years.

A story that is passed down through the family is that General Gaujot required his sons to salute the picture as they entered their home. However, he became loyal to his adopted country. You will find the Gaujot name left on a street and also on an apartment building in Williamson.

The only descendant of the Gaujot family now living in Williamson is great-grandson Graham Smith. General Gaujot died in 1909, six years after the death of his wife. Both are buried in Tamaqua, Pennsylvania.

Author: Nancy P. Smith. See index for additional work by Ms. Smith.

249-001-ST-WV-002-1998

Wells Goodykoontz

Mingo County was not in existence when Wells Goodykoontz arrived by train to begin his life in a new town, around the turn of the century. As a young lawyer, he rode horseback to Logan, the county seat, and to the homes of the justices of the peace to represent his clients. Tall and handsome, Mr. Goodykoontz was a striking figure in the pioneer days as the town of Williamson grew.

He was first called into public life in 1911, when he was elected to represent his county in the House of Delegates. He became an influential Republican leader, going on to serve as state senator. During his campaign years, he was given the nickname "Goody" in a slogan.

He married Irene Hooper from New Orleans at First Presbyterian Church in Williamson, on December 22, 1898. They had no children.

His devotion to the study of great Americans led him to become a much-requested speaker at gatherings, especially on the subject of Presidents Washington and Lincoln. A kindred subject that interested him greatly was the last resting places of our deceased presidents, and in the course of years he visited the tombs of many of them.

Statesman, lawyer, banker, extensive land owner, he remained one of the homefolks, with his interests centered in his town of Williamson.

Son of William and Lucinda K. Goodykoontz, he was born June 3, 1872, in Newbern, Pulaski County, Virginia, and died March 2, 1944, in Good Samaritan Hospital, Cincinnati, Ohio. He is buried with his wife in the Williamson Cemetery.

Author: Nancy P. Smith. See index for additional work by Ms. Smith.

250-001-ST-WV-002-1998

Two Different Worlds

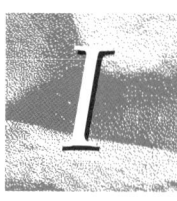

I was born right after the Second World War, one of eleven children born to Ray C. and Wanda Estep Meade in Kermit, West Virginia, a small town founded by my great-grandfather William Thomas Meade in 1910. My parents grew up only half a mile from each other, one inside the city limits and one outside. But that short half mile separated two totally different worlds, and I feel fortunate to have been exposed to both.

Although we moved from Mingo County to Wyoming County in 1950 when Dad found work in the coal mines, my brother and I would visit our grandparents for weeks at a time each summer from the mid-1950s to the mid-'60s, and my love for Mingo County has

CHAPTER 4: METRO VALLEY

never weakened. This story contains some of my fondest memories of my grandparents.

My paternal grandparents were Lorenza Dow and Anna Marcum Meade. I only knew them as Mommy and Poppy Meade. Poppy was a very tall, distinguished gentleman who walked very proudly and upright. He was chief of police in Kermit, but if you met him on the street, you wouldn't have known it. He dressed in three-piece suits and

Anna Meade-Matney, September 29, 1991.

carried a pocket watch that he would often take out of his watch pocket and look at. One of my favorite memories is thinking of how he loved looking at that watch. He patrolled the streets with a smile and a "Hello" for everyone, not with a gun. He was softspoken, but uphold the law he did. He preferred nonviolence, but only spoke once. If he told you to go home and behave, you best go or he would pick you up by the shirt collar like he was a big bear and take you home or to jail.

Now, Mommy Meade was as small as Poppy was big. She was four foot, ten inches and ninety pounds, but when she spoke, everyone took notice, including Poppy. Mommy was very Baptist and lived it. Time spent in Mommy and Poppy's home was quite different than in most homes in those days. Meals were always served in the dining room, with the table set with beautiful china and silverware. When you came to the table, you were to be dressed and well groomed. I can never remember seeing Mommy cook. Like magic, though, when she called you to eat, there was a beautiful table set for a king. Meals were eaten with little conversation, and you had to sit up straight and proper. I was always corrected when I didn't. We could sit at the table for a little while after eating, but when Poppy looked at his watch, we were excused. If it was after lunch, Poppy went back to work. If it was after dinner, we sat on the porch in wicker rockers and enjoyed the evening or visited with a neighbor. The two weeks I spent with Mommy and Poppy went quickly, after helping with some late spring cleaning such as windows, laundry, and floors. I remember that, when my hands were too small to wring out the mop, I would mop as Mommy wrung. Mommy suffered from severe asthma most of her life, and in her later years needed a little help with some of her chores. Now, in my later years, those small things are such wonderful memories.

The day before I was to go to my other grandparents', Poppy would hold my hand and walk me downtown for ice cream. I was so proud that he was my grandfather. The next day I would leave crying as they took me to spend the last two weeks of my vacation with my other grandparents. But I didn't cry for long.

My maternal grandparents were John and Mary Jane Chaffin Estep. The lived on a farm at Burning Creek, Mingo County, just on the other side of the city limits sign. It was time to enter another world. My brother John Dee would always be there when I arrived. We didn't get to see Grandpa Estep very much. He had a severe stroke and was bedfast. We would go in his room and visit just minutes at a time. He was propped up in bed, but tired quickly after talking. I remember how beautiful his snow white hair was. John has the same white hair now. We called Grandma Estep "Big Ma." She almost reminded me of a kettle, short and plump, always wearing an apron that was just a little bit soiled from drying her hands on it all day. Jolly, happy, and a bit loud, she was always glad to see anybody who came by. Visitors had to stay and eat something, even if just a piece of cake, which she always baked well. It wouldn't take me long to get settled in, and I lost my good grooming quickly. The shoes were the first to go.

Big Ma could make you think you were playing when you were really working—slopping hogs, feeding chickens, drawing water, and just about everything that needed doing on a farm. She knew what she was doing. Cooking supper was a family event. After she got that old stove started, she shouted out orders: "Go to the cellar and get me some beans and corn," "Draw me some more water," "Go to the smoke house and get me one of those hams." After everything was cooking, we washed up and set the table. It was set with an oilcloth and odds-and-ends dishes. In the few minutes before dinner, we would talk about our day with Grandpa, but when Big Ma hollered for dinner, he would tell us to go on and eat.

In that kitchen was a feast. Ma loved to eat, and after a hard day's work and play, we loved eating with her. She would have bowls of potatoes, corn, beans, gravy, and platters of ham; jars of canned goods such as jelly and apple butter; fresh churned butter; and of course, big, fluffy biscuits. We would eat until we couldn't walk, then we'd go sit on the porch until our food settled a little. Then it was time to carry water and get the kitchen cleaned up. We loved the two weeks spent on that farm every year. There was no inside bathroom or water. We worked hard, but we didn't know that until we grew up.

I was named after both my grandmothers, Anna and Mary. I have both of their personalities—a little bit city and a little bit country. My brother John Dee was named after both grandfathers. Dee was Poppy's nickname. John has both of their personalities, too. He looks like Grandpa Estep, but has Poppy's way of talking and entertaining kids.

Although my grandparents and parents have long since passed away, I still visit the cemeteries of my first home to pay my respects to the ones I have lost. They are gone in body, but will never be gone from my heart. I have nine brothers and sisters now who have their stories, too. Maybe they will write them down someday.

My Meade lineage is as follows:

Anna Meade-Matney, daughter of (d/o) Ray C. Meade, date of birth (b.) 5/17/1918, date of death (d.) 4/5/1976; son of (s/o) Lorenza Dow Meade, b. 7/9/1883, d. 6/7/1971, wife Anna Marcum, b. 5/29/1889, d. 3/3/1965; s/o William Thomas Meade, b. 10/1848, wife Levisa Spaulding, b. 8/1886; s/o James Alexander Meade, b. 1827, wife Amanda Lowe, b. 6/1828; s/o William Bingham Meade, Jr., b. 4/25/1798, d. 1850/1860, wife Jane Leander Rutherford, b. 3/8/1802; s/o William Bingham Meade, Sr., b. 8/22/1762, d. 2/11/1841, wife Mildred Esther Davis, b. 1776.

My Estep lineage is as follows:

Anna Meade-Matney, d/o Wanda Estep-Meade, b. 1/29/1919, d. 3/27/1970, husband Ray C. Meade; d/o John Estep, b. 1/5/1886, d. 1961, wife Mary Jane Chaffin, b. 4/29/1900, d. 10/5/1976; s/o William D. Estep, wife Missouri Ann Meade; s/o A.J. Estep, wife P. Lester.

Author: Anna Mary Meade-Matney wrote this story in memory of her maternal and paternal grandparents.

251-001-ST-WV-002-1998

Blackberries and Chow Chow

When I was a kid growing up on the Kanawha County side of Montgomery, West Virginia in the 1960s, summer often meant family outings going berry picking. We younger kids weren't allowed to go by ourselves, and Mom, Helen Rosella (Martin) Bainbridge, always gave us warning: "You watch out for snakes." When we made these trips as a family, it seemed that my father, Robert Bainbridge, knew where the best berry patches were located. Only years later did I find out that he had been watching these patches since they first bloomed, just waiting for them to ripen.

If there is ever a "Hall of Fame for Berry Pickers," then it will have to include my father, the berry-picking champion of all time. I can remember waking up many times early in the morning and asking my mother where he was. "Gone berry pickin'," was all she said. Leaving early in the morning to avoid the summer heat, he always took two buckets, one for blackberries and one for raspberries. Returning several hours later with both buckets full, he would sometimes go right back out for more berries.

One time my father came home earlier than usual, soaking wet, and all he told Mom was, "I lost my balance and fell in the river." The amazing thing is that the bucket he was holding landed on dry land, while he ended up in the river. All he did was change clothes and go right back.

The temptation of all those berries in our refrigerator was terrible, especially if there were blackberries. It didn't matter where Mom was in the house, she always heard the

refrigerator door open. "Stay out of them berries and close the door," she would yell.

Our kitchen was non-stop in the summer, as Mom would constantly be making preserves for the winter months. During the winter, we always opened the blackberry preserves first. If Mom would send a couple of jars to her friends, we kids made sure it was raspberry. But it was Mom's blackberry cobblers that were a special treat for the family during the summer months.

I can remember watching her make these cobblers, effortlessly rolling out homemade crust, layering the bottom of the pan, and then cutting the dough into strips and latticing the top layer. Mom always made her cobblers in a 9" x 13" pan, in which the bottom and corners would absorb all the juices, turning a delicious shade of purple. The corners were especially prized pieces that we all wanted, but there are only four corners and there were six of us. Seconds did not exist.

Chow Chow was another of Mom's specialties. She always planted a little garden spot during the summer and, like most mountain folk, she used nearly everything she planted out of necessity. "Let nothing go to waste," she would say as we cleaned up the garden spot each fall. We always had green tomatoes, and my mother's tradition was to use them to make her delicious Chow Chow that I remember so well.

Several years ago I was visiting a local minister and his wife. She had been cooking a pot of beans and asked if I would like a bowl. For a West Virginia boy raised on beans and cornbread, this was like asking a fish if he liked water. While the three of us were eating, I commented, "What I would love to have is some Chow Chow to go with my beans." This prompted her to ask, "What's Chow Chow?"

I thought this to be a strange question at first, until I remembered that she had grown up in western Canada. However, her husband was a southern boy. I looked at him and asked, "You're originally from Virginia aren't you? I bet you know all about Chow Chow?" He answered "Yes" to both questions, and then the two of us began explaining to his wife, "Chow Chow is a form of homemade relish made by many southern families, particularly in the rural areas, as a way of using everything in the garden. Its main ingredients were green tomatoes, onions, peppers, and cabbage. Depending on your taste it could be made sweet or hot."

I always regretted never taking time to pay closer attention to my mother's recipe, but I was just a young boy. I did remember most of the ingredients she used, especially the green tomatoes, but as for the other ingredients, they were a mystery. People just don't can as much as they used to years ago, and it seemed as though, every time I asked someone about making Chow Chow, they were in the same dilemma as me: remembering their parents or grandparents making it, but not knowing exactly how it was made. My older friends were not of any help, giving similar answers.

What I remember about making Chow Chow is that Mom used an old-fashioned hand-cranked grinder. She would chop up the ingredients, and it was my job to grind them into what I always called "the green mush." I remember the green tomatoes most of all because I didn't like the strong aroma. She would say, "I always add a couple of red bell peppers just to give it a little color, but if you want to spice it up a little, add a couple of hot peppers. Some people make it hot by using only hot peppers." Thankfully, Mom only made sweet Chow Chow. She would cook this mixture in a long roasting pan over two burners for what seemed forever.

Many years later, I was at a rummage sale and picked up an old cook book. While thumbing through this book I noticed two familiar words that had been hand written inside the back cover: "Chow Chow." I got all excited as I read this recipe. After nearly twenty years of regret, wondering about those missing ingredients, I had finally found a recipe that was very similar to my mother's recipe. It may not be exactly the same, but it was close enough. The memories it brought back of helping Mom making her Chow Chow can never be replaced.

Chow Chow

1 peck green tomatoes
1 peck peppers
1 gallon onions
3 heads of cabbage
vinegar to cover mixed with water
salt and sugar to taste
mixed spice in a rag

Cook about three hours.

For spices, Mom always used pickling spices, pouring them directly into the mixture. Biting down on one of these seeds was a most interesting experience.

Unless you plan to make a lot, I suggest you cut down the recipe.

Author: Richard Bainbridge is the fifth of six children. See index for additional work by Mr. Bainbridge.

252-001-ST-WV-002-1998

Montgomery (A Smoldering Ember)

Nothing is as sad as watching the city you live in and grew up in die a slow death. As the life blood of a city's industrial base declines, so does its population and services. As each store goes out of business you wonder if things will ever be the same, and know the chances of the city prospering as in times past are not good. Unfortunately, this is the sad fate of numerous small towns across West Virginia's coalfields. Montgomery, West Virginia, where I was born and lived for forty-three years, is one such town. Over the past twenty-five years, I've worked with many senior citizens in Montgomery; this story comes out of my experience of the town, and reflects some of their longer histories there as well.

Montgomery is located along the Great Kanawha River, approximately thirty miles upriver from and southeast of Charleston, on the border between Kanawha and Fayette Counties. Years ago, it had the unusual distinction of being one of the world's smallest metropolitan cities. To understand how a city of only three thousand can be considered metropolitan, you have to realize its significance to the surrounding area. In 1997, around twenty-five thousand people resided within the city and surrounding communities of the Upper Kanawha Valley, but many of these people commuted to Charleston or Beckley. In years past, it was Montgomery that served the valley, and an even larger population base. With its now-empty storefronts and streets serving only as shadows of a once-bustling atmosphere, it is hard to imagine Montgomery as the economic center of the area.

Today Montgomery, home of West Virginia Tech, is looked upon as a small college town, but for most of its history it was a coal town. "Coal is King" in West Virginia, and as the mines go, so goes the city. As the area mines and industrial base developed, especially during the late 1800s and early 1900s, so did Montgomery. For a while the city was known by three names: as Cannelton, its first name, because of the long-burning cannel coal that was mined nearby; as Coal Valley, its second name; and as Montgomery, after the city's first mayor, James C. Montgomery, the name that finally stuck. Conductors aboard the C&O Railroad passenger trains would for a time call out all three names when stopping in the city.

Montgomery was vibrant through the 1940s and still very much alive in the '50s and '60s, with plenty of life left even in the '70s. During those years, the coal mines operating in the Upper Kanawha Valley employed hundreds, if not thousands. The mines in operation today employ a fraction of those numbers. America's declining dependence on coal as a major fuel, along with the rise of strip mining and of automated mining machinery, has cut considerably into the work force. For many years, the C&O Railroad maintained a railyard at Handley, just two miles west of Montgomery, primarily for moving coal out of the valley, but with the demise of the coal industry in the valley, C&O Railroad (now part of CSX) opted to close the yard in the mid-1980s.

Other major employers for the area included Union Carbide's steel plant (now Elkem Metals) in Alloy, four miles east of the city, which once employed nearly three thousand workers and today employs just over three hundred. Until recent years, DuPont's chemical plant in nearby Belle very rarely had lay-offs or cutbacks. Montgomery General Hospital and West Virginia Tech struggle continually to remain open, with officials at both institutions, like other area businessmen, citing the decline in the area's population as part of their dilemma. This decline comes as many of the area's residents choose to move out of the valley rather than to make long commutes to jobs elsewhere. A classic domino effect has taken place: as Montgomery's industrial base declines, secondary business closures have cascading effects on all the surrounding businesses.

Another disappointment that affected the economy, not only of Montgomery but of the entire upper Kanawha Valley, occurred in the late 1980s when Interstate 64 was routed south along the West Virginia Turnpike, rather than following Old US Route 60 through the valley, as one proposal suggested. The whole area still feels the effects of political decisions that sacrificed an entire region for the growth of one city.

However, the problems of the area can also be attributed in part to progress and improvements. Before the better roads, a trip from the Montgomery area to Charleston meant at least a forty-five minute drive. Most area residents preferred to shop in Montgomery, and in its heyday, you could find just about everything you needed locally without having to go outside the area. Now, with improved roads, one can travel to Charleston or Beckley in little more than half the time it once took, and the lure of giant shopping malls has drawn our residents to those cities to shop.

The Montgomery I remember, in the 1960s and '70s, always had people on the streets, with no empty storefronts or empty

Chapter 4: Metro Valley

houses. Finding an apartment or house within the city during those years was so difficult that students at West Virginia Tech would pay rent in advance for the entire summer so that their landlords would hold their apartments for them when they returned to school in the fall.

The centerpiece of the city for many years was the G.C. Murphy Store. Some of my fondest memories are of going to Murphy's for hot dogs. We had bus and train stations, two theaters, a bowling alley, and two large chain grocery stores plus three smaller mom-and-pop–type grocery stores, and the streets were full of variety shops. In addition to the high school (at one time, two high schools) and college, there were also two grade schools and a junior high within the city. Now, besides a couple of small discount stores, two banks, and the college, it seems the type of businesses that are able to survive today—two drug stores, the hospital, and three funeral homes—are a reflection of the area's increasingly elderly population, the residents who have stayed behind and are slowly dying off. Unfortunately, this is more fact than figure of speech, as the area's declining industrial base does not attract new businesses or new residents.

Listening to Montgomery's older residents, you get a feeling for the way things use to be in the city. They speak of the city in its proper perspective as the hub of the Upper Kanawha Valley, even more alive than I remember, growing up in the 1960s. "We had everything the big cities had!" residents say, when asked about the past. "Nice hotels, restaurants, a bakery . . . the old Fayette Boiling Company supplied our dairy needs. All the stores stayed open until 9 PM and were busy when they closed their doors. The C&O trains made several daily stops in the city, and you could almost set your watch by them. There was something happening all the time—celebrations, street dances, always something to do. During the '30s and '40s, all the 'Big Bands' played concerts at the college. The weekends got pretty wild at times, as all the small bars throughout the city kept people on the streets all hours of the night." Some residents proudly remember when the local radio station, WMON-AM, went on the air in 1946, because at the time it was unusual for a city as small as Montgomery to have its own radio station; others fondly remember when Harry S. Truman and John F. Kennedy made campaign stops in Montgomery during their presidential runs. The stories these older residents tell of Montgomery are of a city whose flame once burned brightly.

However, along with past prosperity, these older residents also speak of a darker side to the city's past. Stories handed down by their parents tell of a Montgomery from the 1880s through the 1920s that was as wild as any of the wild west towns. "Weekends were particularly wild," they say, "especially when the miners all got paid. Local residents would come out of all the surrounding hollows and converge on Montgomery's drinking and entertainment establishments. Gambling, prostitution, and gangs were all part of the city as well. Fights were common occurrences during those early years, with things sometimes getting out of hand. If someone didn't come home from the previous night, everyone knew where to find the body." I can remember my mother warning me many times to stay away from the C&O Railroad trestle over Morris Creek on the west end of town. I always thought it was because it was a favorite place for the area's winos to "sleep it off." Not until I learned of this trestle's morbid reputation did I fully understand why she warned me to stay away. The older residents explained, "During those years, the C&O Railroad trestle was beyond the edge of town, and it was a favorite place for dumping bodies of men that had been killed downtown the previous night."

A story appeared in a 1904 issue of *The Cincinnati Enquirer* about the lawlessness of Fayette County, and of its largest city, Montgomery. This article describes the judge of the criminal courts, who was himself under indictment for embezzlement, and the county sheriff, who was convicted of violations of liquor laws. Thankfully for its citizens, Montgomery did improve through the years, but its "wild west" reputation of the past is still spoken of today by its older residents. There is an old story that best illustrates this reputation. It's supposed to have actually happened, but there is really no way to confirm the story. In the 1940s, when the C&O still ran several daily trains through the Kanawha Valley, a rather inebriated man came to the train station in Charleston one night and told the ticket agent, "I want a one way ticket to hell." According to the story, the ticket agent sold him a ticket to Montgomery.

Montgomery may not be hell, but it did burn brightly at one time. Looking at the city streets today, it is hard to imagine how busy they once were and the "wild west" reputation the city once had. When the state prison relocated to Mount Olive, just north of the city, opening in 1994, it was hoped that it would help to regenerate the economy of the area surrounding Montgomery. Unfortunately, one business can not replace the thousands of people who once lived and worked in the Upper Kanawha Valley.

The secondary support businesses that residents hoped to develop around the state prison may never develop to the status of

yesteryear. In this commuter-oriented world of today, the easier access to better roads leading out of the area also makes it easier for workers and goods to come into the valley from outside. The sad fate for the area is that, without its strong industrial base to hold onto its population, Montgomery's once brightly burning flame is only a smoldering ember of memories past.

Hope is eternal. Some residents look for better days, but only time will tell if the winds of opportunity will be able to rekindle the flames once more for Montgomery and the Upper Kanawha Valley.

AUTHOR: Richard Bainbridge. Mr. Bainbridge, like many others, found himself traveling more and more frequently to Charleston for services that were no longer available in Montgomery; he left his home and moved to Charleston in early 1998. See index for additional work by Mr. Bainbridge.

253-001-ST-WV-002-1998

The Red Crayon

I've written this story down in honor of my late sister, Margie Fay Sheets, who always told it at family gatherings and hoped that someday it would be recorded for posterity.

Margie was the oldest of my brothers and sisters, and in many ways she was like a second mother to us younger ones. She always had stories to tell about the family, and one of her favorites about me was about the "red crayon." In actuality, I was too young when this story took place to remember any of the details. But each time she would tell this story, I would always defend myself by saying, "I never said that!"

My mother, Helen Rosella (Martin) Bainbridge, would clean the entire house each summer, which usually meant at least one room would be painted. It was time consuming moving furniture from one side of the room, painting that wall, and repeating the process until the room was finished. On this particular occasion Margie described, the day was warm and humid, so painting took a little longer than usual. None of us younger kids was allowed to help, so each time we came into the room we were told to leave.

After the room had been painted and all the furniture moved back into place, my mother walked into the room an hour later and found me drawing on her freshly painted walls with a red crayon. As in many West Virginia families, when your full name is used, it usually means that you're in big trouble. "Richard Charles Bainbridge!" my mother said. Hearing the tone of my mother's voice, Margie came into the room to see what was happening, and describes the incident this way.

"We just painted this room!" my mother exclaimed. "Why are you marking on the wall with a red crayon?" she asked. Margie said I just stood there motionless and said nothing. Again my mother asked the question, "Why are you marking on that wall with a red crayon? Answer me!" Margie described "this look of fear" that came over my face, adding that, after being asked the same question a third time, I was close to tears. It was at this point that I spoke those famous words that I claim I never said. She described this sad little voice that came out of me and simply said, "Because I didn't have any blue."

After hearing me say this, Margie said, she and my mother burst out laughing. She always ended the story with "You couldn't deny it because you still had the evidence in your hand," laughingly adding, "You were 'caught red handed.' But what you said and how you said it with those sad eyes was so cute that Mom couldn't whip you even though you deserved it."

I only wish I could say this once more to my sister Margie. For posterity, "I never said that." Love, Ricky.

AUTHOR: Richard Bainbridge. He adds that, to this day, his favorite color is the color blue. See index for additional work by Mr. Bainbridge.

254-001-ST-WV-002-1998

Memories of Grandma

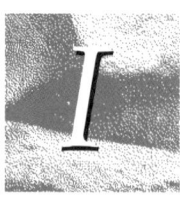

In 1962 it was barely dawn as I slipped out Grandma's back door. Everything was so beautiful, and the sparkling dew that was everywhere tickled my bare toes. The dew ran down my hand as I pulled a deep purple grape from the vines. As the sun peeked over the hill, I listened to the birds twitter awake. Shimmering in the sun, I saw a big spider in her jewel of a web. Alongside was a fence full of the most beautiful smelling flowers.

I think I was only four, living in Springfield, Massachusetts, when I first remember visiting my Grandma Myrtle Scraggs Stone in Marmet, West Virginia.

My memories of her consist of smells of Noxema and roses, a tender smile, and her sitting in the rocker in front of the fire brushing my long hair. To me it was so soothing and loving. While sitting on the front porch stringing green beans we watched the trains go by and tried to count all of the cars. It made me dizzy.

I have memories of delicious smells coming from her kitchen that made my mouth water. I sat on books at the table and always found a treat in the special drawer. My aunts and uncles would gather in the evenings playing the guitar and singing "The Old Rugged Cross." This was fun for everyone. I remember Grandma slipping me cookies and milk. At Sunday dinners, the men would watch ball games on TV, the women would cook and talk, and my cousins and I played in the yard. We ran in and out of the house knowing we would be scolded.

I helped take care of Grandma before she passed away. She wasn't anyone famous or unusual. I loved her deeply and when she died a part of me died with her. The memories she gave me will always live on in my heart.

I guess each of us in our own way loved her. I hope to see her one day and tell her how much I have loved and missed her.

AUTHOR: Kathryn Campbell resides in Dunbar, West Virginia. Her goal is to be successful in a writing career, spoil her three grandchildren, and travel.

255-001-ST-WV-002-1998

E. M. JONES and his trusty .32 calibre "gat" which he used to nab spies. The little Milepost 65 was given to him by his friends when he retired last year at age 65.

Fastest Gun In West (Virginia)

Trackman Caught Spies Like Flies

A November 18, 1960 Chessie News *article recounted Grandpa Jones' spy-catching adventures.*

E.M. Jones: Company Man and Spy Catcher

My grandpa Edgar Matthew Jones was born July 21, 1895, at Merritt's Creek in Cabell County, West Virginia. He worked for the Chesapeake and Ohio (C&O) Railway for fifty years and four months, from age fifteen to sixty-five, as track section foreman. When it snowed, he had to get his crew together and go clean off his section of track, working many hours until the tracks were clear. He wore bib overalls, long underwear, flannel shirts, long wool socks, lace-up boots, and a fur hat that had ear flaps.

Grandpa Jones shot his first rabbit at age eight. He shot it with a muzzle-loader that his grandfather had brought with him from England when he originally came to this country. His grandfather's surname, Jons, had been changed to Jones.

At age twenty, as he was playing shortstop for the C&O baseball team, Grandpa Jones was hit by a line drive that knocked out most of his teeth and caused a speech impediment. He also chewed tobacco and, together with the speech impediment, it was very difficult to understand him when he was talking. He carried a coffee can in his car to "spit in," and his side window and door were always brown with "amber" ("tobacco juice").

Grandpa was about five foot, five inches tall and weighed around 150 pounds. He was very strong. One time during a thunderstorm near Yates Crossing, not far from Milton in Cabell County, West Virginia, a tree fell on him and they carried him home. He was in bed two or three days, and then back to work. To my knowledge, this is the only time in fifty years that he missed any work.

I was four years old when Grandpa and Grandma lived at Yates Crossing. I lived at Fry, and visited them often. One spring night, I was spending some time with Grandpa in his work office, which was behind his gray C&O railroad company house. A big sycamore tree was between the house and Grandpa's shanty work

Grandpa Jones as a contract railroad worker in Ashland, Kentucky at age seventy-five, in 1970.

office. I was tired and I left Grandpa to his work and was passing the tree when out from behind the tree stepped a "ghost," saying, "come with me, come with me." I stopped and could not speak or move because I was very frightened. The "ghost" saw that I was really scared. It was my grandma with a white sheet over her.

My grandma Georgie Hall Jones was a real good cook. She made me a marble cake often when I was a teen. She was born at Hurricane in 1899, and died of diabetes complications at the C&O hospital at Huntington in 1957.

Clearing track was important, but when Grandpa Jones retired in 1960, he was recognized in C&O's *Chessie News* for his finest achievement: catching spies. "Fastest gun in West (Virginia)," he captured his first three enemy agents during World War I. The article read,

> In 1917, the trackman captured a man, woman and a boy together near Cabin Creek Junction as the man illegally snapped pictures of a power plant and C&O structures.
>
> "I followed them through the woods and saw them taking pictures," Mr. Jones said. "That area was a mean place in those days and I was carrying my gun," he added.
>
> "I told them they were under arrest. The man, who was dark and swarthy, went for a gun in his pocket but I beat him to it," the C&Oer remembered.

The man was later convicted. On another occasion, Grandpa Jones caught two men, and later, in 1936, six more men, for eleven spies captured in all. His words on retiring were, "I hope the next one that takes my place will give better service than I have."

After retirement, Grandpa did contracting work for various companies that required railroad work. He did this for fifteen years until age eighty, when an automobile accident slowed him down. Grandpa Jones died of a heart attack in August, 1977 at the age of eighty-two, while putting a new roof on the garage of his Huntington home, and was buried at Ridgelawn Cemetery in Huntington.

AUTHOR: *Arno "Sam" Lucas was born in Fry, West Virginia, on July 20, 1940. He was both the grandson and friend of E.M. Jones. He moved to Huntington, West Virginia when he was a teenager, and attended Marshall University in Huntington. He has resided in several different places, but now lives across the Ohio River from Huntington in South Point, Ohio. He is vice-president of Giorgi Interiors in Chesapeake, Ohio. His mother, Emogene Leach, lives in Huntington.*

256-001-ST-WV-002-1998

Lessons from Mom and Dad

When it comes to West Virginia, there are two things that come to mind that are most important to me. Actually, they are people: my husband and his parents.

I am originally from Wichita, Kansas. One day, my great sense of adventure and my desire to see the mountains got the best of me. That is when I traveled all the way to West Virginia, on high school spring break in 1982, on a Greyhound bus. I'm not sorry I did, because not only did I see some of the most beautiful land in the country, I also met my future husband—now my present husband, Earl. He introduced me to two of the nicest people in the world, Colene and Jim Heim, better known as "Mom" and "Dad."

Let me tell you something about Mom and Dad Heim: no matter what, they always have room for one more. Whether it be at the table for a meal or to spend the night, their house just expands to the size it needs to be.

Earl and I fell in love and got married in the fall of 1982. Jim and Colene took me into their house and welcomed me into their family. We were married on May 24, 1985. Colene coordinated the wedding, which was held at St. Andrews United Methodist Church in St. Albans, West Virginia, where Colene and Jim live. Earl and I were living in Florida at the time and came home to West Virginia for the wedding. We moved back to West Virginia in November of 1985 with our two-month-old son Joshua, and lived in the St. Albans area until our daughter, Chelsea, who was born in June of 1989, was two and a half months old.

I have learned a great many things from my parents-in-law. Here are just a few of them: Colene has taught me how to do things I never dreamed I would do, such as how to can spaghetti sauce and green beans, and how to bake "homemade light bread." She also taught me to make hard Christmas candy and candy Easter eggs. Jim taught me about patience, which he practices so well each time we all come to visit. With four sons, four daughters-in-law, and thirteen grandchildren, he needs it . . . and he has quite a bit.

Most of all, Mom and Dad have both taught me about giving, as they have always been generous about helping us whenever Earl was laid off work. They've also taught me to "hang in there" and keep a strong faith in God during the trying times. Mom will tell me to "keep my chin up and things will get better," and do you know what? They always do! Mom and Dad Heim are about the best grandparents who ever lived, next to my own parents, of course. I am very blessed to have them.

Dad Heim is a retired mail carrier and has since done some truck driving. Mom Heim has been everything from a homemaker to a scout leader. She has been president of the West Virginia State Association of Letter Carriers Auxiliary and president of the United Methodist Women's group at church, and is a retired Realtor.

I would like to dedicate this story to Anita Heim, Colene and Jim's daughter, who lived to be almost twenty-one years old. She died in October, 1981, of juvenile diabetes. I never got to meet her and look forward to the day when I will.

AUTHOR: Diane Heim is a teacher's assistant in Buchanan, Virginia. She and Earl are still happily married and have lived in Buchanan since August of 1989. Earl has worked at various jobs, and has his associate's degree in business management. He is working toward getting his bachelor's. Josh is now age twelve and Chelsea is eight.

257-001-ST-WV-002-1998

Chapter 5

Mountain Lakes

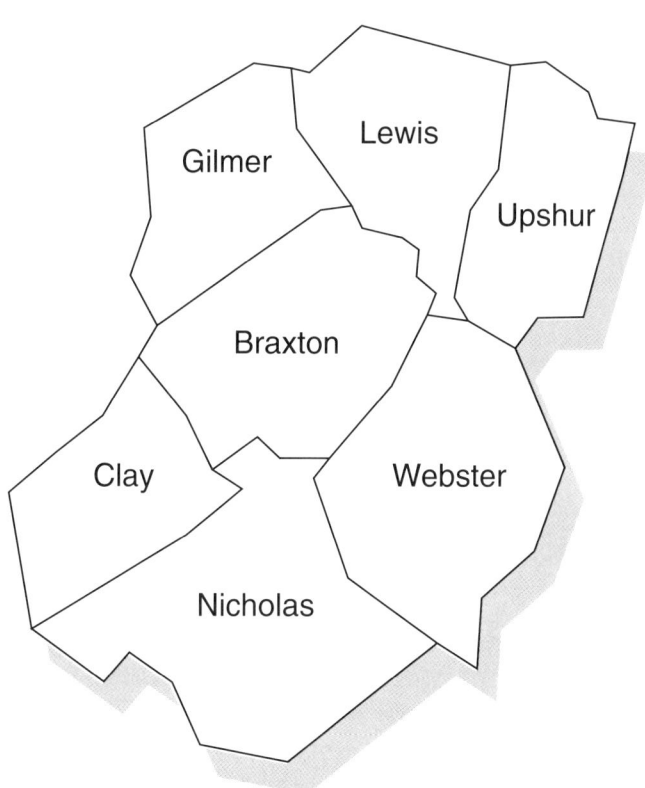

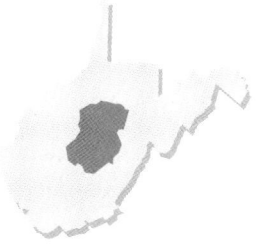

The Honeymoon

We were not expected to show up in Richwood, West Virginia, that night, July 12, 1968. Oh, to be sure, we had reservations at the New Northern, the only hotel in Richwood. So did the other two dozen members of my summer school class field trip to Cranberry Glades. Stan Ash, class instructor, and the others had arrived there that evening in the pouring rain. They speculated, as the hour grew later, that we would not show up. After all, we would have to drive from Huntington to Greenup, Kentucky, back to Huntington, then on to Richwood. Riding with us was another classmate, Miss Susan Ferrell, but we still were not "looked for." We were going to be married in Greenup that afternoon. We were not expected to show our faces in Richwood.

Jim and I had originally not planned to marry until 1970, but my parents had recently decided to move to Detroit, Michigan, for a two-year period. I had not been invited, as they insisted I complete my final two years at Marshall University in Huntington. So we decided to move the wedding forward, unbeknownst to our families. I was not yet of age in West Virginia to marry without parental consent, so Kentucky, where the legal age was eighteen rather than twenty-one, became our target.

So in mid-June, 1968, we had driven to Ashland, Kentucky, to begin the paperwork. But when I said my address was in West Virginia and we were told we could not marry in Kentucky, we decided some deception was in order, along with a drive down the Ohio River to Greenup County. As we drove near Greenbo Lake, we chose a broken-down mailbox, unused in appearance, as my Kentucky address. At the Greenup County courthouse we said the appropriate things, signed the appropriate forms, and were then told the courthouse would close at noon, in a half hour. We must get the blood test completed quickly.

Off to the local doctor's office. When he asked where was the mailbox?, we replied, "Oh, out by the lake." Fine by him. He performed the blood test and sent us back to the courthouse for our license. Little did we suspect that my arm would bruise from elbow to wrist. More deception. I told my future mother-in-law later that week that the bruise resulted from dropping a heavy box as I moved into the dorm for the summer. She said nothing more.

Our thoughts had been to wed on July 19, but we learned that the license was only good for thirty days from the blood test, which meant moving things up a week. That was the date chosen for the class field trip!! No sweat. Not much anyway. What to tell Jim's folks? Jim "elected" to go along on the field trip, which was okay. They were planning to be out of town that weekend. After they left, we raided his mom's bureau for the wedding ring she'd kept for us ever since we'd bought the set and I'd put on the diamond. Then we took the family dog to the kennels, picked up our friend Susan Ferrell, and hied ourselves to Greenup.

The newlyweds, Kay and Jim Hill, in 1968, a few months after "The Honeymoon."

Susan needed a ride to Richwood, and we needed a witness for the wedding, so that fell into place nicely. Of course she knew what was going on and brought a nice outfit along for the occasion. I'd bought one courtesy of a sister's checking account, a pretty white mini-skirted dress, just right for an afternoon elopement. Jim's Aunt Betty had assisted us also, accompanying me to the gynecologist for the pre-marital exam and providing a lovely flower arrangement for me to carry. It seemed that much of Huntington knew our plans.

Judge Lewis McCubbin performed the ceremony and we returned to Huntington for a wedding supper. The food was not well prepared and the three of us were queasy on the rainy drive into the mountains toward Richwood. Susan's only comment was, "All you two do is look at each other."

Near ten o'clock that night we finally arrived in Richwood. The rest of the class then told us they'd long since given up looking for us. After all, they, too, knew we were being married that day. We had not been expected to show up in Richwood that night.

The hotel owner apologized for our accommodations, as nobody had told her we were newlyweds, and the bathroom was down the hall. The New Northern Hotel was a rambling frame building that had arisen from the ashes of the old Northern Hotel a few decades previous. It creaked and the windows leaked, but it sported a lovely wide wooden staircase leading to a spacious lounge on the second floor. All the rooms opened into this area, and all the doors had transoms above. Many of these transoms were permanently stuck open, ours included.

Jim and I escaped into our room as quickly as possible, while classmates remained lounging in the common area well after midnight. We finally became aware of our surroundings and some of their limitations some time later, after a hearty round of applause following what must have been a loud vocal performance from the newlyweds. The open transom had allowed every sound we'd made to be carried to all the folks just outside our doorway!

The night continued along similar lines, but eventually the sound coming into our room was the snoring of Mr. Ash, immediately next door. Finally the night ended. Mr. Ash trudged along the hallway administering wake-up raps on the doors of all the other rooms. He passed us by. We didn't need the knock anyway. We'd never been asleep.

The entire class sleepily walked to Prelaz' Restaurant for breakfast and to order brown bag lunches for the trip into the Glades. I asked for a bacon, lettuce, and tomato sandwich and buttermilk. We picked up our bags as we paid for breakfast, then sauntered off into the heavy mist on the boardwalk leading into Round Glade.

Many hours later, weary from both the sleepless night and the seemingly endless trudging over grassy hummocks, uphill, downhill, across creeks, we stopped on top of Round Hill for lunch. When I bit into my sandwich I discovered yet another round in the continuing comedy of errors into which this honeymoon had deteriorated. I had a cold, greasy, fried egg sandwich, and I have never liked fried eggs! My generous bridegroom gave me the sandwich he'd received and he ate the one I'd been given. I found out much later that he didn't like fried eggs either. The buttermilk was warm, but it seemed delicious to me.

Mr. Ash excused the two of us from the afternoon's hiking and observing, and we returned to the New Northern. A wedding present lay on the bed—but from whom? None other than the proprietor herself. Still embarrassed about our accommodations, she'd purchased a lovely sheet and pillowcase set as her apology. Now, the hotel bill for two nights may have outweighed the cost of the gift, but not by much. The room was only five dollars a night, so we've always been pretty sure she lost money on our stay, or at least did little more than break even.

Thirty years later, still married, three children and one grandchild to boot, we continue to laugh as we remember that weekend. How many other couples begin married life with two dozen classmates, a creaky old hotel, and a fried egg sandwich? But what should we have anticipated? After all, we were not expected to show up in Richwood that night.

AUTHOR: *Kay Hill. See index for additional work by Mrs. Hill.*

258-001-ST-WV-002-1998

Mom and Dad's Best-Kept Secret

My children have often told me that I probably have coal dust and ramp juice in my veins. From that statement, you can gather that I'm proud to be from West Virginia. I was born in a holler (I never call it a "hollow") in Upper Glade, and spent my formative years in Webster County in the 1930s and '40s, back in the good old days when times were bad. My parents, Luther and Eva (Wright) Williams, did their best for their family and their community. They also had the best-kept secret of anyone I know. You see, they never let any of their seven children know that we were poor.

My dad had followed in his father's footsteps, working in the timber business and living in the logging camps. Now, as his family grew, he took a job with the State Road Commission and saved to buy a place of his own. Soon, he bought a few acres in a holler, and built a little house that quickly became a loving home. For extra

Chapter 5: Mountain Lakes

This photo was taken in front of the Upper Glade Methodist Church in Webster County in about 1938. We were very proud of our 100% community involvement in the church.

Front row (l-r): Sammy Given, Denzil Paugh, Wellington Moffatt, Paul Holcolm, Troy McClure, Gerald Springston, Billy Paugh, Chester Johnson, Betty Lou Armentrout, Willa Armentrout, Jacqueline Armentrout, Gloragene Williams (the author), Shirley Ann Williams (author's sister), Phyllis Wright, Harold Wright, Archie Wright, John Henderson, Deral "Dubby" Williams (author's brother), Walter Hinkle, Jr.

Second row: Boy Wright, Junior Paugh, Gordon Hamrick, Lyman Williams (author's brother), Leonard Gross, Ford Williams (author's brother), Jennings Wright, Gerald Coakley, Arden Hissom, Acie McClure, Vincent Gillespie, Gordon Knight, Robert Barger, Loyd Moffatt, Robert Handschumaker, James Clevenger, Bernard Conner, Lowell Williams (author's brother), James Conner, Herman Cogar, Clinton Hamrick, Orville Knight, Charles Armentrout, Philip Cogar, Otto Gross, Elden Handschumaker.

Third row: Norma Hamrick, Shelton Hamrick, Billy Knight, Ruby Knight, Betty Given, Barbara Given, Patty Conner, Ada Jarvis, Evelyn Knight, Hazel Knight, Mary Ellen Stalnaker, Lucy Jarvis, Daisy Jarvis, Von Johnson, Emma Johnson, Aileen Dillon, Georgia Woods, Eulajean Cogar, Phyllis Hamrick, Cecila Case, Flora Dell Williams (author's sister), Juanita Baughman, Agnes Brewster, Ms. Leo Moffatt, Mrs. Clarence Henderson, Dorothy Given, Mrs. Dora Woods, Anita June Johnson, Mary Helen Gross, Harold Gross, Barbara Case, Irma Lou Gross, Marjorie Given, Eileen Gillespie.

Fourth row: Robert Hardway, Fred Jarvis, Roland Miller, Agnes Sexton, Edna Johnson, Ona Lee Johnson.

Fifth row: Verdun Hamrick, Alma Hamrick, Morg Holcolm, Johnny Holcolm, Herndon Given, Phyllis Given, Dan Conner, Frieda Johnson, Wilma Johnson, Frances Matthews, Geraldine Williams, Hazel Moffatt, Goldie Given, Frankie Woods, Faye Matheny, Golda Moffatt, Ruby Coakley, Martha Jean Paugh, Geraldine Miller, Betty Lou Rankin, (skip across to:) Betty Lou Gillespie, Mable Hardway, Harold Gillespie, Leslie Coalton, Ernest Miller.

Sixth row (seated ladies): Mrs. Bill (Bess) Matthews, Virginia Matthews holding Louie, Ada Gallogly, Mildred Holcomb, Mrs. Susan Given, Mrs. Ike Green, Eva Williams (author's mother), Shirley Smith, Mrs. Oris Smith, Helen Smith, Goldie Given with Eunice, Mrs. Verdun (Alma) Hamrick with Elden, Mrs. Ernest Miller, Patty Moffatt, Howard Moffatt, Clarence Henderson, Rev. Andrew Coakley, Virgil Payne.

Seventh row: Charles Paugh holding Joe, Elma Paugh, Mrs. Ted (Marion) Gross, Mrs. Ed (Loretta) Hambrick, Nellie Coakley, Mrs. Conner, Mrs. Gardner, Philip Barger, William Barger, Leslie Wright, George Miller, Dewey Given, Amy Cogar, Ruth Hardway, Dolly Hissom, Owen Miller, Alice Miller, Ted Gross with son Howard Gross, John Sill, Carl Henderson, Hercy Given, Roy Smith.

Back row: Bill Matthews holding Charles, Mrs. Matheny, Mrs. Steel, Mr. Conner, Pauline Barger, Hanse Given, Ben Moffatt, Mrs. Moffatt, Oris Smith, Luther Williams (author's father), Dorr Hardway, B.R. Hissom, George Handschumaker.

money, my dad repaired shoes, having a full set of shoe lasts that had been handed down by his father, Joseph Mayse Williams. He also grew herbs, such as calomel and garlic, which he sold or traded. Dad also had the only patch of Indian Pipe that anyone knew of, and it was pretty much in demand in those days. I always assumed that my father learned the medicinal value of this plant from his Indian ancestors. Supposedly, the juice from the stem would cure almost any ailment; therefore, my dad was asked to share this plant during an outbreak of "pinkeye." This mysterious plant thrived in a dark and secluded part of our woods. It was ghostly white, and had no leaves or green coloring whatsoever. Since that time, I've learned that Indian Pipe, or Ghost Plant, has no need of leaves or sunlight, because it does not use photosynthesis. As a kid, I didn't know about such things, so I believed that the eerie plant was guarding the site of an ancient Indian burial

ground. Therefore, my father's medicinal herbs were left undisturbed by me.

My mother was quite a seamstress for her day. Her sewing was extraordinary, in that she would take old coats, dresses, and other pieces of clothing and transform them into beautiful garments for us or for the neighborhood kids. All of our clothing was "Mom-made," including our winter coats. As cold weather approached, my mom was overwhelmed with anxious mothers who brought their old garments to be cut down and made into clothing for their children. It was not unusual to hear someone ask, "Evie, do you think you can get two coats out of this one?" And, being my mom, she probably did. Many times the only pay was another used garment that would be made into clothing for us. My mom looked through the Sears, Roebuck catalog, and designed our clothing in the latest fashions. We would be the first kids in school to have hooded coats, peek-a-boo dresses, or poodle skirts. Many designs were borrowed from that book before it was relegated to the outhouse. Incidentally, our outhouse was a three-holer . . . nothing poor about us.

I've often wondered how many Upper Gladers remember participating in the Young People's Program that my mother held every Sunday night at the church. All of the young folks attended and sang, read poems, said prayers, or performed in various plays. My mother was instrumental in helping many young people develop their talents. Some really good musical groups grew out of this Sunday night ritual. I remember the Staton Brothers; Floradell and Nellie, a duet; the Knight Sisters; the Cochrans; the Three Bettys; and of course, my family, the Williams Family Singers.

These same talented young people would "put on" some wonderful and sometimes hilarious plays that offered a real show of talent. The church would send away for scripts that my mom requested. Then she would pick the cast, re-writing or adding scenes to accommodate her large group. For these plays, the older kids were required to help the tiny kids make a quick costume change. Imagine their laughter once, when one of them quickly yanked my dress off to reveal my nice new undershirt made from a sugar sack: across my chest in bold black letters were the words "Forty pounds when packed"!

These plays were a huge success in Upper Glade. On several occasions, some of the nearby towns would request that our play be performed there. We were thankful to Hanse Given and Morg Holcolm for loading the entire cast on their flatbed trucks for the trip. My mother was presented with at least three Certificates of Award for her work in the community. In my mind's eye, I can still see these certificates pasted to our newspaper-covered wall in the holler.

After we moved out of the holler and into "town," my brother Ford would set up a "stage" on the front porch in the evenings. There, complete with a microphone and amplifier, he and his friend Hays Johnson would play their musical instruments for anyone with nerve enough to sing—thus the entire community was entertained, or so we thought. The young singers "on stage" included my two sisters, Flo and Shirl, my brother Dub, the Cochrans, the Sandys, and many, many others. Members of my family would often "warm up" the audience for some pretty famous radio personalities who made personal appearances in the area: Ernest Tubb, Buddy Starcher, Roy Acuff, Little Jimmy Dickens, Mother Maybelle and the Carter Family, The Delmore Brothers, and others. Many of these stars, when they heard Ford pick the Wildwood Flower, would urge him to go to Nashville. Looking back, I've often wondered how many of the neighbors living near that "stage" wished for all of us to pack up and move to Nashville . . . or anywhere.

Although there was not always a variety of food, we never knew a hungry day, unlike some "poor" kids that we knew. Dad always managed to provide us with, at least, the staples: pinto beans, cornbread, eggs, potatoes, and gravy. On Sunday, after church, my brothers Lowell and Lyman would catch a couple of chickens and let my little brother Dub chop their heads off. I hated watching the headless creatures run about, but soon all was forgotten as they became a pot of delicious chicken and dumplings. When the cold winter came, and only then, my mother would go to the fruit press and get out a jar of something that she had canned in the summer. For desserts, we could dig apples from their burial hole; munch on dried peaches, prunes, or apples; or pop corn from our huge supply in the granary. As the snow piled higher around our little house, Dad would get out a shoe last and use it to crack black walnuts, giving us yet another treat.

Electricity never made it to our holler, so we read by oil lamp light or firelight and, like most people around, we went to bed early. Our perishables were kept on a rock ledge in a little spring, which was also the source of our fresh water supply. I can still taste that cold spring water. People came from all around to pick huckleberries, blackberries, and apples from our farm. Before leaving, they would usually fill a jug with our clear, cold spring water to take home with them.

In the lazy summer days, we kids would try to earn some cash by selling huckleberries or picking bean beetles. We never

got very rich. Huckleberries sold for twenty cents if we filled a five-pound lard bucket to the brim. As for the bean beetles, any grateful farmer was willing to pay five cents to "buy back" a snuff can full of beetles picked from his garden. I was not adept at filling my snuff can. Every time I would try to add one, two or three would fly out. Finally, my little brother showed me how he did it. He just squeezed the little buggers before he put them into the can. Ugh!! Problem solved . . . and the picky farmers who counted before never bothered to count my beetles after that.

No amount of money could ever erase my memories of growing up in West Virginia and, in reminiscing, I've decided that perhaps I was wrong about my parents' secret . . . I've just realized how truly rich we were.

Author's Note: A shoe last set consisted of an iron stand about twenty-two inches high and many iron foot-shaped forms, or lasts, in various shoe sizes. Once the proper size last was placed on the stand, the shoe to be repaired was inverted over this "iron foot," and the new sole or heel was tacked or sewn on. The set, which contained thirty-two items, cost my grandfather, Joseph Mayse Williams, a whopping fifty-nine cents, from Sears, Roebuck and Company in 1900. In addition to repairing shoes, the lasts were used to repair harnesses and tinware and, of course, to crack black walnuts.

AUTHOR: *Jean Rigsby retired from AT&T Technologies in Phoenix, Arizona. She is the mother of three children—Mike Rigsby, Pam Chernault, and Kim Reynolds—and the grandmother of nine; she lives near Baltimore, Maryland.*

259-001-ST-WV-002-1998

One-room Bailey School on the Bailey Ridge Road, just half a mile from Ruth's home. The Board of Education bought the property in 1967. The school closed in 1968, and the schoolhouse is now used as a community building.

Thoughts of West Virginia

he sun was shining brightly this morning as I looked out my window on the Bailey Ridge Road in Upshur County, West Virginia. A soft breeze sent hosts of leaves fluttering downward from my maple trees. The ground was soon covered with nature's own carpet of reds, golds, browns, and greens. A beautiful sight to behold.

I grew up loving West Virginia. If one were to ask me why, my reasons could fill a book. Its natural beauties, the peaceful community where I grew up, the good people I knew, all played a part in my love for our state.

One vivid memory is of a one-room school I attended on Mulberry Ridge, near French Creek. We dressed warm, wore four-buckled arctics over our shoes, walked a mile over roads often covered with mud, ice, or knee-deep snow to reach the school house. There we stood around a pot-bellied stove to get warm. We carried our lunches in round tin pails. We had two fifteen-minute recesses to play games.

At noon, after eating, we played or went to eat persimmons on the hillside, or pick up chestnuts behind the school.

We sat at desks that showed the scars of time by cuts, scratches, and scribbles. We enjoyed going up to a long recitation bench for each class. Walking up front allowed us to exercise and break the monotony. Now and then the school had box socials.

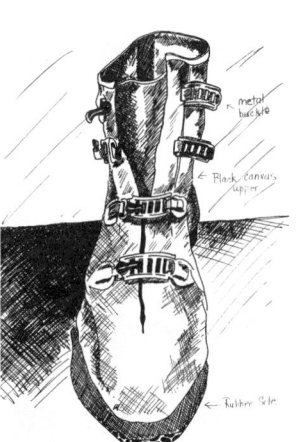

Four-buckled arctic.

Another activity was the telling of ghost stories and folklore tales. As one story goes, a drummer stopped at a store to sell his wares and heard some men talking about an old cemetery at the top of a steep hill far from the village store. The cemetery was thought to be haunted, but no one had the nerve to go see. The drummer said, "I'll go if someone will

The Ensors attended a few schools while growing up, including Slab Camp School, here, February 12, 1918. Front row (l-r): Goff Hefner, Cecil Snyder, Nellie Hefner, Nellie (Sallie Swecker) Bennett, Hallie Heavner (boy holding sign), Milton Snyder (Ada Ensor's brother), Gary Linger and Arlie Linger (Stella Perry was their Aunt and Mollie Linger was their mother), Ada Ensor (Minor Snyder's daughter), Cora Vandevender (married Clyde Cunningham), Clarence Heavner. Second row: Fred Jones (Charlie Jones' son), Tarsie Heavner (Roy Poling's first wife), Laura Heavner, Ora Douglas (teacher), Edith Jones (Charlie Jones' daughter), Blanch Heavner Sayres, Lundie Jessie Gould. Third row: Edwin Hyre, Roy Lanham, Dick Lanham, Guy Davis, Ira Jones, Gary Davis, Amie Hyre (Edwin Hyre's sister), Jud Hefner, Lee Heavner, Minnie Jones (in back with horse), Troy Duncan (holding horse).

go with me." A crippled man they called "Ol' Rheumatick" was sitting in a wheelchair. He said, "I'll go with you, but you will have to carry me."

So the drummer put Ol' Rheumatick on his back; shortly after they reached the cemetery fence, they heard a voice inside the fence say, "Did you get anything tonight?" Another voice said, "Yes, I have two right outside the fence." The drummer said, "No, you only have one." He threw Ol' Rheumatick down, "You can have him, but don't take me," he said. He broke into a run, but when he reached the store, Ol' Rheumatick had already beat him there.

My thoughts just turned back to another page of life, to an eight-room school I transferred to. There was no recitation bench. I was so disappointed, I wrote a poem about the one-room school. Two of its lines spoke of my fond memories:

> We didn't sit back in our seats at class,
> As if too lazy to move.

But I did adjust, and the things that really matter are still here in West Virginia.

Author's Note: I asked an elderly gentleman from French Creek, West Virginia if he had heard of four-buckled arctics. He said "Yes, indeed," that he might have a pair upstairs in the old home place. My daughter, Karen Ensor Brown, did this sketch from one that he brought me. Four-buckled arctics were worn over your shoes. The soles were rubber, and the uppers were some kind of repellent black canvas, because they never leaked. There was a tongue you pushed in, and you brought each buckle across the front opening. The tongue kept the water from getting through the opening and feet stayed dry—fairly warm too!

AUTHOR: *Ruth Ensor. Ruth has been writing poetry since she was in grade school and has been a published poet for several years.*

260-001-ST-WV-002-1998

CHAPTER 5: MOUNTAIN LAKES

West Virginia State Folk Festival, Then and Now

The West Virginia State Folk Festival began in 1950, with the inspiration and foresight of Dr. Patric Gainer. It has since grown, and has become a state tradition, eagerly anticipated each year by West Virginians of all ages.

In 1950, I attended a summer term at Glenville State College. I took a Folklore Class taught by Dr. Gainer. He was collecting folk songs and stories from older West Virginians to preserve our heritage for future generations. It was that summer that he decided to have the first Folk Festival. He had members of the class perform a story, song, or dance in vintage dress. I was asked to sing the ballad, "Barbara Allen." It was just a one-evening event, as I remember it.

In 1957, Belles became part of the festival. Their participation has been a traditional part of it since. The Belles are healthy, independent ladies, at least seventy years old, selected in each county by local groups such as the Extension Homemakers, Senior Citizens, or a Chamber of Commerce. The festival is still held at Glenville State College. While the Belles are on campus they are housed in Pickens Hall.

Helen Garrett (l.) and Estelle Gordon smile for the camera.

In 1996, I was chosen to represent the Lewis County Extension Homemakers at the forty-seventh Folk Festival. It has changed over the years to a three-day event. Many activities have been added. Two of the main events were a luncheon held in the ballroom at Heflin Center, and a parade through Glenville in honor of the Belles. There were also concerts, sings, dances, barbecues, craft displays, meals, and receptions. It ended with a church service at Job's Temple, a very old log church, ten miles from Glenville.

Once again, I had a wonderful time. I am proud to have been a part of the West Virginia Folk Festival from the very beginning. It has been exciting to watch it find a place in the hearts of proud West Virginians, and become what it is today

AUTHOR: Helen Hall Garrett. Helen has lived in Lewis County, Freemansburg, West Virginia, most of her life. She is the fifth of six children born to Claude and Nelle White Hall. She and her husband, John Edward Garrett, have three children—Melinda Garrett Bailey, John Thomas Garrett, and Bruce Hall Garrett—and six grandchildren. Helen retired in 1988 after teaching in West Virginia for twenty-seven years. Her hobbies are traveling, growing flowers, reading, collecting historical material on Freemansburg, and working on her genealogy.

261-001-ST-WV-002-1998

The Sad and the Funny

My parents were Emery and Betty Facemire Burroughs. They were Braxton County natives, my dad from Birch River, and my mom from Carpenters Fork of Little Birch River. They were married in Braxton County, and finally migrated to Clay County in March of 1926, with their three children, Ruby, Nellie, and Ernest. Their fourth, Okey, was born in Clay. My father worked for the Baltimore and Ohio Railroad Company in Clay County at the time. When I was about fourteen years old, my father suffered a stroke. It did not paralyze him but it rendered him unable to continue to work and earn a living.

We lived on a small farm (eighty acres) in Clay County, West Virginia, and from that little farm we earned our meager livelihood. My mother, all eighty pounds of her, worked as hard as any man, as did myself and younger brothers. We carried eggs, milk, and butter to the people who lived in town and worked in the Buffalo Creek and Gauley Railroad shops. This was our only source of cash.

Christmas came and the boss's family owed us ten dollars—the only cash we had to depend upon to buy our Christmas food and gifts. When I delivered their farm products (whatever that was at the time, I don't remember), they *"couldn't"* afford to pay me what they owed us. Needless to say, our Christmas was bleak. Although we couldn't afford the extra goodies, fruits,

October, 1993. Nellie Stephenson, as she shows her catfish she caught in the Potomac River. Her husband, B.H. "Hub" Stephenson, sits by and watches.

and candies that other people might have had, we didn't go hungry. People who live on a farm never go hungry. Our mother, as always, prepared a fine Christmas dinner with chicken and all the "fixin's," cakes and pies, and especially our favorite, "dried apple stack cake." These dishes were always part of our festive meals. The year was 1932, and I was fifteen years old.

The week after Christmas, when I made my delivery to the bossman's family, I was shown all of their nice Christmas gifts. I saw a beautiful tree with an electric train running around it. A lovely satin robe and slippers were among other gifts. The hurt I felt at that time stayed with me for many years. I learned a very important lesson from that experience. Be very careful of the hurt you may bring into the lives of others, especially children. The hurt you may bring into another's life may well come back into your own.

My family survived. My brothers and I graduated from Clay County High School and everyone in our family has led a productive life. My parents asked for help from no one but were always willing to help others when possible.

I grew up! I was married to O.C. "Brownie" Moore and we were the parents of three children, Betty Ann Moore (Husk) of Davisville, West Virginia, O.C. Moore II of Lawrenceville, Georgia, and Jonny Dale Moore of Jacksonville, Florida. Also, a niece, Margaret Burroughs (Stapleton) of Riverside, California, lived with us from age nine through high school.

Times have really changed. Now that my children have all grown up and spread out across the country, we make an extra effort to visit, and keep our family ties strong. It seems we always find something to laugh about. August 1, 1997, I was preparing to visit my son Jonny and his family in Florida. My brother was taking me to the airport which is about forty miles from my home. My flight was leaving at 7:20 AM so we were leaving home quite early. My luggage was sitting in my kitchen, ready to go. A bag of garbage was also there to be taken to my garage.

We arrived at the airport and I was at the ticket counter, checking my luggage when I heard my brother ask, "Do you want this checked through, too?" I turned around and there sat my big bag of garbage. He thought it was something I was taking to my son. He took it back to his home and proceeded to burn the papers that were in it. He accidentally dropped his car keys and the electronic door opener into the fire and burned them—a sad ending to an otherwise hilarious incident.

AUTHOR: Nellie Burroughs Moore Stephenson. Nellie married O.C. "Brownie" Moore January 1, 1938, who died July 13, 1979. She is the proud mother of three children. She married B.H. "Hub" Stephenson February 15, 1986, who died April 9, 1996, and is stepmother to six wonderful stepchildren. June, 1995, she was elected by WV Extension Homemakers Club to reign as Clay County Belle in the Glenville Folk Festival, and October, 1997, she was elected by the Golden Age Club to reign as Golden Delicious Apple Belle Queen at the Clay County Golden Delicious Apple Festival.

262-001-ST-WV-002-1998

I Wanted to Run That Big Steam Engine

In 1918, when I was five years old, I went to live with my grandparents at North Bend, West Virginia, about eight miles above Richwood, in Nicholas County. Their house was at the end of the row, close to the coal tipple, sand house, blacksmith shop, and train dispatcher's office.

My granddad, Joe Williams, was railroad car inspector, and my dad, Luther Williams, was a fireman on one of the engines. When not in school, I spent as much time as I could in the dispatcher's office. This is where the train

Chapter 5: Mountain Lakes

people hung out when they were not on the road. I got to know all of them by their first names and I, being the only boy on the scene from morning to night, became a favorite with them. Most of the time I was with the dispatcher and my granddad. The dispatcher, George Husk, was our next door neighbor.

I made many a trip into the mountain, riding in the engine. I would sit behind the engineer, George Gum. Never once did I think of the wrecks that had happened or could happen. Sometimes the trips were all-day events. I often rode the supply train that came by at 6 AM and delivered groceries to every camp on the line and did not return until well after dark.

I spent many hours with Pat Ball. He was the night man who took care of the engines and made them ready for the morning shift. The first thing that he did was to clean the firebox. I would rake the hot ashes out of the ash pit under the engine. I burned the toes out of many shoes doing this.

After cleaning the firebox, we went to the sand house and filled the sand boxes, both front and back. The coal tipple was next, where we took about nine tons of coal. The water tank was last and it was about a half mile away. I was about seven years old and had learned from Mr. Gum how to run the engine. I told Mr. Ball that I could run the engine to the water tank. He said, "OK, you run it to the water tank and I'll sit and watch." I did and he said I did a good job.

One night after dark we had to go take water and he said, "I don't want you throwing switches out in the dark, but you get it ready and you can run the engine." I got the headlights going and he got his lantern and we took off. After that he did other things while I went to get the water. So, there I was, seven years old and running that big engine all by myself.

Some years later I did work for the railroad, but only for about one year. Many years after this, I visited Mr. Gum at his home in Webster County, where he retired. He asked me if I had forgotten how to run a train. I told him that he was a good teacher and I had not forgotten. He passed away a few years ago, but I will always remember him.

AUTHOR: *Ralph Williams is a retired federal police officer, and at present works for the city of Hurricane as Honorary Caboose Museum Conductor.*

Editors' Note: For those less familiar with the finer points of the railroad and coal industries than many West Virginians, a coal tipple is the structure that loads railway coal cars with coal for transport. The water tank of the engine described in this story held 5,200 gallons of water and could provide steam power to carry the train fifty miles before being refilled, and the sand boxes held sand for application on slick rails.

263-001-ST-WV-002-1998

A Talented and Ingenious Man

Harry George Decker was born November 18, 1897, at Bridgeville, Pennsylvania, and died at Sand Fork, West Virginia, December 10, 1943. He was the first of seven children born to Frank Levi Decker and Clara Keefer Decker.

"Youngest Engineer," a 1911 article in Grit, described Harry George Decker's work at the Eureka Pipe Line Company, when he was age thirteen.

Around 1903, when he was still a young boy, Harry's family moved from Bridgeville to Sand Fork, in Gilmer County, where his father was employed by the Eureka Pipe Line

The Decker brothers' first garage: Harry George in the vehicle on the left, and Frank, Jr., in the one on the right, July, 1916. The author recalls that, when he was a boy, the location of the haystack in the background was occupied for a short time by a downed aircraft. He writes, "it seems that the radiator of the craft sprung a leak in the air and began blowing hot water back into the pilot's face, causing him to make a forced landing. At the man's request, my dad removed, repaired, and replaced the radiator. The man paid him, and then took off for parts unknown!"

Company at the Sand Fork oil pump station. Harry regularly attended grade school at Sand Fork until he was thirteen years old. According to his diary, he then started working for his father's employer, operating the pump station "on his own," working different shifts and attending school when he could. He earned the same rate of pay as his father. A May 21, 1911 clipping and picture from the weekly newspaper *Grit* pretty much tells the story of his early life as a self-taught engineer, encouraged by his father, of course.

As a boy, Harry drove one of the first automobiles in Gilmer County, when an older lady bought one and had no idea how to drive it. He later operated the first auto sales and repair garage with his brother Frank, Jr. In addition, Harry owned and operated an oil and gas well drilling business, and he was also an agent for auto and life insurance.

In the early 1920s, Harry married Floy Blanch Bailey, and to them were born three sons. I am Billy D., and my brothers are Harry Joe and Robert L.

At age seventy-five, I continue to be impressed by the life of my father, an amazing man who had only an eighth-grade education and lived only to age forty-six. In that short time, he accomplished more than most men who lived longer and had much more formal education.

I treasure the early photographs that capture glimpses of my father's time. Included here is one showing my father and his brother Frank doing steady business at their first garage. Frank is also shown here in another photo, making repairs for a friend. Both pictures were taken in July, 1916. This would make Father's age eighteen and Frank, Jr.'s, seventeen. Frank chose to leave the business in the early 1920s for full-time employment with the Eureka Pipe Line Company; however, my father continued to operate the business under the name "Decker Brothers" until his death in 1943.

Another photograph shows the Decker Brothers building, which was constructed in 1922, the year of my birth. Our family lived on the second floor and was indeed fortunate to have electric power and indoor plumbing, the only dwelling in town to have such "luxuries" until West Penn Power became available. Our "power plant," a dynamo powered by a large, single-cylinder, natural gas–powered engine, even supplied power to our local high school for a time.

Our "power" also helped provide entertainment to our community. Dad put a public movie house in the rear of our residence. We showed silent movies, like "Tarzan of the Apes." I sold hot buttered popcorn for five cents, although, being young, I was confused and if you asked me, I sold "hot butter and popcorn." Of course, everybody got a chuckle out of that. Grandma sold tickets at the top of the rear stairs, and we could accommodate about fifty people.

Frank Decker, Jr. (left), making repairs for friend Tony Ferguson at the Decker brothers' first garage, July, 1916.

CHAPTER 5: MOUNTAIN LAKES

The second Decker Brothers garage, constructed in 1922 and pictured here in 1979.

This and many other contributions to our community were made possible because of the talents of my father, Harry George Decker. My two brothers and I agree that we "had it real good" for that day and age, to have been brought up in a small West Virginia town and to have had outstanding parents.

AUTHOR: Billy D. Decker lives in Kingwood, West Virginia. Mr. Decker would like to acknowledge his brothers, Harry Joe and Robert L., who helped sponsor this tribute to their father.

264-001-ST-WV-002-1998

Great-Aunt Shirley and the Cow Pies

y grandmother, Gloria "Jean" Williams Rigsby, often tells me stories about growing up in Upper Glade, West Virginia in Webster County, in the 1930s and '40s. The family consisted of her parents, Luther and Eva Williams, and their children: Ford, Lowell, Lyman, Floradell, Gloria "Jean," Deral "Dub," and the youngest, Shirley. One of my favorite stories is about Shirley.

The entire Williams family walked to church together, to the Upper Glade Methodist Church, the older ones taking turns from one week to the next holding Shirley's hand. It was quite a walk to church—up the hill and across the old cow pasture—and herein lies the problem. They had to go under the fence on one side of the pasture and over the fence on the other side. My great-grandmother would admonish whichever sibling was holding Shirley's hand that week, "Be very careful, I don't want her stepping in a 'cow pie' again!" All of the brothers and sisters swore that they never once saw her step in a cow pie, but somehow, she always did.

This church holds beautiful memories for my grandmother. She told me of a lighthouse bank that the children would put their collection pennies in. It would light up with each coin that was dropped into it. This was one of the highlights of the day for the young ones. She often tells me too of the golden bell Preacher Coakley kept that was used to bring the congregation to order.

Upon arriving at the church, the preacher, Andrew Coakley, would welcome each and every one of the people and take his place on the pulpit. After ringing the bell three times, he would say, "Now let's all turn to page fifty-one (or whatever) in your hymn book, but first, Shirley, would you please go outside and wipe your feet?" And sure enough, there would be evidence that Shirley had stepped in another cow pie!

Whichever sister or brother was responsible for Shirley that day would be scared and my grandmother's parents would be very embarrassed. Since my great-grandmother felt she couldn't trust any of the children to watch Shirley, she decided one week to show them how it was done. She held Shirley's hand all the way—up the hill, under the fence, over the fence, and through the village all the way to the church. Preacher Coakley welcomed each and every person, took his place at the pulpit, rang the little golden bell three times, told the congregation to turn to page fifty-one (or whatever) in their hymn books, and said, "But first, Shirley, would you please go outside and wipe your feet?" And, as usual, there was evidence that Shirley had stepped in another cow pie!

From that day forward, none of the older siblings got into trouble for letting Shirley step in cow pies, but my great-grandmother did say that, when Shirley got to Heaven, she was sure St. Peter would be standing there at the golden gate with Preacher Coakley and she knew he'd say, "Come on in, Shirley, but first, go outside and wipe your feet!"

AUTHOR: George Poulos is fourteen years old and the grandson of Jean and Bill Rigsby, formerly of Upper Glade in Webster County. He lives in Joppatowne, Maryland, where he attends Joppatowne High School. George says that writing seems to come naturally to him, as he is from a family of writers.

265-001-ST-WV-002-1998

Maybe the Rain Was a Good Thing

We had been blessed with good camping weather on the first four days of our June, '97 vacation. Today, it either rained or threatened to rain all day. My wife, Rae Jean, and I packed up our gear at Watoga State Park in Pocahontas County early in the morning before it really started. We headed to nearby Cranberry Glades and walked the meandering circle on the new boardwalk in a light mist or drizzle, dressed in ponchos that somehow seemed unnecessary, fascinated with how the fragile ecosystem seemed to have been transplanted from some tundra up north to southeastern West Virginia. As we drove out to Route 55, I mentioned that in twenty-one years as a transplant to the state, I had never seen a bear. I had been thinking that not many people were out on a rainy morning, and it was still early. I swear that this sort of thing does not happen to me often, but no sooner had I mentioned this fact than I looked off to the left and saw a black bear about 100 yards away watching us drive by. We stopped and had time to snap a picture before he loped back into the shelter of the woods.

Maybe the rain was a good thing.

Lucky for us, the weather at Cranberry Glades was so bad that the park was empty and this bear was out.

It rained on and off as we drove to Summit Lake in Greenbrier County, about ten miles east of Richwood. We had done a little fishing at Watoga, but the small lake there was still pretty muddy from the flash flood that had passed through not long before. Summit Lake was much bigger and looked like a good place to paddle our canoe, which we'd lashed to the top of the 1985 Toyota. Even though clouds were visible in the west, the sun was shining; we decided to put the canoe in. Knowing next to nothing about canoeing, I listened to Rae Jean, who has extensive experience canoeing rivers and lakes in the Pacific Northwest. We stayed pretty close to the shore in case a thunderstorm might blow in. In several of the little inlets, we stopped to fish. In spite of her boating experience, Rae Jean had done little fishing before, so it came as a big surprise that first I caught about a twelve-inch bass, and then she caught another one. That was the extent of our "luck," but we both felt lucky anyway.

It was getting to be about three o'clock in the afternoon, and we knew that we needed to make it to Hinton by evening. We also wanted to cook the fish outside, another first for Rae Jean. We had paddled nearly halfway around the lake when we heard thunder in the distance. Knowing how fast a storm could be there, I suggested we shorten the trip back to the boat launch area by cutting across the lake. Against her better judgment, Rae Jean agreed. We reached the launch just as it started to sprinkle. As Rae Jean put our gear in the car, I cleaned the bass and put them in a plastic bag. In the ten minutes or so that passed, the rain steadily picked up. We threw what gear was left into the car and got fairly wet lifting the canoe upside-down on top of the car. At just that point, one of those several-times-a-summer West Virginia downpours hit with a vengeance. We dove into the car and waited for nearly half an hour while it rained so hard that the entire parking area was variously covered with up to an inch of water. Tired of waiting, I finally put on my sandals, donned my poncho, went out, and tied the canoe down. We drove in moderate to heavy rain all the way to Richwood.

We had already decided to stay in a bed and breakfast for one night in Hinton for a comfortable bed and nice shower, glad we were not going to have to pitch our tent in the rain. After filling up with gas in Richwood, we decided to get something warm to drink. We asked where a good restaurant was and were immediately directed to C&S Restaurant on Oakford Street. It was still pouring when I parked in front and, still wearing sandals, stepped out into a couple inches of water running down the side of the street. We went inside and sat at the counter to order some hot chocolate. I looked at the menu of home cooked meals and desserts and suggested maybe we should just eat dinner early here.

Rae Jean asked, "But what about the fish?"

Susie Strader, who owned and ran the restaurant, overheard our conversation and asked me, "Are the fish cleaned?"

CHAPTER 5: MOUNTAIN LAKES

Rae Jean at Lake Summit. She smiles in anticipation of catching "the big one."

"Yes," I answered.

Without hesitation, "Go get them, and I'll cook them for you," she offered.

How could we refuse? I waded back to the car and got the two bass from the cooler. I gave them to Susie, and she took them to the kitchen.

We ordered some a la carte items from the menu and waited for dinner. In the course of the wait, we talked to Susie and some other "regulars" about Richwood, and even about a story that one of the *Mountain State Stories of the People* authors had written about the town. Susie said that she cooks fish for folks like us often. Her reasoning was simple: if one of her children was traveling somewhere in the same situation, she hoped a friendly restaurant proprietor would treat them the same way.

The fish and all the fixin's were delicious.

Maybe the rain was a good thing.

AUTHOR: *Ken St. Louis. Ken and his wife Rae Jean Sielen live on twenty acres up the Cassville Hollow, about six miles west of Morgantown.*

266-001-ST-WV-002-1998

Growing Up in the Country
Rural Braxton County, 1934–1952

Growing up on a farm out in the country was not an easy life. Everything we ate had to be raised on the farm. The produce raised was preserved in a variety of ways: canned, pickled, smoked, dried, or put in holes in the ground.

Some vegetables and meats were canned, for example, tomatoes, beans, corn, peas, wild berries, and pork. The pickled vegetables were cucumbers, cabbage, beans, and corn.

Fruit was gathered each year. Apples were made into applesauce and apple butter, and the peel was cooked. The juice was then used in blackberry, raspberry, and sometimes huckleberry jelly. A berry cobbler was a special treat.

On hog-killing day, neighbors helped, as it was an all-day job. The water was put in wash tubs the night before, and the fire started before daylight. After the hog was killed, it was put in the boiling water so the hair could be scraped off. Whoever helped always took a "mess" of meat home. All the meat was used—nothing was wasted. Hams and bacon were either smoked or sugar-cured. The skin was taken off and rendered into lard. The head was cooked with the liver and heart, and made into sowshead. The meat was mixed with salt, pepper, spices, and cornmeal—it was very delicious when fried. Sausage was also made. It was usually canned and the grease poured over it.

A flock of chickens was kept for eating, as well as for eggs. The eggs were used at the store to get sugar, flour, baking powder, and other items.

A cow or two was kept for milk, butter, and cheese. The cream would rise to top of the crock of milk, and was skimmed to make butter. It seemed to take forever to churn butter.

Some milk was put in a pan and set on the back of the wood stove to make cottage cheese. Butter was used at the store for goods. Money was scarce in those days.

Hay was cut twice in the summer months and put in stacks around a pole. It was used to feed the animals in the winter. We usually had chickens, hogs, cows, and horses. There was a large field of corn that was shucked to be fed to the animals. The corn stalks were put in shocks to use as feed.

The first lights I remember were oil lamps. If you went anywhere in the evening, a lantern was carried. The gas lights used mantles, which were very hard to light because they were fragile and easy to break. Electric was unknown in our area until 1946 or 1947. It did not get to the hollow (holler) until after I grew up.

There was no running water unless you ran and got it in a bucket. Our water was a deer lick spring. It was cold even when the spring was in the sun.

AUTHOR: *Colene Heim. Colene is a housewife and retired Realtor. She grew up in Braxton County, West Virginia, and now lives outside of Charleston, in St. Albans. She is the mother of five and grandmother of thirteen.*

267-001-ST-WV-002-1998

Chapter 6

New River / Greenbrier Valley

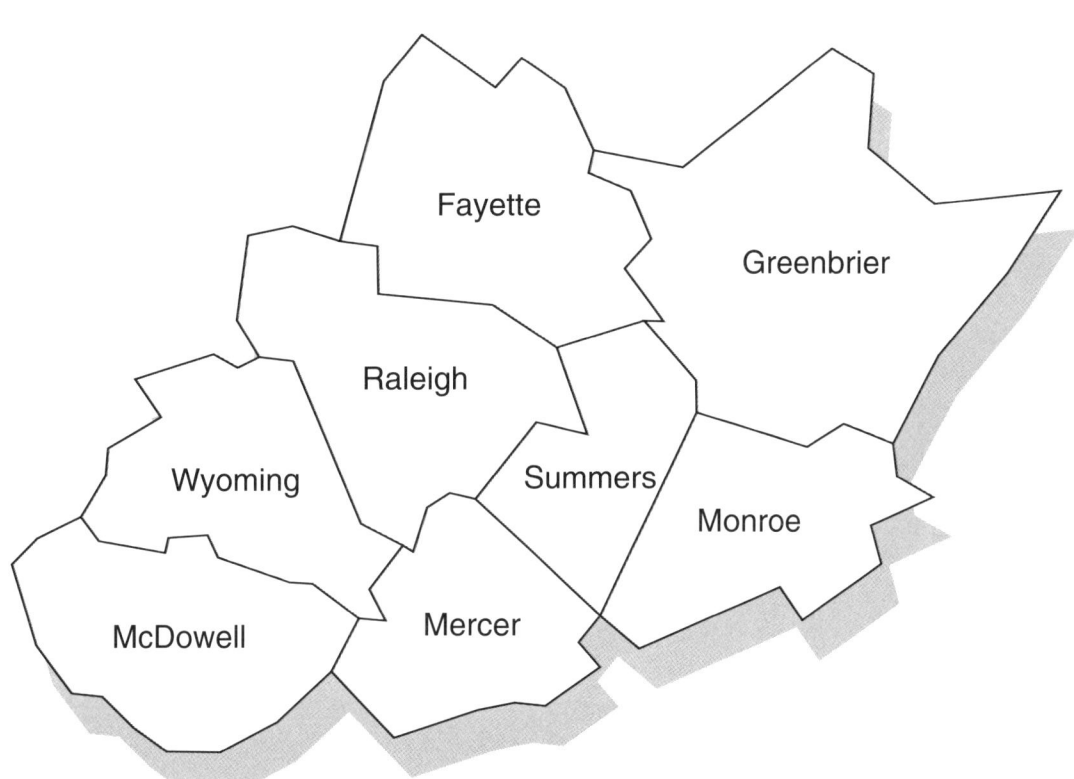

You Don't Miss What You Never Had

On October 29, 1929, Black Tuesday, the US stock market came crashing down. Even though this was not the fundamental cause of the Great Depression, it certainly marked the beginning of the most traumatic economic period of modern times. So what did the future hold for a child born on this day in the Mercer County coal camps of West Virginia? Velva Billings was such a child. She had this to say.

"Naturally, being born in 1929, I didn't really suffer the hardships that a lot of people suffered, but I grew up *from* 1929, in that period of time when people were working hard to get it together again. It was a very trying time, but being the only life I ever knew, I didn't miss what I never had.

"I never rode a school bus. The old saying, '. . . walked ten miles, one way, in the snow, barefoot' would almost apply, except for being barefoot. In the fall each year, Mommy would place an order with Alden's mail-order catalog for snow boots. They bought us one pair a year. We were so proud of those shoes! We took real good care of them 'cause when the shoes wore out school was over. Sometimes they lasted through the whole year, but many times we had to quit until the weather got warm again. Then we could go back to school barefoot.

"In school the teacher would always ask, 'What would you like to get for Christmas?' Most girls wanted dolls; boys new wagons. When she asked what I wanted, I said a BIG BOX OF CORNFLAKES. I had eaten it once at my aunt's house and thought it was the greatest thing. Daddy always had a garden and kept livestock. Mommy canned. We never went hungry, but there was something about Cornflakes. Besides, I always worked the garden, tended horses, and milked cows; I didn't have time to play with dolls.

"'Round about that same time the preacher was forevermore preaching on going to that land where the milk and honey flowed. Well, my daddy had bees and we always had plenty of honey. I remember many a time taking a cold glass of milk out of the springhouse and I'd pour honey in it, stir it up, and drink it. Gosh, I loved it! But after a while, I got tired of it. And I thought, 'Why couldn't heaven have something besides milk and honey? Why couldn't they have Cornflakes?'

"It was a joyous time! There were days filled with playing chase around a one-room school house, being chased through the house and on to a second-story roof by a mountain goat, jumping the creek, and too, days of hard work. There was also the time spent gathered around the radio listening to the 'Lone Ranger' or 'I Love a Mystery.'

"We were a happy family; grew up well together," Velva says of her dad, Burette; mom, Oma; and her eight brothers and sisters: Buster, Flora, Delta (who died before Velva was born), Raymond, Ellen, Colena, Roberta, and Buddy.

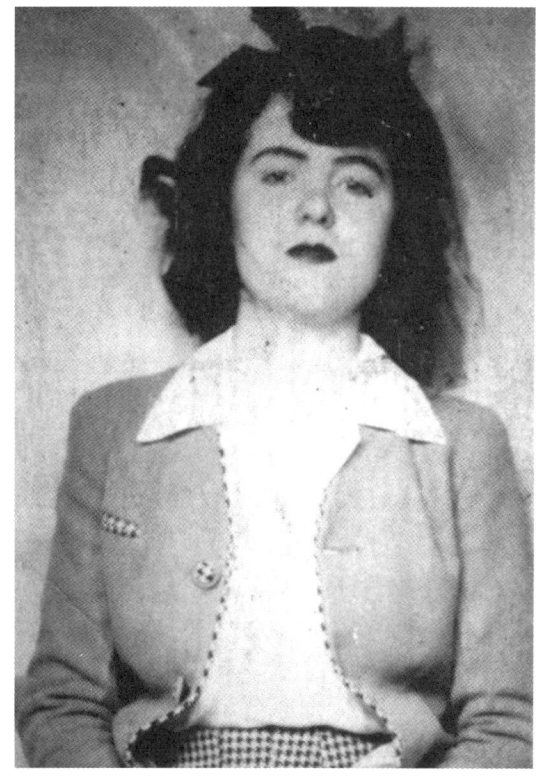

Velva Iris Billings in 1944, at age fourteen.

While the nation was focusing on a New Deal, Velva was anxiously awaiting new shoes. W.K. Kellogg survived the Depression, much to the delight of this young girl in Hiawatha, West Virginia, who thought Cornflakes were "the greatest thing" in heaven or on Earth.

Yes, it was called the Great Depression, but actually, life did not necessarily mean growing up low in spirits, dejected and suffering. Velva stated it best: "You didn't miss what you never had."

AUTHOR: Glenna G. Carroll. Velva Iris Billings Boyles is the mother of the author and the grandmother of Velva Iris Boyles Anderson. While in the fifth grade, Iris Anderson, who is now twenty-three years old, had a homework assignment that required her to tape an interview with an older relative about his or her life. Mrs. Carroll states, "I am so glad the tape survived this many years in Iris's care, and that Mom gave her approval for this story to be told in the same manner she told it then."

268-001-ST-WV-002-1998

My Country Church

My country church, Salem Presbyterian Church, is located on Route 219, nine miles south of Lewisburg, and four miles south of Ronceverte, in the community of Organ Cave, West Virginia. Salem Church was organized in 1860. This makes it 138 years old. A celebration was held in 1960, when the church was 100 years old. Salem Church is not only a landmark in the community, but is a lighthouse that has sent rays out to people near and far.

Salem Church has been housed in three different church buildings. All have stood on the same lot. The first, erected in 1860, burned. The second was built in 1875. That church grew until it became inadequate for the needs of its members. Nevertheless, churchgoers continued to fill the building for about thirty-five years. Salem Church burned again on a Sunday morning, May 20, 1910. All that was saved from the fire was a pump organ, which in later years was electrified and now stands in the sanctuary of the church.

Salem Presbyterian Church. Organized 1860.

Ollie Jackson Hoover on her eighty-second birthday, January 31, 1997. She is with her two great-grandchildren. Alex was six years and ten months, and Emily was nine months old.

The present church has been renovated several times. A basement was dug and has a kitchen, a large dining room, and two restrooms. More Sunday school rooms were built with two restrooms upstairs. There have been preachers, school teachers, school principals, bankers, historians, nurses, electricians, Sunday school superintendents, engineers, secretaries, court clerks, Extension workers, sheriffs, store clerks, Presbyterian Youth Fellowship leaders, 4-H leaders, and a host of farmers in Salem Church. Also, three women from Salem Presbyterian Church have represented Greenbrier County as Extension Homemaker Belles: Mrs. Charlotte Mason Dickson in 1974, Mrs. Ollie Jackson Hoover (myself) in 1988, and Mrs. Margaret Rodgers Boone Shanklin in 1990. Since 1920, ten pastors have served Salem Church. The present one is Reverend William H. Dent, Jr.

My country church has survived and grown in spite of the test of time and the ravages of fire. This is a testimony to the spirit of community and the dedication of its members. I look forward to continued membership in my country church, Salem Presbyterian Church.

AUTHOR: *Ollie Jackson Hoover. Ollie was a resident of Organ Cave, West Virginia for seventy-five years.*

269-001-ST-WV-002-1998

Edwin and I

When I was asked to be the Monroe County Belle, the first thought that came to me was, "This will be great! I was married during the war in a short dress, and now I will enjoy the Belle celebration in a long purple dress from around the Victorian era."

My fiancé, Edwin Sibold, had served two years in the Forty-fifth Infantry Division when we decided to get married, February,

CHAPTER 6: NEW RIVER / GREENBRIER VALLEY

1943. Our wedding was beautiful, held in my church at Pickaway, West Virginia. I was working in Roanoke, Virginia. We only had a weekend to come home and get married. I was wearing a navy short dress with shoulder epaulets to blend with the groom's military uniform. I wore a white straw hat with a short navy veil and white long cuff gloves, and had a small Bible in hand.

The large crowd of friends made our wedding so very, very special, as did the soloist singing "I Love You Truly." At the close of the ceremony, Edwin and I stood at the back of the church and spoke to all our guests. You could feel their love and concern (War!), but you had to live and love each day you had. Then we were on our way in Edwin's old Chevrolet, parked in front of the church, when a friend said, "Wait! I must get your picture." That was the only picture taken of our wedding. We received lovely letters afterwards, one in particular was from an older man—Dr. Hodge, saying, "That was a perfect kiss."

On to Camp Pickett, Virginia. Previously, Edwin had found us a room in the lovely home of an elderly couple in Kembridge, Virginia. Now commissioned as Warrant Officer, he had more responsibility and preparation for the overseas duty that I knew was ahead of him. Officers were not allowed to tell when orders would be given to be shipped out. He didn't have to tell me; I knew. We had three months together. The last morning was a very sad time. Not knowing where he was overseas for two months was also very difficult, and in that time we had received word that my brother, Elwyn, a captain at age twenty-three, had died in Tunis, North Africa. Elwyn, being such a jolly, lovable person . . . makes you wonder why!—and would Edwin make it?

It was through my brother that I had met Edwin. Elwyn brought him home from school as they were planning a double date. Elwyn pitched Edwin's trousers and shoes down the back stairway and said "Sis, will you please press Edwin's pants and shine his shoes as we're in a hurry?" I must have done a good job as the next Sunday he asked me for a date.

The Forty-fifth Infantry Division originated from the Oklahoma National Guard, where Edwin served at Camp Berkley in 1941. Edwin couldn't tell me where he was—ever, so I subscribed to the Oklahoma Newspaper thinking that they would know. I found out the Forty-fifth Division landed in North Africa and went on to Sicily, Anzio Beach Head, and southern France. It was a long, hard three years as I spent my time praying, writing to my husband overseas, and working as a secretary for the Monroe County superintendent of schools.

Newlyweds Edwin and Eloise Sibold, February, 1943.

He made it home, and the celebration lasted forty-two years. It began by his going back to college so he would be certified to teach in high school. To give you an idea of the times, we had to take our zinc tub and washboard. That is how I did our laundry! It was a short year and soon Edwin was back to the classroom and being a six-man football coach. He loved being with his students.

We soon made our first purchase—a home with sixty-two acres of land. The baby lambs and "chicks" were a joy. The old storage building was used as the beginning of our dairy with two cows. I stayed home with the farm problems and a hired hand while Edwin taught school. He also taught me to not tell the hired man what to do in a problem situation. I was to say, "Edwin said to do so and so," or I was to call. That was one way of keeping the hired hand for thirty-seven years. When Edwin would arrive home from school I would often follow him to the top of the steps—sit there and tell him of the day's problems or joys as he changed into his work clothes.

We celebrated our forty-fifth wedding anniversary on a Sunday in 1988. It was a great day and night. The next morning at six-thirty, he was gone. Edwin was a kind man and loved to laugh, he lived a full life, and you never heard him speak harm of anyone. He would have been so proud of me as a county Belle, dressed in a long, purple, flowing dress, and a black straw hat with purple trim and feather.

After Edwin died, it was time for me to fulfill OUR dream, which was to take the grandchildren on tours—"that special time with them." It was 1993 when I took our two older granddaughters on a Royal Caribbean Cruise to St. Thomas, Puerto Rico, and beautiful Bahama Island. It was our first time to snorkel in the great waters. My girls loved it. There were dress-up occasions and food elaborately decorated and displayed. Next, a tour to Alaska in 1996, for the older boys. It covered all the means of transportation that the boys had never experienced: airplane, bus, train, and small ship, a thrill within itself. They finished at Valdez, climbed Mt. Healy at Denali National Park, and toured picturesque Fairbanks. Now, where shall I take my three younger grandchildren, two boys and a girl, to complete Edwin's and my dream?

AUTHOR: Eloise Allen Sibold. Eloise lives in a beautiful farming community called Pickaway, and stays busy with community activities, being the church pianist, reading to school children, spinning wool, knitting, tatting, weaving rugs, quilting, picture framing, and pottery.

270-001-ST-WV-002-1998

called Pearl Harbor!" A lot would change in our peaceful life during World War II, as uncles would go off to a war around the other side of the world. My father was a coal miner, and he stayed here to work for much-needed energy during the war. A miner's pay was very little back then, and times were hard for everyone. My mother would crochet

Danford Earl Bragg, Sr., November, 1986, at Twin Falls State Park in Wyoming County, West Virginia.

Reflections of Yesterday

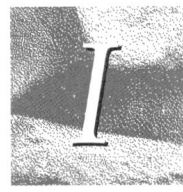

I entered this world on March 17, 1939, at Hatcher, in Wyoming County, West Virginia. I'm the son of Lloyd E. (Hager) Bragg and Rita I. Elkins-Bragg. I grew up in a large family of eleven children, as follows in order of birth: James, Patsy, Danford, Carol, Hubert, Judith, Barbara, Dennis, Fredrick, Jimmy, and Kimberly, who was adopted.

We lived on a farm near my maternal grandparents, Denny W. Elkins and Corby Stewart-Elkins, and I have a lot of memories of growing up there. I remember my grandfather coming around the hill carrying a lantern saying, "We are at war! The Japanese have bombed a place

doilies at night, and I would ride my horse and sell Blair mail-order pudding and pie filling mixes and my mother's crochet work to help make ends meet.

I miss my grandfather a lot. He was my best friend. He always called me Dan Patch. He died October 9, 1950.

I joined the air force in 1955 and served in San Antonio, Texas and Great Falls, Montana. I served in the 150th armored cavalry, West Virginia National Guard, rank of sergeant, in Welch, West Virginia. I worked for Vecillo and Grogan building Route 99 on Kopperston Mountain from 1964 to 1967, and I worked for Paramount and Pacific as they built R.D. Bailey Lake and Dam. I was an employee of Eastern Gas and Fuel at Kopperston; US Steel at Pinnacle Creek; and finally at Island Creek Coal, at Elk Creek #10 tipple.

My hobbies are hunting and fishing. I believe my love of outdoors to be part of my mountain heritage, from my ancestorial grandfathers such as John Cook, Sr. and Captain Ralph Stewart. History books tell that Captain Ralph was a scout and an Indian fighter. The books also tell how John Cook found this land on a scouting and hunting trip, and that he and his sons would later settle on it as a land grant awarded Cook for service in the Revolutionary War. This is a part of the land I grew up on, as did my mother, her father, his mother, and her father, back to John Cook, Sr. I feel a great sense of pride for my ancestors.

I am a disabled coal miner, a twenty-five-year member of the United Mine Workers of America, and a member of the Wyoming County Genealogical Society. I'm also a member of the Grayson County, Virginia Genealogical and Historical Society, as my great-grandmother Della Myrtle Mae Francis-Stewart and other ancestorial grandparents were from there. I belong to the Lincoln County, West Virginia Genealogical Society as well, as my paternal grandparents Everet E. Hager, s/o (son of) Enock Adam(son) Hager and Lavina Adkins-Hager, and Lottie Spears, d/o (daughter of) Hamilton Spears and Jerusha Spurlock-Spears, and also my step-grandfather Albert Bragg are all from Lincoln County, West Virginia.

My lineage in Wyoming County, West Virginia goes very deep, as my maternal grandparents go back to John Cook, the first settler in and founder of Wyoming County, as follows: Danford Earl Bragg, s/o Rita Elkins Bragg, d/o Denny Elkins, s/o Serrilda Cook, d/o Thomas Green "Doby" Cook, s/o William "Doby" Cook, s/o Thomas Cook, s/o John Cook, our progenitor, born in London, England about 1752.

He is also my maternal grandfather as follows: Danford Earl Bragg, s/o Rita Elkins-Bragg, d/o Denny Elkins, s/o Serrilda Cook-Elkins, d/o Margaret "Peggy" Brooks-Cook, d/o Elaender "Nellie" Cook-Brooks, d/o John Cook, Jr., s/o John Cook.

Captain Ralph Stewart, who, like John Cook, was a Revolutionary War veteran, and who was also a veteran of the War of 1812, was my maternal grandfather, as follows: Danford Earl Bragg, s/o Rita Elkins-Bragg, d/o Corby Stewart-Elkins, d/o Austin Rice Stewart, s/o Charles P. Stewart, s/o George P. Stewart, s/o Captain Ralph Stewart and Mary Clay-Stewart, who is the daughter of Mitchell Clay and Phoebee Belcher Clay.

William Brooks, also a Revolutionary War veteran, is my maternal grandfather, as follows: Danford E. Bragg, s/o Rita Elkins-Bragg, d/o Denny Elkins, s/o Serrilda Cook-Elkins, d/o Margaret "Peggy" Brooks-Cook, d/o William Brooks, s/o Richard Brooks and Peggy McClancy.

Also a maternal grandfather is Richard Bailey, Sr., born in England, also a Revolutionary War veteran; our relationship is as follows: Danford Earl Bragg, s/o Rita Irene Elkins-Bragg, d/o Denny Elkins, s/o Serrilda Cook-Elkins, d/o Thomas Green "Doby" Cook, s/o Chole Bailey-Cook, d/o James Bailey, Sr., and Margaret Stinnett-Bailey, s/o Richard Bailey, Sr., and Annie Belcher-Bailey.

I am also a descendant of James Brown and Mary "Millie" Vance-Brown, d/o Abner Vance and Susanna Howard-Vance—yes, the same Abner Vance, a Baptist preacher, who was hung for murdering a Dr. Horton in defense of his daughter's honor. This is in the fact-filled book by Virgil Carrington Jones, *Hatfields and McCoys*. My connection is as follows: Danford E. Bragg, Sr., s/o Rita Elkins-Bragg,

The author's family, taken in 1986. Seated (l-r): Danice Lilly Bragg, author's daughter; Sylvia Acord-Bragg, author's wife. Standing: Danford Earl Bragg II, author's son; Danford Earl Bragg, Sr., author.

d/o Denny Wirt Elkins, s/o George Elkins, s/o Virginia "Jensy" Brown-Elkins, d/o James H. "Harley" Brown and Nancy C. Toler-Brown, s/o James Brown and Mary "Millie" Vance-Brown.

I'm also a descendant of Jacob Webb and Mary Austin-Webb, included in the *Webb*

Families of Virginias by Ronald Ray Turner, as follows: Danford Earl Bragg, s/o Rita Elkins-Bragg, d/o Corby Stewart-Elkins, d/o Austin Rice Stewart, s/o Emily Webb-Stewart, d/o Austin Webb, s/o Giles Webb, s/o Henry Webb, s/o Jacob and Mary Austin-Webb.

There are too many ancestorial grandfathers to name at this time. I will save them for another story.

My first marriage was to Flora Mae Daly in 1958 in Great Falls, Montana. We have one daughter, Debra Ann Bragg-Cagg, of Indianapolis, Indiana. She has two daughters, Helen Cleone Stewart and Tonya Renee Cagg.

On January 24, 1961, I married my wife of thirty-seven years, Sylvia Ann Acord-Bragg, d/o Robert Acord, Jr., and Myrtle Lilly Hager-Acord, in Oceana, West Virginia. We have two children. Our daughter, Danice Lilly Bragg of Charleston, West Virginia, has three children: one daughter, Danielle Elizabeth Wooten, and two sons, George Fred Wooten, Jr., and Travis Aaron Wooten, all of Lynco, West Virginia. My son is Danford Earl Bragg II. He and his first wife, Kelli Harbour-Bragg, have one son, Danford Earl Bragg III, of Cross Lanes, West Virginia. With his second wife, Angelia Sue Robinson, he has one son, Cody Shawn Bragg, of Man, West Virginia. And with his third wife, Barbara Ann Short-Bragg, he has one daughter, Taylor Ann Bragg, of Oceana, West Virginia. My first great-granddaughter, Destiny Danice Wooten, was born in January, 1998.

AUTHOR: Danford Earl Bragg, Sr.

271-001-ST-WV-002-1998

Childhood Mountain Memories

I, along with two brothers and two sisters, Lawrence Mills, Elmer Mills, Elsie Mills, and Ellen Mills Sneed, was born in the mountains of West Virginia, in Camp Creek, Mercer County, of a German Baptist mother, Mary Louvenia Foley Mills, and a non-Christian father, Charles Wesley Mills. We were poor-poor-poor in material things but had lots of love-love-love, especially from Mommy. Here are three memorable incidents that happened in the early 1920s.

My older sister Elsie, who also married a Mills, one day decided she would ride one of the cows on our farm. The rest of us children directed the cows along a nice little shady road in the woods. The cow with the bell around her neck was the lead cow, with me walking at the rear of the herd. My sister climbed a tree, or sapling as we called it, one that would bend. However, she decided to wait for the second cow in the procession. She then jumped out of the tree, landing on the cow's back. The cow jumped "over the moon" and so did Elsie. Elsie then landed on the sandy ground all sprawled out, face first, and the cow kept on running. I'm laughing as I write this.

Mary Magdalene "Maggie" Mills Porter.

Poppy, as we called our dad, always had bees and bee hives. Sometimes they would swarm and leave before he could save them for another hive. So, he was always looking for bee trees where the bees made their homes. Sunday afternoons were wonderful times for the family. Poppy would say, "All right, let's go cut the bee tree." He would take his bee hive, which was sometimes made from a dead hollow tree, or one in which the hole had been pecked by woodpeckers. He would cut down the tree where the bees were, so that tree would fall into his hive. If he was lucky enough to capture the Queen Bee, the other bees would follow. That, and finding chestnuts in the new fallen leaves, was such fun for us.

We five children went to a one-room school, Barn Elementary, which held grades one through eight. Each Friday was recitation time. On one particular Friday, all the kids in the school started arguing about politics. I was nine years old at the time, and don't remember what the argument was about, except that it was between the Democrats and the Republicans. Before we knew it everyone was fighting. One boy hit me in the eye and I ran him in the spring house, hitting him with my lunch bucket. My sister Ellen had dragged a girl to the creek and pushed her into the water. The next day the teacher was about to punish everyone in school. However, my sister Ellen ran home and the teacher's comments were, "Let her go, she has a head and horns of her own."

Chapter 6: New River / Greenbrier Valley

Author: Mary Magdalene Mills Porter. Mary is eighty-seven years of age. She was married to Robert Jackson "Jack" Porter, who passed away four years ago. They lived in Lashmeet, Mercer County, West Virginia, where they raised their children, Patty Kay Porter Grace, Thomas Michael Porter, and Mary Jane Porter Childers. After her husband retired from the coal mines, they spent twenty-three winters in Florida, fishing, touring, and enjoying friendships with neighbors. Mary now lives in Glenwood Park, Princeton, West Virginia, in Mercer County. Her hobbies are collecting baskets, placemats, and sand from around the world. She has sand from the River Jordan, Sea of Galilee, Spain, France, Hong Kong, Korea, Japan, England, Monaco, Australia, and many more countries.

272-001-ST-WV-002-1998

Growing Up in Greenbrier County

I was born February 14, 1924, as Sarah Vena Coughlin, the fifth child of Michael L. and Flora Jane Coughlin, on a farm in Greenbrier County, between Springdale and Dawson, West Virginia. There were ten children. One boy died at about three years old, and a sister died at birth. The other eight were raised on this farm. Times were hard as it was the Depression. We didn't have much, but we never went hungry or cold, and were clothed by my mother, who made as much as she could for us. One thing we did have was lots of love for one another. Oh yes, we had our quarrels and little fights as all children do, but we would also fight *for* one another. We had our work time, as each one had a job or errand to do, but Mother and Dad saw that we had play time too. In winter we played games out in the snow. One game that stands out in my mind was "The Fox and Goose." This was a big circle made in the snow, and then there was a path made across the circle both ways. One person was chosen as the Fox, and the rest were the Geese, and the Fox chased the Geese to home base, which was a small circle drawn in the center of the big circle. Sleigh riding time was a big time for us, and all the neighbors' children would come and we would take turns sleigh riding.

My oldest brother, Alvin Coughlin, made a big sled called a bobsled. It was two parts: the front part was short and fixed for guiding, and it was attached to a big long sled behind. Six or seven would pile on and ride down the hill. Lots of fun!

In the summer we had different kinds of parties, and played ball and other games with the children. A great fun time with lots of laughs was when Dad would cut the hay and then he would hang up lanterns on posts and have what we then called lawn parties. This was for all ages: parents, children, boys and girls, and courting couples. One game that I have never forgotten was "Cross Question and Silly Answers." There were two lines: boys and men on one side, and girls and women on the other side, facing one another. One side was given the question and the other side the answer. This was all made up and no one knew what the question or answer was except the one it was told to. The girl facing her partner would ask the question and the boy would give the answer. This was to be done three times without laughing. If they laughed, they had to go to the end to start over again. This was really funny as the questions and answers were of a funny or silly nature. Mother would have refreshments after it was over.

Five generations of the Coughlin family (l-r): James Mortin Dunn, grandson; Vena Rose Walthall Dunn, daughter; Vena Coughlin Walthall, author; Christina Rose Dunn, great-granddaughter; and Michael (Mike) L. Coughlin, father.

My school days were in a one-room school, Lowery School. It went from primary through eighth grades. Students sat on seats with chairbacks serving as the desk for the student seated behind them. There was a potbellied stove for heat in the center of the room, and in the winter, we rotated around the room to keep

warm. Water was kept in the water cooler, a large container with a spigot on the bottom. We all drank from a water dipper until there were some kind of cups given. There were no inside facilities, so we were to ask the teacher when we could leave to go to the outhouse. My first year in school we had a book called the primary and we had to go through it before we went to the first grade. By the end of the year I was promoted to the third grade. My teacher was the greatest—Harold Quillen of Dawson, West Virginia. For having perfect attendance and not missing a day, he awarded me with the prettiest dress I had ever seen. It was blue, with ruffles and lace on it. I was so proud of that dress, for I had never had a store-bought dress. I showed it to everybody who came in.

Another thing I have to brag about is another teacher that I had, who was very strict, and believed in reading the story as it was supposed to be read, with all the punctuation marks put in. One such well-known story in the reader was, "Chicken Little." It had a lot of exclamation points, commas, and periods, and I had to read that story over and over until I got it just right. I had to read it with great feeling. The teacher was so proud of me that she would have me read it to everyone who came by our house, as she was a boarder at our home. Her name was Miss Effie Forren of Dawson, West Virginia. We all loved her, for she was a great teacher.

Another highlight of my life was when I was married to a wonderful husband, James Willis Walthall, on January 11, 1944. We were married fifty-four years as of January 11, 1997. A happy time was when a baby girl was born to us on September 24, 1946, named Vena Rose Walthall, who is now married to Morton Dunn of St. Albans, West Virginia. She and her husband live in Springdale, West Virginia.

Vena and Morton presented me on October 17, 1970, with a beautiful granddaughter named Christy Ann Dunn. Then, on June 21, 1974, I was presented with a grandson named James Mortin Dunn. This made me a very proud and happy grandmother. But not all times are happy times. We have sadness too. A great hurt came to me on March 22, 1987, when the only granddaughter I had was killed instantly in a car wreck. My grandson was in it too and we almost lost him, but God saw it fit to spare him. Their really close friend was also with them. He lived six months, never really regaining consciousness, so it was a loss of two children. We grieve a lot for them, but time is helping us deal with it.

My mother died in November, 1978. My oldest brother, John Alvin Coughlin, died in 1989. Another brother, Michael Lake Coughlin, died in April, 1991. A sister who lived the last two years of her life with me, Mary Emma Coughlin Hutsenpillar, died April, 1992. My oldest sister, Opal Lorena Coughlin Robertson, passed away April 10, 1995. My brother, James Neal Coughlin, was sick just three weeks with cancer before he passed away March 12, 1998. He was buried Sunday, March 15, 1998.

This leaves me now with one brother, William Clark Coughlin; one sister, Hazel Mae Coughlin Franklin; and my father, Michael L. (Mike) Coughlin, still living at 101 years old. His health is very good, and grandchildren and children can sit down while he tells us things that happened in his lifetime. The changes that he has seen come and go are amazing. Dad started to work in the woods, logging with a team of horses when he was thirteen years old. He worked for one man for twenty-three years, who helped him get his first car. He tells us he was so used to driving a team of horses that, when he got to the gate, he hollered, "Whoa! Whoa! Whoa!" but the car went on through the gate. What a laugh we had!

The last highlight of my life was when my grandson met a nice young girl, Kelly Sue Johnson, of Rupert, and married her, and now I have a beautiful two-year-old great-granddaughter named Christina Rose Dunn. This makes our lives complete.

AUTHOR: Vena Coughlin Walthall. Vena lives in Springdale, West Virginia, with her husband on a three-and-a-half acre plot of land. Her daughter and son-in-law live beside them, as well as her grandson and his wife, and her great-granddaughter. Vena's husband raises a big garden every year, and Vena cans the vegetables and fruits and makes her own jellies and jams. She also makes hot sauce, spaghetti sauce, and sandwich spread, the way her mother taught her. Vena has lived in the Springdale community for fifty-four years, and is active in church and community. She also likes to travel.

273-001-ST-WV-002-1998

Three Incidents in a Boy's Life

My grandfather, Oliver Quenton Fox, the third son of Houston and Della Fox, was born on October 25, 1907, and lived to the age of eighty-two. His brother John is still living, but Emmett, William, and Faye have also passed on. They grew up living with their family on a mountain farm in Summers County, near Brooks, West Virginia.

Della and Houston Fox of Summers County, with children (l-r) William, Faye, John, Emmett, and Oliver Fox, circa 1917. Oliver is the author's grandfather.

These are three of my favorite stories of the many told by my father, Jerry David Fox, about his father's childhood. I've written my version of his stories, while keeping some of his dialect. These incidents are from the years 1915 to 1920.

When my grandfather was about eight years old, he was too small to help with heavy work on the farm. His father decided he could ride on Gin, the mule, and take grain to the mill. Two sacks were filled and slung over the mule's neck, and my grandfather was lifted onto Gin's back. Now, with the mule going along at a walking pace, the sacks were slipping on account of one being heavier than the other. I can say, that young boy was scared! If the grain sacks fell, he couldn't lift them. If he got off the mule, he was too short to jump back on. How did my grandfather get to that mill? Well, he inched up onto Gin's neck and put one foot on the lighter sack. Yes, that's how he rode that mule, till the men at the mill could help him get down.

Growing up on a farm, one way to earn a little money was by trapping animals and selling their hides. One winter, my grandfather caught a skunk in one of his traps. While skinning that skunk he cut out its stink sack, put it in a cork-stopper bottle, and put the bottle in the cellar on a beam under the kitchen floor. Now that old bottle was forgotten until a mouse ate the cork. I'm told my grandfather got the hardest thrashing ever over that skunk sack!

What can you do for entertainment when living in the country? During the winters, my grandfather and his brothers would sometimes go to a neighbor's house. Hunting tales, ghost stories, and the like were how they passed the time. Once, after the kids went up to the attic room to sleep, my grandfather's older brother Emmett pulled a trick on him. Just as he was almost asleep, my grandfather felt his covering slowly being pulled off. He pulled the blanket back up and was nearly asleep when something began pulling the blanket again. This happened many times, until his brothers had to bust out laughing! How it worked was, Emmett had seen that the beds were close enough together so that he could reach his brother's blanket with his foot. He had been pretending to be asleep while pulling the blanket off with his toes!

AUTHOR: Steven Fox is the son of Jerry David Fox and Imogene Waybright Fox. Mr. Fox is an amateur archaeologist of historic and prehistoric sites. He is a 1997 West Virginia History Hero, honored for donating to the West Virginia State Museum his collection of bottles manufactured by the four West Virginia factories of the Owens Bottle Company and the Owens-Illinois Glass Company.

274-001-ST-WV-002-1998

My Accent

Where were you born? People often ask me that question, saying they detect a little accent but cannot really identify it. I tell them I was born in southern West Virginia, so close to the Virginia border that I have neither a West Virginia accent nor a Virginia accent, but a mixture of both. My father, Robert Jackson "Jack" Porter, was a coal miner who migrated from Virginia to the coalfields of southern West Virginia. There he met my mother, Mary Magdalene "Maggie" Mills, who is part Cherokee Indian, when she was still in high school. Their courtship was a long one, more than five years, because my mother went away to Charleston, West Virginia, to college. In those days, to travel

one hundred miles on West Virginia roads was too long of a trip for either of them.

However, the courtship lasted, they were married in 1934, and two years later I was born on an Easter Sunday morning. The snow drifts were so high, the doctor hardly made it to the house before I did. Yes, we lived in the country, because my father refused to bring his children up in the coalfields. This small wide place in the road, of approximately eight hundred people, was called Lashmeet, in Mercer County, West Virginia. The Indians cured their meat by hanging it and then lashing it with leather straps, of which we found some evidence on our property.

Patty Kay Porter Grace, 1996.

As the saying goes, "the acorn does not fall far from the tree," and I went to the same high school as my mother. College was a different thing, as I was sent in 1953 to a small teacher's college about thirty minutes' drive from my home.

I was then married to a fellow in the US Navy, Julian Seigle Beamer. We lived in Norfolk, Virginia, then in Bermuda, where our daughter was born. Of course, my accent was questioned many times by the English and Portuguese people on the island. We moved back to Virginia, then to Terre Haute, Indiana, and from there to Columbus, Ohio, where I spent the next twenty-five years.

My first husband passed away. Some time later, I married a wonderful man, John Joseph "Jack" Grace, who was raising three pre-teen children, and that could be another story. The two of us formed a screen-printing business, Fraternity Sportswear Sales Company, retail, and Famous Sportswear Sales Company, wholesale, of Columbus, Ohio. We sold soft goods and party favors to the college market—fraternities, sororities, and college bookstores—and to department stores. Soft goods are T-shirts, sweatshirts, jackets, and jerseys printed with the college name or fraternity or sorority insignia. In traveling over the United States representing this company, I was also questioned many times about my accent, and met many new people in this way.

We sold this company and retired nine years ago to spend our time in Fort Lauderdale, Florida. Since living in Fort Lauderdale, I have been involved in selling real estate with The Prudential Florida Realty. I also spend much of my time doing volunteer fundraising for cancer research, for the Florida Philharmonic Society, and for the Broward Center for the Performing Arts.

My accent has brought me many new friends at the places I have lived and visited. No one away from West Virginia has ever guessed that I am from West Virginia, but everyone tells me they love the way I say anything. I know now that when someone says "where were you born?" it is usually because of my accent and I could be on the way to making a new friend.

AUTHOR: *Patty Grace. Ms. Grace grew up in Mercer County, West Virginia, as the eldest of three children. Now in very active retirement in Fort Lauderdale, Florida, she enjoys volunteer fundraising, as well as sewing, golf, tennis, bridge, and spending time with family.*

275-001-ST-WV-002-1998

My Rear Windows

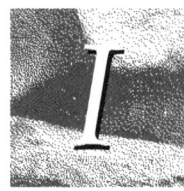

I am fortunate enough to have been born in the beautiful little town of Oceana, West Virginia, nestled deep in a valley of the Appalachias, and this was no accident. God guided my ancestorial grandparents here so they could hunt, fish, trap, farm, and raise their families in the peace and tranquility of Wyoming County. Only the Lord could have created something as beautiful as autumn in the Appalachian Mountains, snow on the pines at Christmas time, or a peaceful summer day swimming in Laurel Fork. And there is just no way to describe the feeling and beauty of spring as it awakens. How blessed we are to live in a place such as this.

I am a member of the Wyoming County and Lincoln County Genealogical Societies in West Virginia, and the Clay County, Kentucky Historical and Genealogical Society. It was to Clay County that my ancestors, including Davidson, Potter, Hays, Campbell, Smith, Callahan, Hollingsworth, Boulton, Herbert, Eltonhead, Brock, Connelly, Stewart, and Wilson, went by wagon train from North Carolina, Maryland, and Scott Coun-

Danford E. Bragg, Sr. and Sylvia Acord-Bragg, 1986.

ty, Virginia, according to *The Strong Family* by J.C. Hurst. The wagon train migrated to Kentucky in 1800–1801. I am also a member of the Grayson County, Virginia Historical and Genealogical Society. This is where my Allen, Blankenship, Lafferity, Jamison, Daniels, and Smith relatives left when they came to Wyoming County.

My parents, Robert Acord, Jr., and Myrtle Lilly Hager-Acord, were married December 21, 1944 in Oceana, and to this marriage eight children were born, of which I am the eldest: Sylvia Ann, Betty Jo, Myrna Catherine, Nancy Carol, Virginia Lee, Stallie Elizabeth, Robert Edward, and Mary Helen. I was born on April 15, 1946 at the home of my maternal grandparents. I wonder if my grandmother, Sylvia Belle Davidson-Hager, felt the bond that was to be between us that I still feel today. She left me her typewriter and desk in her will. She was very special. My father was a muscular man with blue eyes and blonde hair; my mother had dark brown hair and brown eyes, and sometimes when I look in the mirror I see her eyes looking back at me.

My Acord lineage, through my father's father: Sylvia Ann Acord-Bragg, d/o (daughter of) Robert Acord, Jr., s/o (son of) Robert Lee Acord and Mary Eva Ann Allen-Acord, s/o Ben Henderson Acord and Nancy Allen-Acord, s/o John "Old Jack" Acord and Nancy Harper-Acord. Old Jack was said to be a colorful character and a teller of tall tales who lived 107 years. He was the progenitor who settled in 1824 on Acords Branch near Glensfork, Wyoming County, according to *The History of Wyoming County* by Mary Keller Bowman. He was the son of John Acord, Sr., and Rachel Combs, married 1788 in Pennsylvania, s/o Andreas Lawrance Acord, who arrived in Pennsylvania in 1753 from Hamburg, Germany on the ship *Snow Good Hope*.

My Allen lineage, through my father's mother: Sylvia Ann Acord-Bragg, d/o Robert Acord, Jr., s/o Mary Eva Ann Allen-Acord and Robert Lee Acord, d/o Henley Allen and Juliet Ann Blankenship-Allen, s/o John "Crap" Allen and Elizabeth Lafferity-Allen. John "Crap" Allen was killed in the Civil War. He was a Confederate soldier captured by Union soldiers en route to a prison camp, and was killed on Walnut Gap near what is now Kopperston, in Wyoming County. He was the son of John R. Allen, Sr., and Nancy Daniels-Allen, s/o William Allen, Jr., a Revolutionary War veteran. His first wife was Agnes and his second wife was Ann; no last names are known for them. He was the son of William Allen, Sr., and Mary Lewis-Allen. In 1698, William, Sr., was born in York Colony, Virginia. In 1676, the Allens came from Scotland.

My Hager lineage, through my mother's father: Sylvia Ann Acord-Bragg, d/o Myrtle Hager-Acord, d/o Watson Riley Hager and Sylvia Belle Davidson-Hager. Watson was a veteran of World War I and World War II. He was also in the Battle of Blair Mountain, which occurred during the 1920–1921 struggle for organization of the United Mine Workers, of which he was a forty-year member. Watson was the son of Claibourne Hager and Mary Arabess "Arispa" Price. Mary went by Cooper, as she was reared by her grandparents William Cooper

Front row (l-r): Watson R. Hager, author's maternal grandfather; Sylvia A. Bragg, author; Sylvia B. Davidson-Hager, author's maternal grandmother; Myrtle Hager-Acord, author's mother. Back row: Danford E. Bragg, author's husband; Robert Acord, Jr., author's father; Kemper Cook, married to author's mother's first cousin. Taken at Palm Memorial Gardens at Matheny, West Virginia, Easter, 1967.

and Elizabeth Smith-Cooper. Both were born in Greenbrier County, Virginia, later to become Lincoln County, West Virginia. Arispa was born in 1868 in Lincoln County to Andrew Price, s/o William and Sarah Price, and Clarinda Cooper, d/o William Cooper and Elizabeth Smith. They were married in 1866 in Boone County, West Virginia. I have found no trace of them after Arispa was two years old, but will continue to search. Claibourne Hager was the son of Phillip Hager and Rebecca Lovejoy-Hager, s/o Lewis Hager and Sarah Bias-Hager, s/o Michael and Martha Hager. The Hagers came from Germany.

My Davidson lineage, through my mother's mother: Sylvia Ann Acord-Bragg, d/o Myrtle Hager-Acord, d/o Sylvia Belle Davidson-Hager. She was married in 1922 in Lincoln

County, West Virginia. She used the alias Belle Hensley because she had run away from home in Wildcat, Clay County, Kentucky, at age fourteen, and knew the authorities were looking for her. She was the daughter of Blevins Davidson and Ellen Roumania Potter-Davidson, s/o Silas Davidson and Sarah Hayes, married 1848, s/o John Madison Davidson and Polly Campbell, married 1827, s/o Daniel Davidson and Elizabeth Smith-Davidson, married around 1773. He was a Revolutionary War veteran and was born in 1753 in a colony of Virginia. He was the son of Samuel and Margaret Davidson, s/o William Davidson, born in Ulster, Ireland. William crossed from Northern Ireland with his father John Davidson to America in the year 1720.

Sylvia Ann Acord-Bragg.

Now I have told you of some of my ancestorial grandparents, whose backgrounds are quite a mixture. They all made me Sylvia Ann Acord-Bragg, wife of Danford Earl Bragg, Sr., mother of Danice Lilly Bragg and Danford Earl Bragg, Jr., grandmother of Danielle, George, Jr., and Travis Wooten, and of Danford Earl III, Cody Shaun, and Taylor Ann Bragg, and great-grandmother of Destiny Danice Wooten.

AUTHOR: Sylvia Ann Acord-Bragg.

276-001-ST-WV-002-1998

Teaching School in Rural Appalachia

A Salute to Juanita Austin Basham

In the fall of 1932, a small blond woman with the determination to become a teacher entered Concord College, in Mercer County, Athens, West Virginia. With two dresses and thirty-two dollars borrowed from a cousin she entered a two-year teaching program which granted her a Standard Normal Teaching Degree. In September 1936, this young woman was given her first school, a one-room building, which was located at Pleasant Hill. This community was located in Mercer County, West Virginia, between Elgood, West Virginia, and Glen Lyn, Virginia. This small woman, wearing a size four shoe and a girl's size ten dress, would walk the seventeen miles to her destination on Monday morning, boarding all week in the community in order to teach, and then would walk back to her home on Friday afternoon. The students, who filled seats in grades one through eight, were as large as or larger than their teacher. Children in this community didn't know what a book, pencil, or scissors were used for. This teacher took the time not only to teach formal education, but she taught the girls to do embroidery, sew, and make themselves a dress. She taught the boys how to make towel racks and other things using hammers, nails, and saws.

From there this loving, gifted, and understanding teacher moved on to the Cunningham School in 1941. This school is located between Dot, West Virginia, and Igeria, West Virginia, in Mercer County. When she arrived there, all the kids used the word "can't." The first assignment given to those twenty students was to write the words "I can't" on a small piece of paper. Each student folded their piece of paper, and placed it in a glass jar; all went outside to a large oak tree, dug a hole, and buried "can't." The word can't was never used again in the Cunningham School while this teacher was there.

In 1948, this teacher was asked to go to Butler School, between Pettry, West Virginia, and Hilltop, West Virginia, then to Pine Grove School at Lerona, West Virginia. From there she moved to Suck Creek School, Summers County, near Little Bluestone, West Virginia in 1956, where she taught until it closed in 1961. This teacher was the first to initiate the hot lunch program in her school at Ellison Ridge, West Virginia, and was one of the first special education instructors, as well as one of the first Head Start teachers in the 1960s program. For over thirty-eight years, her teaching was an example. Through her leadership, her

Juanita Austin Basham.

dedication to others, her compassion, and her generosity for others in her community, Juanita Austin Basham was named Outstanding Elementary Teacher of America for 1973, for the state of West Virginia.

For her role as a wife, parent, teacher, and community volunteer, as a loving and kind woman who sees goodness in those around her, and one who has given so freely of her time and talent, Juanita was nominated to represent the Nimitz-Jumping Branch Extension Homemakers as Belle from Summers County, West Virginia. It is with great honor and love that her family writes of her accomplishments over great odds, and it is her faith in God that allows her love to shine, touching those whom she has encouraged, supported, and given knowledge to, making the world a better place.

Author: Wilma Lilly Rodes. Mrs. Rodes is Mrs. Basham's daughter. She has two children, Shannon and David. She says her family is "forever bonded through ties of love, honor, and our heritage of being West Virginian."

277-001-ST-WV-002-1998

An Embarrassing Moment

Recently, I noticed my violin in the corner of my closet, and got it out. I opened the case to reveal my violin resting on the plush yellow velvet lining. As I lifted the violin and put it under my chin, I recalled my first recital, when I was about six years old.

My violin teacher was Mr. A. Ben Lowe. I had been practicing my number for several weeks. Finally, a lady who would accompany us on the piano came, and we went through it several times. The recital was the next day at the First Baptist Church, in Beckley, West Virginia. I walked calmly to my place and began to play with the pianist. Then I got excited, and I began to play faster and faster. When I got to a certain place in the music, the pianist was supposed to turn the page and continue. When I realized she hadn't caught up with me yet, I put my violin under my arm and waited. When she finally turned the page, I put my violin under my chin and finished the number with her.

Virginia Bonds.

Author: Virginia Bonds. Virginia still lives in Beckley, West Virginia, where her first violin recital was held. Her composure in the face of embarrassment allowed her to continue with her violin lessons. She went on to play in her school orchestra from seventh to twelfth grades, in Beckley Junior High and Woodrow Wilson High, and for a year in the Marshall College orchestra, in Huntington, West Virginia.

278-001-ST-WV-002-1998

Chapter 7

Potomac Highlands

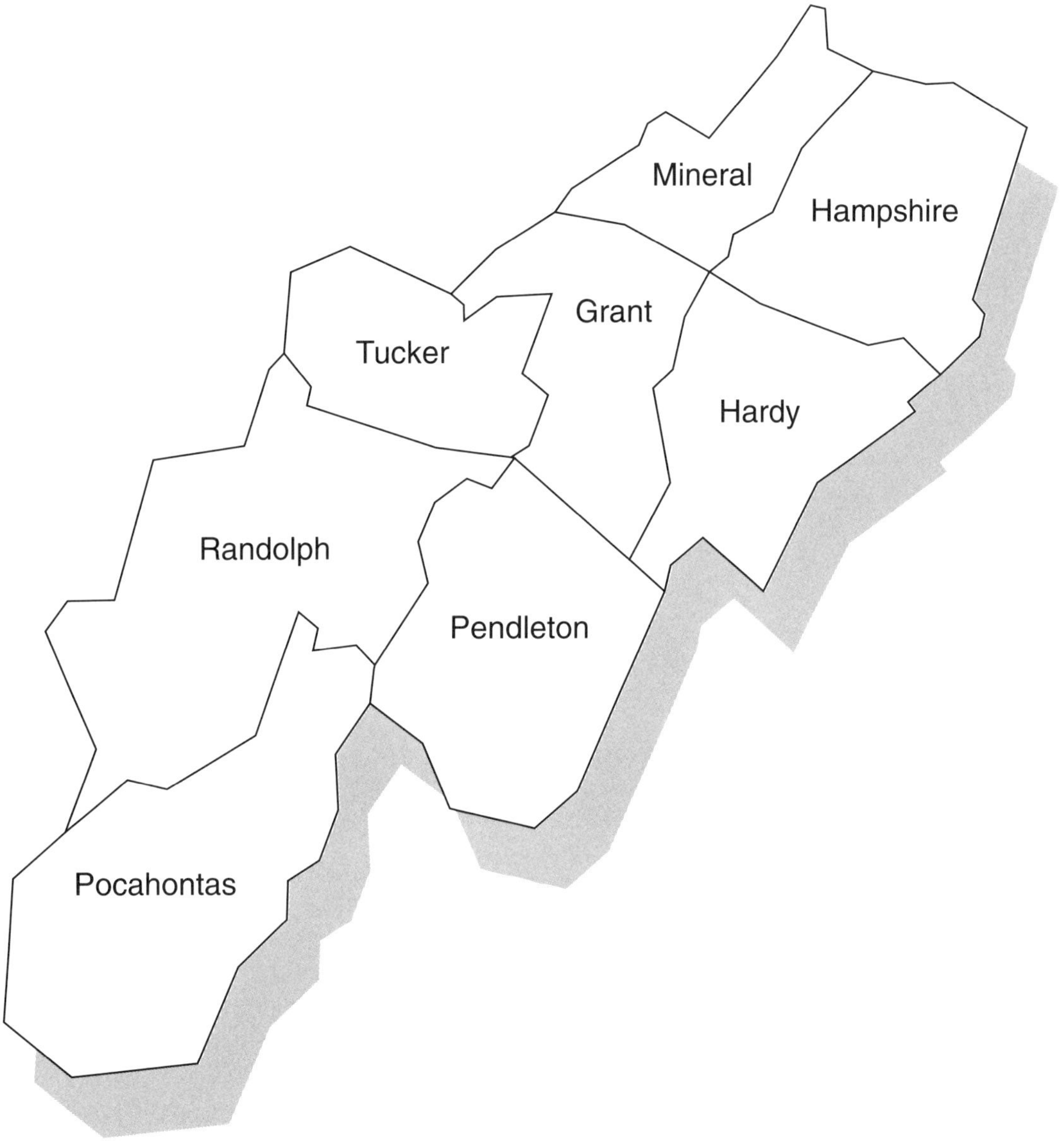

An Ode to the One-Room Schools

C'lang, clang, clang. The hand-held school bell was heralding the start of school in five minutes, at nine o'clock. We dashed out the door and ran approximately 500 yards down past the garden and were in our seats in time. You see, we were fortunate in living near the little one-room school.

The school was Old Rough Run One-Room School, in the Rough Run area eight miles from Petersburg, in Grant County. The original building had burned in 1925, and a new one was built. By state regulations, the new building, facing west, had to have all the windows on the south side of the room, making the light come in over our left shoulders. A nice vestibule had shelves and hangers for caps and coats—left side for girls and right side for boys. A common water cooler occupied a table in the vestibule. Directly above was a cabinet for our individual cups. A treat of the day was going to a neighbor's house for a pail of water.

On the west end of the room hung two blackboards complete with chalk, erasers, and framed pictures above. A choice duty was being asked to go outside and clap the erasers together to clear the chalk accumulation.

The teacher's desk was directly in front of the room. Teachers assigned to the school came to the community and roomed and boarded with a local family. A recitation bench occupied space across the room. Contrary to today's standards, all eight grades were in the same room and were called to the bench at separate times for recitation and instructions from the teacher.

Two rows of double desks completed the furnishing—smaller desks in front and larger ones towards the back. Desks were complete with ink wells, a groove for pencils, and a shelf beneath for books. A big burnside stove in the center of the room provided heating and could be used to heat soup or anything else a pupil brought in their tin dinner bucket.

Morning and evening flag raising was a ritual complete with the Pledge of Allegiance. A Bible verse and prayer was the opening exercise. We considered it a privilege to be asked to read the morning Bible verse. Strict discipline was maintained, and was needed for the twenty-plus pupils in one room.

Now, don't think it was all work and no play. At 10:15 and 2:15, teacher would announce recess, which started a mad rush outside to play tag, prisoner's base, fox and geese, ring around the rosy, drop the handkerchief, etc. Baseball was played with a homemade flat bat and a ball made by wrapping twine around a wad of inner tube. Don't laugh—that was our playground equipment!

Every Friday at 3:30, all the upper grades lined up around the room for a spelling bee. We spelled for head marks and turned down if we missed a word. A top prize was given at the end of the year for the most head marks.

"Teacher and student body at the Old Rough Run One-Room School, which I attended." Circa '20s.

Our schoolhouse was the social center for the community. Programs were held at holidays, and a couple times a year a box supper was held if we needed funds for a special purpose. The girls would decorate a lunch box and fill it with goodies to be auctioned off. The fellows would bid for the chance to share the goodies with his "girl." Sometimes a little brother would "tip off" which was his sister's box.

All eighth-grade students took the diploma test to be eligible for high school. Going to high school meant leaving home and boarding near a school in the city. Consequently, few young people took advantage of higher education.

Our Mountain State Heritage

"All dressed up and ready for church. I'm in the middle in the front seat of this Model T. Ford." Photo taken approximately 1919.

Believe it or not, we did survive without school buses, hot lunches, computers, electricity, and indoor plumbing, but basic principles were learned in those little one-room schools which produced teachers, nurses, doctors, lawyers, pilots, and others of whom we justly can be proud.

Author's Note: When my father, Jessie N. Sites, married my mother, Nettie Catherine Getz, he received farm acreage and built our home around 1912. Six children were born. One died in infancy. The Old Rough Run One-Room School, which is still standing, was constructed in 1925, on a plot of our land. All five of us kids attended this school.

AUTHOR: *Edna Post adds, "My husband, Clay Post, and I will celebrate our fifty-eighth anniversary in September, 1998. We have one son, Daniel. My husband and I are retired and living in Petersburg, West Virginia. We are active in the community and in church. Daniel and I are state 4-H All-Stars, and I was the Grant County Belle in 1996." See index for additional work by Ms. Post.*

279-001-ST-WV-002-1998

A Real Cold Idea—How It All Came About!

On our farm in Grant County, an Ice House was constructed with double walls approximately twelve inches apart to be filled with sawdust for insulation. There was a creek running through the farm which led to a pond, used as a swimming hole in the summer. The Ice House was ready for the cold winter weather when the pond would freeze solid across, with ice six to eight inches thick.

A side benefit of the Ice House was added—a pipe had been built through the wall at the floor level. A concrete trough erected in an adjoining room caught the cold, dripping water as some of the ice would melt. Milk and butter were refrigerated in that manner.

"Forget about fancy parks and pavilions for a picnic! At these family picnics, the food was spread on the ground as shown. My mother, Nettie Catherine Getz Sites, is in front on the left with her back to the camera, and I'm eighth in the row—just in front of the lady standing."

Neighbors would gather to assist in the ice cutting and hauling to the Ice House. My dad would chop off the ice in big squares to make it easy to pack in the Ice House. A two-horse wagon was used to haul it to the house. Now, the house had a loading platform in front of the main opening. The ice was handed up to one person—then he would layer sawdust, ice, sawdust, and more ice, until the building was full of sawdust-covered ice. This took an entire day to accomplish. Afterwards, there was always a big, hot dinner awaiting the workers, who really enjoyed it and the chance to warm up beside the big stove in the dining room. Of course, those workers expected a big bag of ice in the summer if requested.

Everyone in Edna's family looked forward to delicious homemade ice cream. Look at these smiles of anticipation!

At a given time, usually on a Sunday afternoon, someone would say, "How about some ice cream." That was the sign to go into action. The men and boys climbed up a ladder to the opening of the Ice House and dug ice out of the sawdust, rinsed it off with water, put it in a burlap sack, and crushed it with a mallet. In the meantime, I was in the kitchen "mixin' the fixin's." Milk was warmed, sugar and Junket tablets were dissolved in the milk. Favorite flavors were added which usually consisted of vanilla, strawberries, peaches, raspberries, or whatever we had.

The ice cream freezer was ready for this preparation. The mixture was poured in the freezer can and ice packed around it in the wooden bucket. A generous amount of salt was added to the ice to aid in the freezing process.

After closing the freezer bucket, it was turned till the preparation was cooled, then it was opened and a goodly portion of real country cream was poured in. (Cream could not be added earlier as it would have turned to butter.) The freezer can was closed and plenty of ice and salt added—then the real work began—turning until the ingredients stiffened. Then the ice and salt were scraped from the lid so it could be opened and the dasher removed. The kids usually got a premature tasting by licking the dasher. Then it was packed down with extra ice for about an hour to "ripen." Then the delicacy was dished out—um, um good.

Author's Note: One year, one of the helpers gathering ice smoked cigars. He discarded one and my eight-year-old brother picked it up and chewed on it. Evening came and he was nowhere to be found. Mother and Dad went down by the creek searching. But, no boy! When we finally found him, he had come home and sneaked upstairs to bed—the cigar had made him sick.

AUTHOR: *Edna Post. See index for additional work by Edna Post.*

280-001-ST-WV-002-1998

"Cool"

have come to the conclusion that Webster will have to revise the Dictionary or else my copy is outdated. The vocabulary of this generation is not easily understood by myself, an old lady in her seventy-fifth year.

Growing up during the Great Depression, I have firsthand experience with depression and recycling, and I know what "cool" is.

Depression in the '30s meant a state of the economy. It meant doing without; it meant sharing; it meant wishing for a nickel for a candy bar, or a bottle of pop. And, yes, recycling went right along with the Depression. Recycling was saving the cotton from an aspirin bottle. It meant trading outgrown clothes with anyone who could wear them. Many small children had clothing made from the legs of a worn-out suit. Bedclothes were made from usable scraps from worn clothes. Laundry soap and labor were even saved by doing laundry only once a week. One of my sharpest memories is the starched underwear made from cotton feed bags (starched to make them stay clean longer). I can still feel the chafing.

Now, I can't get over the use of the word "cool." I hear my teenage granddaughter answer a friend who has made a remark such as "We won the game tonight," with the reply, "cool." That has absolutely nothing to do with my interpretation of the meaning of "cool."

I worked my way through college at Potomac State College and landed a job in 1942 as a clerk for Farmers Home Administration in Franklin, Pendleton County, West Virginia. I was now living in town with all modern conveniences. The Great Depression was only a memory. Soon I met a young man who lived in the country, also in Pendleton County. His name was Woodrow Wilson Hartman. We courted for a time; he told me about his farm home with air conditioning even in the bathroom, and finally, December 1943, we got married.

Alice B. and Woodrow W. Hartman, 1996.

We went on a short honeymoon, came back late at night, and went to his farm. The temperature was ten below zero. I got ready for bed, and, as most brides do, put on a sheer nightgown and looked for the bathroom. Not being able to find it, I asked my husband where it was. He got the kerosene lantern down from the shelf and lit it with me looking on, not knowing what to think. He then told me to put on my coat and follow.

Having said I would obey, I did just that. We trotted through the garden out to a little building out back. "Cool" is the cold air coming in from all four sides and up through the bottom.

AUTHOR: Alice Branson Hartman. Mrs. Hartman has been married to Woodrow W. Hartman for fifty-five years. They have one son, William (Bill), and one granddaughter, Hiedi Jon. Alice and Woodrow pioneered in the TV cable industry and own Hartman's Furniture, in Franklin. Alice currently serves as mayor of Franklin, West Virginia.

281-001-ST-WV-002-1998

old towels were cut into squares and hemmed for washcloths. Remaining pieces were saved for bandages. Newspapers not needed to start the coal stove were used to clean windows with a solution of vinegar and water. Used laundry water was poured on the garden. Everything had a use.

Mom made every piece of clothing her nine children wore. She also made her dresses, and aprons and bonnets with the scraps. Mom always wore a bonnet in the sun to shade her face and neck. When she died at age eighty-eight, she never had a wrinkle.

Wrapping cord was crocheted into dishcloths. Anything made of wool and worn out was cut into squares for quilts, which were stuffed with worn out blankets. It took a lot of quilts to cover nine children.

Dad's trousers tended to wear out in the front panel first, around the knees. Mom would take good back panels and sew them down the fronts of his new pairs to make them last longer. Even one of her old aprons had a use as a denim work cap for Dad.

Once Mom wanted to wallpaper over the plaster. She tore rags into squares and dipped them into paste made of cooked flour, and smoothed over the holes in the wall. The next day she made more paste and was ready to wallpaper.

Mom used baking soda in her bath water as deodorant, and also saved money by baking all our bread. She baked twice a week. Our sweet treat was homemade bread spread with jelly. To us it was better than cake.

AUTHOR: Betty Waller quit school and was married at age sixteen, during World War II. She and her husband had three daughters. Mrs. Waller worked for W.T. Grant Co. for twenty years, and for Stone & Thomas for ten years. At age fifty-seven, she got her GED and then enrolled at Fairmont State College, all while working full-time. She graduated at age sixty-two with an associate's degree. Mrs. Waller is now retired, and has seven grandchildren and six great-grandchildren.

282-001-ST-WV-002-1998

Recycling by My Mother

Living in Elkins, West Virginia during the Depression, my mother, Ethel Shrover Miller, defined recycling. When a sheet wore out in the middle, she took the good corners and made pillow cases. The worn parts became handkerchiefs for Dad, Floyd C. Miller. Good parts of

Never a Dull Moment

There is never a dull moment in the life of an elementary school teacher. I recall that my first year teaching was quite an experience. Because I was born in a small town and attended school half a block from our residence, as a child I never experienced the fun of being in a one-room school. Due to my family's politics, when I became a teacher, the president of

CHAPTER 7: POTOMAC HIGHLANDS

Maypole at Parran School, May 17, 1935.

the local Board of Education sent me to teach in a one-room school, five miles from town, on a nice, narrow, clay country road.

I remember that, my first morning, I made the mistake of picking up the children I passed on the way, who were walking to school. Soon, the old Dodge sedan held thirteen children, believe it or not! Arriving that first morning with "my load," I was greeted by as many arriving from the other direction as I had transported. I remember that first day so vividly. And every morning after, the children wanted a ride.

There stood the small white building with four windows on one side, and the other wall blank. It was Parran One-Room School, located five miles south of Moorefield, West Virginia, on South Fork Road, in Hardy County. There were two little buildings out back, one for the girls and one for the boys, and a lean-to woodshed attached to the building to house the wood to be burned in the stove that sat in the middle of the room.

On opening the schoolhouse door, there was a small hallway with hooks for the children to hang their coats. To one side was a shelf holding a granite water cooler and a bucket beside it, for water that had been carried from about a quarter of a mile away, for drinking and sanitation. Every child was supposed to have either a glass or tin cup, or a folding cup for drinking water. Rows of larger desks were in the back of the classroom, with the seats getting smaller toward the front. The teacher's desk was a small homemade creation with a tilt top lid, with every teacher's name written on it since 1903, and space to keep the records. In back of the teacher's desk was a blackboard (now called a chalkboard). On the windowless side of the room was a homemade bookcase, which was the school library. Beside it was a pump organ, used for church services held in the building. Since I could play, it provided music daily, after the Bible reading and flag salute.

It was a wonderful year! We had parent-teacher meetings on the last Friday of each month, with a program presented by the children. Then to bring the year to an end, there was a big picnic given by the parents with a Maypole and a program by the children.

How times have changed! These good old days will always be remembered.

Author's Note: At the end of the school year, the children and their parents all looked forward to the big May Day celebration. May Day has been celebrated on the first day of May since the earliest times, as an out-of-door festivity. On this day, our school would erect a Maypole with brightly colored streamers or ribbons attached at the top. Originally, men and women were the dancers, but, as in our school, children eventually became the dancers. The girls wore different colored paper dresses, which added to the beauty of the dance. Each child held the end of a streamer in one hand, while dancing around the Maypole. They wove in and out, creating intricate patterns, wrapping and unwrapping the pole, all in time with the lively march of a Victrola.

Ella Bergdoll, 1960.

AUTHOR: Ella Bergdoll. Ella retired after teaching for forty-five years. Her parents were Thomas Jefferson Bergdoll and Patsy Harper Bergdoll. She has one sister, Virginia Bergdoll Whitesell. Ella lives in the house she was born in. She is active in the Methodist Church, and has sung in the choir since she was fourteen. She had a column in the WV Education Association School Journal, called "Ella's Tips," and was active in national, state, and county education, holding offices in each association. She enjoys tatting, crocheting, and knitting, and has done a lot of traveling, having been in all fifty states as well as Europe, Japan, China, and Korea.

283-001-ST-WV-002-1998

The Turkey Almost Caught

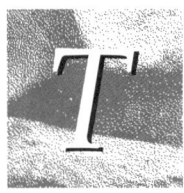

This exciting incident (at least it was to us) took place at Chert Mountain Orchard, our home. It is located in Mineral County, in the Eastern Panhandle of West Virginia. At that time the orchard was owned and operated by Ed A. Leatherman, Jr. To add an interesting historical fact, a four-county stone is located here; namely, Hardy, Grant, Hampshire, and Mineral. One is able to be in four counties at once.

The following is a true story about my nephew, Roy Arthur Stickley, known as "Artie," and myself. This experience happened one Sunday in the fall of 1952, or thereabout.

When my husband, James (Jimmy) R. Stickley, and I went to Sunday school and church, our niece and nephew liked to come home with us after church to visit. This particular Sunday, Jimmy had to work, so Artie came home with me. After dinner we decided to go for a drive through the orchard. It was always so pretty this time of year with so many apples, red and yellow, along with the colorful trees joining and surrounding the orchard. As we came towards the upper line fence corner where Mineral County borders Grant County, we saw three or four wild turkeys.

Chert Mountain Orchard home, in the winter of 1972 or 1973.

Needless to say the two of us were quite excited, even though Artie was only five years old. I said to Artie, "I'm going to pull the car down a piece below and we'll sneak back and maybe we could catch one of those turkeys." (Dumb me.) Of course Artie, being only five, agreed. So we proceeded to close in cautiously on those turkeys, having picked the biggest one to catch.

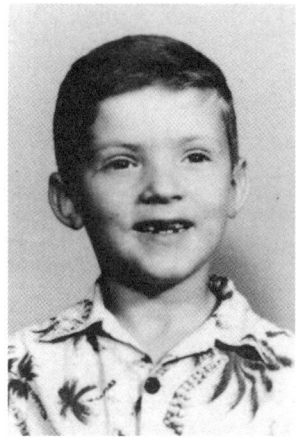

Roy Arthur "Artie" Stickley, 1953. Artie was six years old and in the first grade when this photo was taken. He is a native of Hampshire County and at present is still living at the same residence, in Purgitsville, West Virginia.

Those doggone turkeys took off just like a helicopter, straight up into the air. I'm sure our mouths must have popped open in amazement. I know we surely were disappointed.

When we returned home in the evening we had quite a tale for Artie to tell his Uncle Jim. Anyhow we learned later, had we been able to catch one we may have been hurt. All's well that ends well. I guess the moral to this tale is an old one: "Never count your turkeys before they're caught."

AUTHOR: *Louise Leatherman Stickley Malcolm. Louise was born in Pennsylvania but has been a resident of West Virginia for sixty years. At present, she is living in Keyser, West Virginia.*

284-001-ST-WV-002-1998

When We Became West Virginians

Remembrances from the 1930s

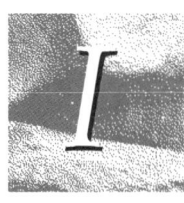

I share the same 1928 birth year with Shirley Temple and Mickey Mouse. "Queen" Elizabeth was then a toddler of two, and Shirley, Mickey, and I would be three when Elizabeth Taylor and Jackie Bouvier (Kennedy) were born. Calvin Coolidge was president, the thirtieth, but within six months Herbert Hoover was presiding.

In the year 1934, the nation was in the middle of the Great Depression. The New Deal, a plan of action, was taking shape under President Franklin Roosevelt, who died in office during my senior year in high school. Europe was experiencing the beginning of World War II in 1939, and the United States entered the war on December 7, 1941, after the bombing of Pearl Harbor in Hawaii. During this span were my grade school

CHAPTER 7: POTOMAC HIGHLANDS

years. Before these years, my parents had each weathered World War I; now, as parents in the depression era, they were full of despair, anxiety, and hope for us to be happy, and to plan for a peaceful and prosperous future.

I was born Miriam Louise Steele at New Kensington, Pennsylvania; my sister, Dorothy Jean Steele, was born two years later in 1930. We are the children of Alfred Reyburn Steele, born in 1899, who resided at Hoboken (now Blawnox), Pennsylvania, and the former Mildred Hendrickson, born in 1900 at Springdale, Pennsylvania. In my very early years we remained in the Pittsburgh area.

My dad, timekeeper for the Vang Construction Company of Pittsburgh, was injured on the Ohio River Boulevard job in 1933—his ankle crushed by the fall of an iron steel beam. He was hospitalized for two years in Pittsburgh. Sam G. Polino and Company, of Elkins, West Virginia, was doing a sublet job in Pittsburgh when Dad was injured. Sam G. asked Dad to get in touch with him when he was able to work. And so we Pennsylvanians found ourselves in West Virginia in 1935.

This is the way I remember my life when I was a child.

Our first West Virginia home: Philippi, summer 1935

Miriam Steele, the author, as a first-grader in Springdale, Pennsylvania, before moving to Philippi, West Virginia in the summer of 1935.

We lived in Philippi during that summer of 1935, just after my first-grade year, with Dad supervising the construction of Route 92 from Belington to Nestorville. It was his first job since the accident, and he was maneuvering around with the help of a crutch.

Our apartment that summer was the second floor of a residence owned by Mrs. and Mr. George White. They and their son occupied the downstairs. Located at 126 Main Street, the house has since been razed, and Hardy's is now located next door. The Methodist Church was on the corner, and across the street from the church was the brick Philippi Grade School, also since razed.

Beside the grade school was a very large, beautiful Victorian home. On occasion I played with the Teters' granddaughter, who was visiting from Elkins. While later attending Elkins High School, my friend Jane Teter and I giggled when we realized that we were these little girls.

An elderly gentleman of sport, also named White, who lived three houses up the street, rode his dapple gray horse for the morning trek to the post office. Accompanying him on several occasions sat an excited Miriam high in the saddle.

Across the street in another lovely, large Victorian house lived the Smiths. Marjorie, Eleanor, Buddy, and Ned were close to our ages. The Smiths owned the Rexall drug store, and Mr. Smith, an artist, painted the previews of coming attractions for the movie house. The Smith children had a high old-fashioned two-wheel bicycle, and this was the summer that I learned to ride. I remember us kids crowding under the Smith's player piano to eat the butter and sugar sandwiches Mrs. Smith served.

A field and pasture extended to the Tygarts Valley River behind the Smith's house. Cow dung was abundant in the field, and we had fun ducking the sailing disks.

Dad bought a new fishing rod, and I was the proud recipient of his old telescopic rod and creel. Very early I was Dad's fishing buddy, and learned to put the split shot on the line and wiggly worms on the hook, and to wet my hands first before touching the fish when removing the hook from its mouth.

Sugar Creek on Route 92 was the site of Sunday afternoon recreation: Dad washed the car, and my sister and I waded while Mom read the paper.

On Labor Day we permanently left Philippi, and routed the car to Springdale, Pennsylvania. I stayed there with my grandparents for several months to start the second grade, while the rest of the family packed a few things in the 1934 Ford and headed south in the fall of 1935 for a long journey to the unknown—which proved to be a cold, snowy winter and a very rainy April in the mountains of West Virginia: Marlinton.

Marlinton, our second home in West Virginia, 1935–1936

"When are we going to be there!! Where is this town?"

I surfaced in the mountain town of Marlinton after the Thanksgiving holiday via a long and hard trip with my parents.

Perhaps you can visualize the Ford with running boards and lack of comfort. It was a long, long trip, with very, very few filling

stations—and I always held a paper bag on my lap for car sickness. At the top of each mountain was a watering trough, probably supplied and kept filled by the Civilian Conservation Corps. As cars were exhausted and overheated from traveling to this level, the side hoods were raised, the steam would hiss, and water was carefully added to the radiator. (A watering can was a must!) Even when the roads were two lane, all of the bridges were one lane, and most of the roads—gravel, blacktop, dirt, brick, and fords—were narrow and windy. Flat tires were frequent, and we learned very early on that the best method to change a tire was to remain absolutely silent during the change and for the next two hours up the road, praying that the patch work on the innertube was a super-secure job. An innertube kit was standard car equipment, along with a full can of gasoline.

Finally we entered the valley that would be my home through the coming winter. Marlinton always weathered cold winters and deep snows. Considering the freeze and thaw factors, the winter road conditions in and out of Marlinton in the mid-'30s were almost impossible—once one was in the valley, one stayed until after the spring thaw. The winter of 1935–36 proved no exception.

Just east of Route 219, one entered downtown Marlinton after crossing the Greenbrier River bridge. As I recall the first block, the Presbyterian Church was on the right, and across the street were the hospital and doctor's office. In the second block, on the right, was a clothing store on the corner, and then a bar, other businesses, a grocery store, and Johnson's restaurant next to the end of the block, with our apartment upstairs. Across the street there were an A&P (Atlantic & Pacific Tea Company), the Alpine Theatre, and a corner drugstore opposite our abode.

The restaurant that we lived above did not serve colored people in the front restaurant, only in the rear lot. The entrance to our apartment was on the east side of the building and up many steps. In the front of the building were two rooms rented to other tenants, and on the west side were rented rooms and a community bath. The wide hall served as a community kitchen. Privacy was certainly not part of the plan!

Although our time in Marlinton was short, we were active in town. We saw a "new" movie at the theater every Tuesday. The piano player was situated on the stage and accompanied the silent action by playing to echo the drama of the movies. (I might add that the piano player was a permanent fixture until the '40s. In Elkins, the piano player was Lillian Henry.) Since Dad's construction job took him out of town, he would pick up the Warner's movie reel at Durbin or Richwood on Mondays and deliver it to the next movie house on Wednesdays, so we got to go for free.

We attended the yellow brick Marlinton Methodist Church. Dot and I would walk to Sunday school and then ride home with our parents after church. During basketball season, Mother and I were loyal supporters of the high school team for the home games.

The author and her Philippi, West Virginia playmates, August, 1935 (l-r): Miriam Steele (the author), Buddy Smith, Dotty Steele (the author's younger sister), Eleanor Smith, Ned Smith, and Marjorie Smith. When it came time for Mr. Smith to gas up the family car, Miriam, Dotty, and all the Smith children would pile in for the three-block drive to the filling station.

I made the trips to the post office and grocery stores. On one occasion, I came home in tears holding each item. The grocer had asked me if I wanted "a poke"—the mountain term, I learned later, for a paper bag.

That winter, the dining room was where the "action" was, because the coal stove, our best heat, was there. I remember that, during Christmas, we just sat down to dinner when the electric failed. Dad opened the door to the coal stove and we ate by "coal light." Gas fuel had not yet been introduced to this area. Santa brought me a dollhouse that year. It was a green two-story house with a red roof, and had real stairs. The dollhouse and a roll-top desk from Santa in 1934 were always my greatest childhood possessions.

I entered second grade at Marlinton Grade School mid-term. My mother never conquered our kerosene range so, at the age of seven, I got ready for school and proceeded downstairs each morning to the restaurant for a hot cereal breakfast. After breakfast I walked the two blocks to the huge, brick grade school by crossing the railroad tracks. Along the sides of the tracks was a grassy area where two staked cows grazed. Near the tracks there remained standing a fifteen-foot part of a dead tree. An older child told me that George Washington had slept in it. In our classroom I would look at the portrait of our first president and imagine George hanging in that tree trying to find a comfortable position to sleep.

My teacher was a Mrs. Stella Moore. I believe my giggles got me in a lot of trouble with my teachers, especially Mrs. Moore. While I was attending a gathering on Droop Mountain in the late '60s, a lady approached me and asked, "Miriam?" I must have looked the same and of course Mrs. Moore hadn't aged a day either.

The school kids I remember are Earl; the blond Kirkpatrick twins, Maxine and Max; and Jewel. My best friends at this time were Louise Knapp, who lived coincidentally by Knapp Creek, and Betty Waugh, who lived near the funeral home.

Mom read to Dot and me each evening. We listened in awe to *The Five Little Peppers and How They Grew* and *Aesop's Fables*, and we recited by heart Robert Louis Stevenson's *A Child's Garden of Verses*.

When winter finally passed, Marlinton was hit hard by the infamous April flood of 1936. All winter it had snowed; in the spring it melted during the rains, and water accumulated in the valley. To help the walking students escape the rising water, the principal, Mr. Johnson, took us home in his car.

Marlinton was the hub for the Civilian Conservation Corps, or CCC. It was a Depression-era program approved and funded by the US Congress to help alleviate unemployment. At that time, between 1933 and 1942, it was one of the few available opportunities for 250,000 young men. The CCC focused on averting the destruction and neglect of natural resources through reforestation and land reclamation, and on constructing access roads. The corps operated as the army: uniforms, housing, meals, military vehicles, and small wages. As we lived on the main street, I can remember the tobacco "spit" all over the sidewalks. This is also the period of time that my sister was learning to roller skate, and she came in contact frequently with the sidewalk.

Dad was now overseeing the surfacing of Route 39 from Marlinton to Minnehaha Springs, and a new Route 39 from Mill Point to Richwood. He was still using one crutch. During the spring when the weather was warmer, we would pile in the car on Sundays and proceed to inspect the weekly road progress on Route 39 along the Cherry River. Sometimes Mom and kids enjoyed time at a country church beside the road, which we found unlocked. Mom played the piano and we sang hymns, while Dad washed "the Ford in a ford." We also had another place to wash our car: a ford on Campbell Creek at Campbelltown.

As became a tradition, I was to spend that next summer, 1936, with my grandparents and relatives in Springdale, Pennsylvania. As we drove near Huttonsville, West Virginia, on our way to Pennsylvania that spring, Dad pointed out in the cornfields the prominent trenches that had been used by the troops during the Civil War. Some of the trenches were still visible even in the early 1950s—almost a hundred years later.

A game Dad and I enjoyed in the car was to follow the old twisty parallel road and stream crossings. As new roads were being built, along with a one-lane bridge, he tested my eye for the topography of the land and the fords on the streams. Still today I eyeball the sides of the road for past trails and roads, and watch them crisscross the newer, straighter paved surfaces.

While in Pennsylvania during vacation that summer, my future was decided: the family moved to Belington more permanently in the fall of 1936, and we were to become West Virginians.

AUTHOR: Miriam Reyburn-Steele is retired from the US Army Corps of Engineers in real estate acquisition, and resides on St. Simons Island, Georgia. Her daughter, Cynthia Phillips Kolsun, and family reside in Elkins, and her son, Rod Steele Phillips, and family have a home in Seattle, Washington. Ms. Reyburn-Steele recalls that, on her last trip to Marlinton, in 1970, she had the honor of escorting Pulitzer Prize–winning West Virginia author Pearl S. Buck in the Pocahontas County Pioneer Days parade.

285-001-ST-WV-002-1998

Chapter 8

Eastern Panhandle

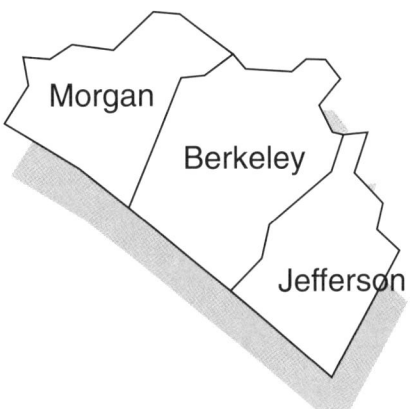

The Court House at Midnight

I came here at midnight
    to watch you alone
As you staunchly stood guard,
    your foundation of stone

Embedded in freedom,
    your walls standing fast
With your face to the sunrise,
    your pillars to last

Through centuries,
    guarding the history within,
The recording of deaths
    and the births and the sin

Of humankind misery,
    joy and defeat
And the records of lovings
    and deeds of conceit.

The Jefferson County courthouse, in Charles Town, West Virginia, as shown on a city brochure.

My heart swelled to see you
    alone in the dark
With your courtyard defining
    your place in the park,

Your wrought iron fence
    with the spires stretching high
Like an army of strength
    as they reached for the sky.

The breeze in the boxwood
    swayed gentle and near
As the clouds overhead moved
    so calmly and clear.

The moonlight shone down
    on your vigil tonight
In your solitude,
    waiting for day and the light,

Again in your walls
    will be stories gone by,
Those of who gets to live
    and who is to die,

Of freedom for some
    and a sentence for those
For whom justice decided
    that wrongly they chose,

Of human life living
    and human life dead,
Of a dignity silent
    and dignity said

In speeches that nobody
    wanted to hear.
Of a monument wordless
    and tower austere

A mirror of life
    at its glorious best
And the worst one could tell
    about all of the rest,

Dismay of upheaval
    and wonder and shame
And the dashing of morals
    and standards and name,

Gone hither in history,
    echoing halls
With your majesty hoarding
    the tales in your walls.

Oh Court House your records
    containing the tears
Of the triumphs and tragedies
    down through the years,

I went there at midnight
    and stood on your hill.
When the clock tolled the twelve stroke,
    I waited until

The last tolling
    had rung out its knell.
Then I stood 'til your silence
    had nothing to tell.

    So sleep in the moonlight,
        oh Court House of old
    With your records of conquests
        and histories told,

The clock tower at midnight
has sung out our praise
As your heartbeat is handed us
down through the days.

AUTHOR: *N.J. Lewis. Ms. Lewis lives in Charles Town. After an adult lifetime away, she has finally "come home to West Virginia."*

Editors' Note: In 1748, Lord Fairfax sent surveyors to map his holdings in what is now Jefferson County, West Virginia. Young surveyor George Washington was so impressed that he later purchased land in the area; brothers Lawrence, Samuel, and Charles, for whom the county seat of Charles Town is named, joined him.

The county's population grew over the following century, and the small 1803 court house was demolished to make way for a larger one. This second building, constructed in 1836 in the Greek Revival style, has served as the site of two famous sets of treason trials.

John Brown's well-known October, 1859 anti-slavery raid against the Federal Arsenal and Armory in Harpers Ferry resulted in six arrests by troops under Col. Robert E. Lee. The conspirators were tried in Charles Town for murder, for inciting slaves to rebel, and for treason against the Commonwealth of Virginia. All were convicted and hanged.

Many years later, in 1921, coal miners in West Virginia's southwestern coalfields attempted to unionize Logan County. The resulting Battle of Blair Mountain escalated to the use of machine guns and aerial bombardment, and ended only with the intervention of two thousand federal troops. Seven hundred thirty-eight indictments were returned, and Jefferson County was chosen as the venue for the high profile treason and murder trials that followed. State police occupied Charles Town and national and global media watched as the first trials brought an acquittal, two commuted sentences, and one conviction; the remaining indictments were eventually dismissed.

The 1836 Jefferson County Court House has seen many important changes in our society, and continues to serve the interests of justice today.

(Adapted from "A Brief History of the Jefferson County Court House," by Judge David Sanders.)

286-001-ST-WV-002-1998

Fourth-Generation West Virginia Gal

My name is Dorothy Michael Crouse. I was born September 15, 1910, in Morgan County, West Virginia. I have lived my whole life within five miles of my birth place. I'm a fourth-generation West Virginian. I grew up on a farm inherited from my grandfather, Andrew Wilson Michael. My parents were William Elsworth Michael and Daisy May Stewart Michael. I had three brothers: Harley Calvin Michael, James Andrew Michael, and Paul William Michael; and four sisters: Laura May Michael, Lesta Francis Michael, Vietta Belle Michael Stotler, and Alma Estella Michael Hawvermale. Growing up, my chores were feeding and caring for the farm animals, gardening, and housework, including dishes.

On our farm, there were acres of corn, wheat, and tomatoes. When wheat ripened, a horse-drawn binder cut and bound the stalks in bundles to dry. A thrashing machine separated the stalks for straw to use for bedding for the animals and stuffing for our bed tickings. This ticking became dusty in time. In the late thirties, the government gave us batting and ticking for mattresses. This was a part of the Homemaker program. Our local Homemakers club met at the apple packing shed in Sleepy Creek to make the mattresses. My husband and I, along with other families, helped to make the mattresses.

Sleepy Creek bordered one side of the farm, providing a good fishing hole. Catfish were plentiful. Thus the name "cat hole." This was the swimming pool in summer and skating rink in the winter. Ice sometimes became several inches thick. It was cut in blocks, covered with sawdust, and stored in a building called "the ice house." Ice was used in the summer for homemade ice cream. What a treat!

Dorothy Crouse, 1983 Morgan County Belle.

My grandfather helped to build the first rural free school in the community. The school was named Mt. Trimble School. It opened in 1886. My father attended this school, as I did later. This one-room school was replaced in 1926 with a two-room school. While I was attending the one-room school, I had my first experience in teaching. The teacher, Lester Olie Stotler, who later became my brother-in-law, gave me the opportunity to teach a fourth-grade history class. I was a sixth-grade student. This was the beginning of what later became my career.

CHAPTER 8: EASTERN PANHANDLE

The school had a pot-bellied stove in the middle of the room. The stove was surrounded by three or four inches of sand, held in place with planks. The sand protected the oiled floor and kept the dust down. We also kept the ink bottles from freezing at night by placing them in the sand while the fire in the stove was banked for the night. The sand retained the heat well. The boys and girls sat on opposite sides of the room, but they would join together when their grade was called to the front of the room for class participation. The bathroom was an outside toilet with a Sears catalog for the students' convenience. My children, Robert William Crouse, Darrell Walter Crouse, Daisy Marie Crouse Fox, and Mary Jo Crouse Crolley, attended the two-room school until it closed in 1946.

Stonesifer reunion, 1939. Seated at far left: Mary Stonesifer, author's mother; seated, center, holding child: Pauline A. Hockensmith, author, holding daughter Margaret Ann Hockensmith at age one month; seated next to them: Fannie Christine Melhorn Higgs Hockensmith, author's mother-in-law; seated in very front, facing group: Mary Frances Hockensmith, author's daughter, at age two.

AUTHOR: Dorothy Michael Crouse. Dorothy is still an active member of the Homemaker club, the oldest club in Morgan County. She learned to knit, and made a blanket for her only granddaughter, Aleva Lynn Crolley, daughter of Dennis and Mary Jo Crolley. Dorothy enjoys the fellowship and monthly meetings, the lessons and the contributions that the Homemakers make to their community. She was honored when asked to represent Morgan County as the county Belle in 1983. The time spent there sharing with other Belles and enjoying the entertainment is time she will not forget.

287-001-ST-WV-002-1998

I Lived Through the "Great Depression"

he Great Depression began with the October, 1929 stock market crash and ended several years following the end of the Second World War.

When I graduated from Taneytown High School, Taneytown, Maryland, in June 1930, a job of any kind was hard to find. When I accepted a bookkeeping-secretary "position" at the Spahr Lime and Stone Company near Thurmont, Maryland, for ten dollars a week, I thought I was lucky! I paid four dollars a week board and lodging. I would stay with my parents back home on the weekends. My boyfriend, Robert A. Hockensmith, of Harpers Ferry, West Virginia, on his way home from weekend "courting," usually dropped me off back at work on Sunday nights, saving my father the nine-mile trip. Soon my pay was increased to twelve dollars and fifty cents a week, later still to fifteen dollars. I tried to save five dollars a week. Then all the banks in the nation were CLOSED, including my Detour, Maryland bank, tying up for years all my saved funds. Then my company went out of business and I was jobless!

Robert A. Hockensmith, author's husband. Taken in Shenandoah Junction, West Virginia, in 1956.

Pauline (Polly) Hockensmith, taken in the spring of 1997.

Bob and I were married on December 10, 1932, by the Reverend Guy P. Brady, in the "Preacher's house" in Taneytown, Maryland, six miles from my home in Keysville, Maryland. It was a cold, snowy, blizzardy night and my grandmother predicted Bob would never make the hour-and-a-half trip in his little green 1928 Ford—but he did!

Twin Ridge Orchard Company, Incorporated. Orchard harvesters, circa 1936. Robert A. Hockensmith, author's husband, is standing in the center.

Our marriage was typical for the skimpy times—formal weddings happened in the movies. Elopements happened often; judges' quarters and preachers' houses were popular choices, with immediate-family church weddings a rare event.

No "honeymoon" was planned. We had not been home from the preacher's long when my friends performed the SHIVAREE, a mock serenade to a newly married couple, using a "horse fiddle," horns, kettles, and pans as noisemakers. It was such a cold windy night, we didn't let them work too hard or long before inviting them in to receive their congratulations. My mother, Mary Stonesifer, was prepared with many kinds of cake and cookies and drinks for refreshments.

The first year of my married life was spent living at the home of my husband's parents, Mr. Samuel J. Hockensmith and Mrs. Fannie Christine Melhorn Higgs Hockensmith, two wonderful people. My husband was manager of Twin Ridge Orchard Company, located at Shenandoah Junction, West Virginia, about seven miles distant. The house on the property was available a year later, and we moved in. It was furnished with second-hand things from sales and attics; the two new things were a Home Comfort range and a three-piece living-room suite—the latter to please me! Water for drinking, cooking, and filling the range reservoir came from the outdoor well house. Kerosene lamps needed filling, wick trimming, and globe washing, and to be carried from room to room and upstairs at night! No bathroom facilities, just a path to the outdoor "necessary." We did have a battery-operated radio with earphones. It was a great day when we got a radio with a built-in speaker.

Mary Stonesifer, author's mother. Taken at Keysville, in Carroll County, Maryland, 1936. Mary kept chickens, as did her daughter Pauline.

CHAPTER 8: EASTERN PANHANDLE

My husband's salary was $700 a year, which was considered very good at the time. (Workers on the orchard received the going wage, ten cents an hour.) It may seem impossible, but we tried to save at least one-half of the salary, spending only for big things—like a second-hand car! We supplemented by raising hogs and chickens for meat and eggs, and by keeping cows for milk and cream. The cream was sold weekly and whatever it brought—from two to three dollars—was used to buy the week's groceries! A garden supplied potatoes, and tomatoes and green beans for canning; also cabbage, onions, beets, peppers, and corn. We had peaches to can and plenty of apples!

Pleasures were found in visiting and entertaining family, friends, and neighbors; fried chicken Sunday dinners; parties with refreshments; cards and "Rook." We raised two daughters, Mary Frances born in April, 1937, and Margaret Ann in May, 1939. We were regulars at the Saturday night movies followed by shopping at the Charles Town five and ten cent store! We attended church and Sunday school every Sunday, at the Charles Town Presbyterian Church in Charles Town, West Virginia. It was a hard but good life!

It all changed for the better, with all our neighbors too, when electricity came to our neighborhood. Now we had a new kitchen, bathroom, electric lights, electric stove, refrigerator, and electric iron. The Great Depression, for me, was over!

Pauline A. Hockensmith at a picnic with family, friends, and neighbors, circa 1945. Here, all keep their distance as she participates in a rolling pin–throwing contest!

AUTHOR: *Ethel Pauline (Polly) Stonesifer Hockensmith celebrated her eighty-fourth birthday July 27, 1997. She is a widow, surviving her husband Robert, who died June 9, 1992. She has two daughters, four grandchildren, and seven great-grandchildren. She has turned her garden into a flower and bulb showplace, saving small spaces for tomatoes, cucumbers, squash, onions, and green beans. She has traveled the world over, writes short stories and poetry, enjoys modeling, and is a Bible student.*

288-001-ST-WV-002-1998

Chapter 9
Mountaineer Country

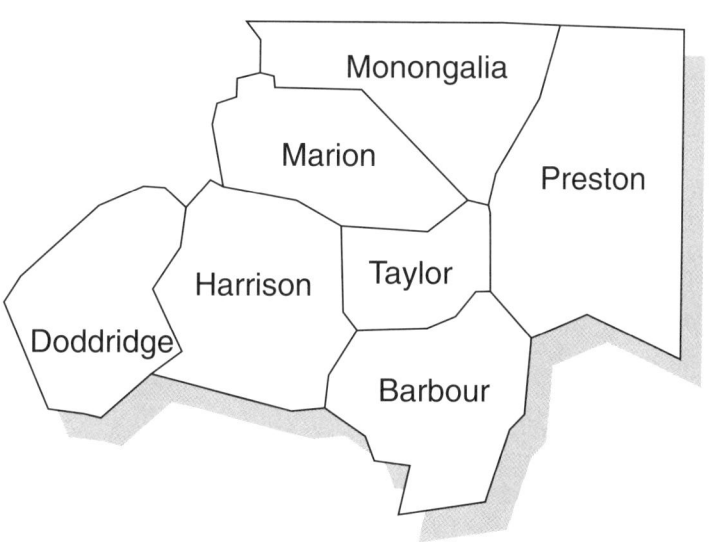

Chapter 9: Mountaineer Country

Saved from the Auction Block!

The Krenn School was built in the spring and summer of 1897, with local labor and materials according to the style of that day. It stood on about one-fourth acre of land purchased for twenty five dollars by the Cove District School Trustees, Doddridge County, West Virginia, from John and Adeline Krenn of St. Clara, West Virginia, according to the deed registered in the Doddridge County Court House dated December 22, 1896. The school, grades one through eight, opened for classes in the fall of 1897, and continued in use until 1942, when it was closed because of low enrollment.

After the school closure, the Doddridge County School Board allowed the St. Clara Community to continue using the building for its meetings. The St. Clara Organized Community is a group of concerned citizens, formed by a county agent in the '40s. Although unchartered, this is an organized group that meets for regular monthly meetings. It is because of the continuous care and maintenance by a dedicated community that the Krenn school building remains today, in good repair inside and out.

Few changes have been made during the building's 100-year existence. For instance, a covered porch and two cloak rooms were added in the early '20s. One cloak room was later converted to a "kitchen" with a hot plate and a single wall cupboard. The windows were modified in the 1930s for better lighting, but the original long-handled pump and two slant-roof, unpainted privies at the far end of the property still stand. The interior remains very much the same as when the last class was held. The slate blackboard extends along one wall. Student desks with ink wells and carved initials are from the '20s and '30s. The original gas lights are intact, although the building was wired for electricity in the '40s. Many pictures and maps on the walls are original. A pot-bellied stove, identical to the one which once heated the room, has recently been added although the building has been heated by natural gas since shortly after the turn of the century.

The "empty" one-room school building served as a community center until 1988, when the school board voted to rid itself of the liability of this last remaining one-room school property at public auction—their only means of legally disposing of the property. My husband and I, recently retired to the farm on which the building stands, decided not to allow this unique bit of educational history to be lost without an all-out effort to save it. We immediately developed plans. Through the cooperation of the school board, Dr. Alton Childers of the Doddridge County Historical Society, County Commissioner Oral Ash, and West Virginia Delegate James Willison, action was taken by the state legislature by which the property could be sold to the Doddridge County Historical Society for one dollar. After that, my husband and I, with support from others, made an application to get the one-room Krenn School listed on the National Register of Historic Places. This request was granted the following year, 1989.

The historic one-room Krenn School now serves as a permanent focal point for community meetings and other functions in St. Clara, West Virginia. Thanks to foresight and community cooperation, the one-room Krenn School was saved and will be preserved.

Author: Hazel Gallien Wysong. Mrs. Wysong, a retired reading clinician (Arlington Public School, Arlington, Virginia), lives with her husband, Bill, of forty-seven years in a restored ancestral homestead in St. Clara, West Virginia. During the past year, Hazel Wysong headed a committee of "Friends Of The Krenn School," which obtained a two thousand dollar grant from the Claude Worthington Benedum Foundation for installing a "self-contained biological toilet system" in part of one cloakroom.

289-001-ST-WV-002-1998

Krenn School, 1897-1942. The Krenn School building and original contents exist as a turn-of-the-century rural one-room school museum because of the foresight and efforts of Bill and Hazel Wysong, and a cooperating community called the St. Clara Community.

A Tail of Black and White

After coming home from the hospital after surgery a few years back, I found my little dog J.R. very ill, and he had to be put to sleep. I decided not to get another pet, but just two weeks later I changed my mind. It was so lonesome.

I thought about what kind of dog to get. I knew that border collies have a lot of energy and need space to run around. They are originally from Scotland and are bred to herd sheep. They are intelligent, protective, and territorial. Since I live on a farm, I decided it had to be a border collie. The search began, and it was not an easy one. Finally, through a friend, I learned of a litter of puppies in Pennsylvania. They had a very good bloodline, which I wanted so that I could get a female to breed. Then, when the time came, I would have those lovable little puppies.

I went to Pennsylvania and bought the prettiest pup the Chambers had. She looks exactly like every border collie picture you see: black with a white ruff around her neck. I named her Megy. I thought this sounded like a good name for a border collie. After choosing this name, I received Megy's official papers, including records of her bloodline. I discovered that one of Megy's ancestors had the same name!

Megy went through all the typical puppy stages of playing, running, and chewing. As she grew, however, and it got close to breeding time, Megy became very aggressive—downright mean. She growled and snapped at everyone, except for two men, my brother-in-law and my daughter-in-law's father. She loves both of them. I made the decision to have Megy spayed, knowing that if she had puppies, I probably couldn't even get near Megy or her litter.

Megy will be three years old in April. It has been about a year since her surgery (we're both doing fine!), and her disposition has changed some for the better. She still doesn't make up with strangers, but she tolerates those she knows and is more loving to me. We have some quarter horses, and she enjoys spending time with them, too. She'll lie down near them for hours at a time, as if she's guarding them. It's in her blood. She loves her ball, her Frisbee. She loves chewing my kitchen chairs, but I still love Megy.

AUTHOR: *Mary Harr Morgan. Mary and her dog Megy live on a farm that sits in both Taylor and Harrison Counties.*

290-001-ST-WV-002-1998

One of the few pictures Mary has of Megy, because Megy is camera shy. She hates to have her picture taken.

Life at Home

I was the fourth in a line of nine children. I was born Dixie Lee McAtee in Chiefton, in Harrison County, West Virginia, on March 30, 1945. My second oldest sister, Eunice Rae, died of pneumonia soon after birth. There was only one boy, David, among all of us girls. I don't know how he survived, but he did.

I was the "tomboy" of the family, climbing trees and riding stick horses all of the time. My "horse" was just a stick about three feet long that all the kids had and rode as though they were real. But in our childlike imaginations, they were real. Back then, we made our own fun.

Times back then were rough for us, but my dad, Harry McAtee, Jr., was a hard-working man. He worked at the Adamston Flat Glass Company for many years. He worked two jobs most of his life just for us to have the things we needed.

With us being such a large family, my mom, Barbara Lamm McAtee, who stayed at home, was forced to be the disciplinarian. In a family the size of ours, you could expect a fight to break out almost instantaneously, and we fought better than anyone else I knew. For example, when we did the dishes, one child would wash and another would dry. Yet we could not even do that without an argument. So Mom had to make us do them separately—that is, the one assigned to wash the dishes washed alone, then one of my sisters, Alice or Terry, came in to dry them. Measures like this helped keep peace in the family.

One fight that I recall occurred one Christmas morning. Neither my brother David nor I liked doll babies, but of course our sisters—Sharon, Alice, Terry, Denise, Pamela, and Janice—did. I recall that every Christmas morning my sisters received dolls as gifts, but then there was one morning when David and I decided to do something about those annoying dolls. We grabbed them up, carried them out to the road, pulled their heads off, and threw them over the hill. Our sisters screamed and cried to us not to do it, but we did it anyway. Today I don't remember exactly what Mom and Daddy did to us, but I'm sure our punishment was as severe as it should have been.

Another squabble that I remember was between my sister Sharon and me. We had a sewing machine in our dining room, which my sister Sharon climbed onto. I'm sure she thought she was safe there. She was kicking at me to protect herself. However, she was also laughing at me, and I hated to be laughed at when I was mad. So, in my frustration, I grabbed her legs and pulled her off the stool and onto the floor. My sister screamed, "She broke my back, she broke my back!" And I was really concerned that I had hurt her badly, but fortunately I hadn't. When I asked Mom recently what that fight was about, she didn't even remember, because we all fought so much that she eventually just let us duel it out ourselves until it seemed that someone might get hurt. I don't remember what the fight was all about either, but I believe that was our last big one.

My dad was a very compassionate man. One of my favorite memories about him is what happened when any one of us fell ill: he would come home with ice cream and bring it up to us along with a cool washcloth for our face. He was so comforting in those times. I will always remember that now since my dad went to be with the Lord on August 8, 1994. He is very much in my everyday thoughts, and also in those of my mother, as they were married for fifty-five years.

Today it is amazing as I look back at my childhood and my family to know that we all turned out okay. I'm sure that sometimes my mom probably thought we were going to kill each other, or she may have even hoped that we would, after her millionth headache.

We didn't have many of the luxuries that are commonplace today, but we never felt for a minute that we were poor. Of course, entertainment was never an issue, as we had our imaginations, and if that failed, one could always pick a fight with the nearest sibling, who was probably just arm's length away. Yet now as I chuckle over all those fights and quarrels, I realize that I really was raised with a lot of love. To think of all the sacrifices my parents made for us makes me feel very fortunate to be a part of my family. I thank God for my life and for who I am because of those days.

Author: Dixie L. Thornhill, homemaker, mother of two, and grandmother of two.

291-001-ST-WV-002-1998

Dixie, smiling a toothless grin at age seven, stands near the family home in Chiefton, Harrison County, West Virginia, 1952.

Called to West Virginia

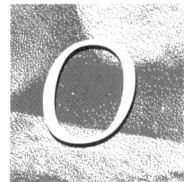

ld ties and long ago, it seems. Why else would these hills and deep gullies call me so forcefully? Their wild, fierce beauty, their haunting loneliness and isolation, their peace and solitude true companions indeed.

I remember my first car trip to Beckley from Morgantown, around 1965. It took forever. The superhighway south of today is no match for those roads of thirty years ago. Today I sit in speedy comfort and with little thought calmly maneuver my car over ribbons of concrete and asphalt at speeds of sixty-five or so. Not then. Each turn was deliberately negotiated. And around each sharp bend in the road waited a new surprise, completely unanticipated because completely unseen. As the day turned to night, the headlights exposed silent specters traced in the rocks, guarding the passage south into unknown and forbidden territory.

We jumped off at Beckley and entered a little coal "camp" called Slab Fork. Underneath the quiet manner of those originals lay a pride of place in their humble town. No need to apologize. My origins trace to a coal "patch" in southwestern Pennsylvania called Ralph, a name alluding to family fortune rather than hard geography. Perhaps the two go together, hard geography for some and family fortune for others. We have a lot in common after all.

I didn't mind the long and winding road because I sat next to my love, long since gone from my life. And now I find, in the WVU alumni memorial, gone from this life. It seems that every important event in my life is living itself out in this state, save for a few. Why does this place call me so? And how do I return its love?

Author: Gail Means Pope Bossart lives in Morgantown, West Virginia. She has worked as a teacher, editor, manager, and parent, and currently has a private practice as an energy healer.

292-001-ST-WV-002-1998

Gail Snyder was a member of the Daughters of the American Revolution (DAR). Friends from the Morgantown, West Virginia DAR chapter joined her for her 100th birthday celebration.

Tribute to Gail Snyder

he was born on January 20, 1890, in Reedsville, West Virginia, Preston County, the daughter of the late Thomas J. Watson and Launa Shuttlesworth Watson. She is the only survivor of her immediate family. Her father served in the Civil War for the Union army, where he lost one arm and was detained in a prison camp for months.

Gail married David G. Snyder while still in her early twenties, and is the mother of six living children and one deceased son. They lived and raised their family on the original Snyder homestead of 125 acres near the Lynch Chapel community in Monongalia County. The farm is now rented but will always be home to her.

Gail taught school for twenty-three years, mostly in the one-room schools, with eight grades per school room, and traveled to work by horse and buggy or horseback in the early years. Laurel Point School, near Morgantown, built around 1865, is one of the schools she taught at.

Her family of six children, thirteen grandchildren, and eighteen great-grandchildren wish her the happiest 100th birthday, and invite family and friends to honor her on January 21, 1990, at the home of her daughter and son-in-law, Conrad and Elva L. Kennedy, in Wooster, Ohio.

Author: Gladys L. Snyder Shackelford Eddy. Mrs. Eddy submitted this excerpt from her mother's 100th birthday celebration invitation as a tribute. Gail Snyder died in 1992, a month short of her 102nd birthday.

293-001-ST-WV-002-1998

Gail Florence Watson Snyder celebrating her 100th birthday, in January, 1990.

The Girls of '54

e were the children born in the latter Depression years. Many of our families' roots were to the 1770s settlers of the hillsides and banks of the Tygart Valley River system of Taylor County. Our folks worked at the B&O Railroad, Carr China Pottery, Hazel Atlas Glass, West Virginia Reform School for Boys, the small farms, the coal mines, and the small businesses and professions supporting these workers.

Except for the displacement of some, caused by World War II—an event of our early grade school years—our extended families and their friends were among these hills and deep valleys of West Virginia. Yet we were to become the generation that was scattered to far away places and lands, a result of the 1950s economic decline of our area.

Chapter 9: Mountaineer Country

The cloud of gloom began on June 16, 1952. The Carr China company closed its doors. During the decade to follow, Taylor County suffered the loss of over 1,000 jobs!

As the Grafton High School (GHS) Class of 1954 began our junior year, we were amazed to see classmates staying behind to be with us as their families moved away . . . but many classmates left with their families and were gone! The adults around us told us to plan to "Go." For many, go we did, leaving behind our beautiful hills and warm, supportive people.

Displaced by choice or chance, we became the "newcomers" to the big cities, the small villages and towns throughout America, learning to adjust, trying to fit in and being proud to defend our Appalachian Mountain culture and heritage. With our migration came the human need to connect, to belong. Yet, the gnawing sense of the loss of "home," our people, and our lifelong relationships prevailed.

Luckily, from 1955 through 1992, Grafton High School alumni reunions were held ten times. Uniquely, graduation classes of all years met simultaneously over a three- to four-day weekend in Grafton. These special gatherings served as the glue that bonded the Class of '54 together through our years of college, military service, marriages, babies, careers, address changes, divorces, grandchildren, and retirement. Ten times we came home to be together, then returned elsewhere to go on with our lives . . . the Class of '54!

In 1992, indications that these reunions were unlikely to continue prompted a plan. The GHS Girls of '54 decided to meet every two years. All are welcome. The site will always be in West Virginia.

The Girls of '54's Thursday-through-Sunday events have been held at Lewisburg (October, 1993); Canaan Valley (May, 1995); and Harpers Ferry (September, 1997). Each event can best be described as a 1950s slumber party held by a bunch of sixty year olds!

Initially intended to be exclusively "for the Girls," the event has proven to be irresistible to the husbands, many being previously gathered in our "far off" places. These men who tagged along with us through the years to the alumni reunions have seemingly bonded, too, as friends. One of them even wrote lyrics for our song. Its tune is that of an old Boy Scout marching song.

We are the GIRLS OF '54 you hear so much about.
The people stop and stare at us whenever we go out.
We're not a bit stuck up about the clever
things we do.
Most everybody likes us and we hope you
like us too.
When we go marching and the band begins to P-L-A-Y.
We can hear them shouting, "The GIRLS OF '54
are on the way."

And every other year, on the way we are! . . . on the way to West Virginia, our home of long ago!

AUTHOR: *Charleen Evans-Thomas, Ed.D., Grafton High School Class of 1954, is a retired educator and businesswoman. She lives at McHenry, Maryland and Ormond Beach, Florida, with her husband, James Spurgeon Thomas, formerly of MacArthur, West Virginia.*

Lyrics: *G. Thomas Bartlett III, GHS Class of 1954. Mr. Bartlett recounts performing, at age twelve, as standard bearer during a Boy Scout presentation at Valley Forge National Jamboree. President Truman, he recalls, stood within ten feet of him, and General Eisenhower gave the keynote address. The scout song that was adapted years later by Mr. Bartlett for the Girls of '54 was performed at that jamboree.*

294-001-ST-WV-002-1998

October, 1993 gathering of the Girls of '54, at Merry Hill Mansion in Lewisburg, West Virginia. Seated (l-r): Roberta Withers McAvoy (MI); Charleen Evans-Thomas, author (MD); Mary Jane Currey Ford (WV)*; Libby Murray Newharth (FL). Standing: Anne Lawson Shaw (WV); Billie Bott Williamson (WV)*; Joan Goff Rush (FL); Janet Boylen Ward (WV)*; Suzanne Lawson Miller (OH); Roberta Coberly Bistany (NC); Charlotte Stilwell Atha (MD)*; Barbara Wagoner Bartlett (HI/MD)*.

* *Lived elsewhere, then later returned to West Virginia.*

Home Is Where the Heart Is

Reflections on my Harrison County home

A house is just a dwelling, but a home is so much more. To each man, it's his castle, though humble it may be. It's that special place that we create and make our very own. Where we store up all our treasures, dream tomorrow's dream, and make so many memories. Where we find our peace and comfort from a long and weary day, lay down all our burdens and cast worries all away. When we're sick or sad or lonely, it's where we want to be, to cry our tears in private and soothe our aching hearts. We can scream and shout in anger, but she never says a word. Like a loyal friend, she listens and keeps our secrets from the world.

It's where families come together to laugh and work and pray. Where our minds and bodies learn and grow to become who we are today. Here we find that warm and cozy bed when we hear those cold winds blow, for she shelters and protects us from all life's cares and woes. That special place we long for when we're far, far away. She's a beacon in the darkness when we feel we've lost our way. Where the welcome mat is always out as she waits for our return, like a mother waiting for her child, she waits so patiently; our candle in the window, "please hurry back to me."

In 1942, on the Sunday before he went into the army, Andrew Drumpus, the author's father, posed with his wife, Edna. Andrew served most of his service time with the infantry in Le Havre, France. He passed away in 1991. Edna turned eighty-three years old in September, 1997.

AUTHOR: *Judith Drumpus Bennett. Mrs. Bennett is a retired employee of Anchor Hocking Glass Company. She says there is nowhere else she would rather call home than our very own "almost Heaven" West Virginia. One of her favorite Bible passages is, "For where your treasure is, there will your heart be also."—Matthew 6:21*

295-001-ST-WV-002-1998

The Drumpus home in Reynoldsville, west of Clarksburg, circa 1950. Once a chicken hatchery, this was home to the author until 1957, when she was a senior in high school and the house was sold by the owner. Until that point, the family had been paying $15 a month in rent. The home and its seven acres, including an apple orchard, was the site of many family picnics, wiener roasts, and neighborhood ballgames.

In 1991, the Drumpus sisters posed for a group picture. Standing (l-r) are Carole Lee Flowers of Clarksburg and Lois Jean Neff of Los Angeles. Sitting are Myra Lou Sienkiewicz of Charles Town and the author, Judith Bennett of Clarksburg.

For no matter where we travel
Or what wondrous sights we see
Home is where the heart is
For it's where we love to be.

The Wonderful Memories I Have of "Grams"

My grandmother is Nancy Rebecca Straight Layman, who lives on the Sugar Grove Road near Morgantown. "Grams," as I call her, is a really good friend of mine and always has been. Even as a little kid, I stayed with her for a week at a time and tried to help her with things. She is a really fun person to be around, and we do a lot of fun stuff. Sometimes when we go to the grocery store we'll make weird noises and talk in gibberish and make people think we're talking in a different language. We go just about everywhere together—the mall or comic book store and other places like that.

Almost every Sunday, we get up early and go to the flea market and look around; then we go home, get ready, and go to church. After church, we go home and she and "Pap"—Chauncy Layman, my grandpa—make a big breakfast for everyone. She is a really great cook and knows just what to fix for everyone. Since she lives just across the road from me, she packs my lunch (the biggest and best lunch in the school) every morning, and meets me at the driveway to see that I get on the bus. If I oversleep, she calls to wake me. I also love to ride my bike over to "Gram's" and grab some "Ho-Hos" and chocolate milk.

We like to go to Hagans, the community where my great-grandfather's old home place is. We walk around in the empty house and talk about how it could be fixed up and we could live there sometime. There is a two-seated commode and a stairway that goes up to two big rooms upstairs. Half the roof is gone, but downstairs there are three rooms and a pantry. The kitchen still has a stove and sink. We like to walk about the property and look through the old barns.

"Grams" is really interested in all my sports and is always there to cheer me on at basketball, wrestling, soccer, and track. She helps make sure I have what I need for my sports and my school clothes. She takes me to all my events. She always took me to karate class twice a week and stayed to watch me practice. She made time to stay for my tests. After karate on Mondays, we went with my good friend Mark Vannin and his dad to the Dairy Queen for treats. Last Halloween she helped my mom and grandpa make my costume of Boba Fett, a Star Wars character. She is a good seamstress, and sewed and hemmed some pieces and helped me buy the other pieces.

Nancy Rebecca Straight Layman, December, 1994.

She is a big help in all my 4-H projects and helps me select, tame, and groom my animals and sees that I get to the fair and to the sales for feeder calves and market lambs. She makes sure I have my books completed and demonstrations ready for the meetings; she helps with my posters and slogans and contests.

"Grams" is a really wonderful grandma who goes out of her way to help others. I'll always have good memories of our times together.

Author: Brian Hoxter. Brian is an eighth-grader and he likes to wrestle and draw. He has one brother, Major, and one sister, Miranda.

296-001-ST-WV-002-1998

Saved from a Terrifying Experience

That night in August, 1985, I knew it was raining unusually hard. The next morning, however, I did not realize that there was flooding and that my drive to work was going to be an experience that would affect me for the rest of my life. I lived in Mount Morris, Pennsylvania, at the time, and worked for Summers Auto Parts in Morgantown. In ten years, I had never missed a day or been late for work.

I made it as far as the post office in Pursglove, West Virginia, in north central Monongalia County. On the drive, I had seen some gravel strewn across the road, but nothing serious. Then I noticed that, ahead of me, Emergency Medical Services was towing a woman out of water that had stalled her car. Scotts Run was flooding fast. The water soon reached me, and EMS came and told me to wait for them. But in a matter of seconds, almost immediately after they left, muddy water engulfed my car. It rose incredibly quickly, and began squirting in the windows of my new Thunderbird. Where had it come from? I was scared to death and knew I couldn't wait—I had to do something. The force of the water was so strong, I had to push with both feet to open my door. The water quickly claimed my shoes. I tried to stand, but the water kept knocking me down, bruising my legs on the road and on the debris that constantly rushed past me. I inched my way to the back of my car, but had trouble holding on. I was hysterical. A crowd had gathered on the bank, and I started screaming for them to help me. One man did. That day a young stranger saved my life at the risk of his own.

Evelyn Howdershelt, 1997 (photo courtesy of Gerson Studio).

Homer Wilson, now of Jere, waded into the fast-moving and fast-rising waters and out to my car. The water kept knocking him down, but he made it to me. He grabbed my car keys and opened the trunk. We both climbed in, but the car started to move and the water was still rising. He yelled for someone on land to throw a rope. They improvised with a garden hose. Homer tied one end to the hinge of the trunk, and someone tied the other end to a sturdy mailbox. Homer's plan was that he would slide out over the back fender while holding on to the hose; I was to slide between his arms and grab the hose.

Once we were out, Homer held the hose with both hands; I was between his arms, gripping the hose tightly. Neither of us could touch the ground due to the force of the water—essentially, we were being pushed by the rushing waters to a horizontal position, parallel to the road. As we attempted to go hand-over-hand to the bank, the hose stretched and I went under water. We were also being shoved hard in one direction, then another—the water was pounding my legs against the ground and twisting my arms as I struggled to hold on. It was like being in a washing machine. Homer tried pulling me up twice, but both times, trying to gasp for air, I inhaled muddy water. I remember at one point trying to grab on to Homer and seeing blood on his neck. The third time I came up, a board hit me on the head, forcing me sideways and breaking my lower arm. I was resigned to death, and thought only of my daughter Dana. I decided to give up!! I let go of the hose and felt sure I would die. What I didn't know was that Homer wasn't going to give up so easily on me. He let go of the hose too, snatching on to my coat.

We were carried by the powerfully churning water for I don't know how long. I was unconscious. Somewhere near the Shack Neighborhood House, Homer managed to pull us out of the water using a concrete barrier for leverage. I came around briefly in the parking lot and noticed that the flood had taken not only my shoes, but my pants and wedding rings as well. I couldn't breathe and had a terrible pain in my arm. Homer and the EMS workers took me to a local home. It was not yet possible to drive me to the hospital. I remember the EMS saying I was in shock and calling for oxygen. When I coughed muddy water across the living room, they knew they had to get me to the hospital.

Interstate 79, high above the river on concrete pillars, was the only road not flooded. Homer and five others cut the eight-foot fence behind the Pursglove post office and carried me on a stretcher up a steep hill of rock to an ambulance waiting on the interstate. Homer then contacted my family in Mount Morris, and located my car a mile from where I had originally been swept away and pulled it out. My family had been looking for me, spurred by a premonition-induced call from my mother in New Hampshire. She said she just had a feeling something was wrong.

I've never publicly thanked Homer for saving my life. He is a friend of mine and of my daughter Dana, who was twelve years old at the time. I cry almost every time I see him. He truly has a heart of gold, and the courage of ten men.

AUTHOR: *Evelyn Howdershelt. Since the flood, Evelyn has nursed a fear of water, and a greater belief in the goodness of mankind. She is West Virginia state Business and Professional Women president for 1998–99.*

297-001-ST-WV-002-1998

Christmas as It Used to Be

Sometimes while reminiscing,
   I think I'd like to see
A real "old-fashioned" Christmas
   as Christmas used to be.

A time before Nintendos,
   computers, and TVs;
When values were more simple
   and people easily pleased.

The mail would bring large boxes
   with gifts from far away,
And greeting cards from loved ones
   arrived most every day.

The carols on the organ
   would make the old house ring,
And often friends and kinfolk
   dropped in to help us sing.

Glass ornaments so fragile
   were handled carefully,
And ropes of colored paper
   would decorate the tree.

Our tree came from the hillside—
   our wreaths from boughs of pine;
The strands of silver tinsel
   gave off a brilliant shine.

So much that I remember—
   the crisp and glistening snow;
The programs at the rural church
   where country folk would go.

We'd practice many hours
   to get each poem just right;
Then all dressed up, we'd nervously
   perform our parts that night.

And Santa'd pay a visit,
   with gifts for every guest;
(Although his velvet outfit
   was not the very best!)

A special treat was helping roll and
   fill the pies to bake;
And Mom's own special chocolate fudge
   that she would always make.

On Christmas Eve before the fire,
   we'd pop Dad's home-grown corn,
And hang our cotton stockings
   to open Christmas morn.

We'd read the Christmas Story
   and "Visit From St. Nick,"
And warm ourselves for one last time—
   then off to bed, and quick!

Next morning in the stockings,
   we'd find a toy, brand-new,
A candy cane, some apples,
   and nuts and hardtack, too.

But years from now, our grandkids
   may look back on today,
And wish for such a time as this
   when life was mostly play.

For Christmas is so many things
   held fast within the heart,

Teagarden family home in Sugar Grove, West Virginia, still the site of family dinners and get-togethers.

And many loved ones now are gone,
   who played a special part.

No matter what our age is,
   our memory holds the key
To a real "old-fashioned" Christmas
   as Christmas used to be.

AUTHOR: *Evelyn T. Kennedy. Mrs. Kennedy writes, "Of all the remembrances of growing up in the 1930s and 1940s in Sugar Grove, a small rural community eight miles from Morgantown, the most precious memories are of celebrating the Christmas holidays. It was an uncomplicated time of simple pleasures, strong morals, family traditions, and celebrating the birth of Jesus with family and friends. The poem is a tribute to the late Fred and Mary McDonough Teagarden, my parents."*

298-001-ST-WV-002-1998

A Country One-Room School

Garner Valley School is located on Route 92 in Barbour County, about one mile from the Preston County line at Dent. In 1919 my brother Howard and I made our first trip from our home on the farm to that white country schoolhouse, a mile and a half over a steep hill. The school had a metal roof and was made of good planed lumber with smooth finished interior walls. Each of the side walls had three double windows of twelve panes of glass. On the back of the school lot were the outhouses, and in the front was the building for wood and coal.

Ada M. Guthrie, left; Nala Shaw Dugan, Ada's mother, on her 100th birthday; and Howard Dugan, Ada's brother. Nala Shaw Dugan lived to be 106 and a half years old.

Students sat on twenty double seats, large to small. Two benches at the back of the room stored our lunch pails and a large container of drinking water. Our coats and headgear were hung on nails on the wall above. Heat was provided by a pot-bellied stove. A stand in the front of the room held a large dictionary, and in a front corner stood a large bookcase with a glass door. The blackboard across the front of the room was the biggest attraction and we enjoyed writing with chalk and erasing. A long recitation bench adorned the front of the room along with the teacher's desk and chair. Some grades would fill the whole bench.

We had six wonderful teachers the years I was there, teaching ten different classes: WV History, Geography, Civil Government, Agriculture, Arithmetic, English, Spelling, Reading, Writing, and Hygiene. Our two vacation days were Armistice Day and Christmas. The pupils presented a Christmas program for which we practiced for several weeks. Special activities, such as ciphering and spelling matches, were held on Friday afternoons. To make a little money for the school, pie and box socials were held. For the latter, the girls each made a pretty decorated box with food in it, and it was sold to the highest bidder. Then they would eat together. We also had cake walks, another fundraiser, for five or ten cents a walk.

One of our lady teachers taught the girls to crochet during the noon hour, a recreation I still enjoy. We also learned to make bead necklaces. When the weather was pretty in the fall, the teachers would let us go up on the hill and get persimmons and mountain teaberries.

I had a lot of fun those days in the one-room school, but we had to study and learn so we could pass on to the next grade. After I took the eighth grade exam, which was set up for two days, I went on to high school, graduating in 1930.

The schoolhouse is still standing, and it brings back many memories when we pass by. My brother graduated the year after I did and went on to high school and then college, where he earned a teaching degree. He taught his first two years in Garner Valley, the same one-room country school where we began our education.

AUTHOR: *Ada M. Guthrie. Mrs. Guthrie was born in Barbour County some eighty-seven years ago, and spent thirty-five years on the family farm. She left the farm in 1945 and eventually retired as an employee of the state Food Service Department. In 1983, she was Monongalia County Belle for the Extension Homemakers.*

299-001-ST-WV-002-1998

Christmases and Other Things

There is so much I'd like to tell and pass on, I could fill half a book myself. I recall sitting and listening to Dad relate history and facts from his young life and from his father and grandfather. I'd think, "I should get some tapes and record this." My next thought was, "No, I don't need any tapes, I'll remember these facts as long as I live, I've heard them often enough!" But we find we can't remember and things need put down. Dad liked to repeat things that meant a lot to him, things that happened before the first gray hair, way before the first wrinkle formed. I once heard a young person say, "Oh, I don't know, she probably has

Alzheimer's, she repeats things a lot." I smiled and remembered Dad. He died at ninety-one, but could tell things word for word and he'd repeat them over and over to anyone that'd listen.

Before I wandered down that side road, I intended to talk about the Christmases of the 1930s. How different they were! We thought any old tree we could find was the prettiest tree ever. It was trimmed with popcorn, paper chains, and most anything homemade. One thing we used was burned-out radio tubes. My brother Ralph, who was much older, built radios in wooden boxes. When the silvery tubes burned out, we saved them for the tree. They were our bulbs.

We had a Santa at school when I was six. He took off his face and under that was a worse face than the first. I was so scared and shocked that I still don't like any kind of make-believe or Halloween costumes, puppets or fantasy. Real people are much more intriguing and likable than any fairy could ever be. No air castle could ever compare with the wonder and beauty around us or the earth beneath our feet. What the Lord visioned and created for our enjoyment far, far surpasses anything our poor powers could ever dream up or imagine.

Your reasoning tells you Santa is a myth when your stocking isn't bulging on Christmas morning. You learn to make your own luck, with the Lord's help, and fall back on your own ingenuity.

When I arose one Christmas there was a tree that reached the ceiling, and presents under it. The only thing I remember about the gifts was that Dad received a pen and pencil set. I liked to write and thought that was the greatest gift ever. My sister told me later that Ralph's wife, Thelma, had helped with the planning and got the gifts. Ralph must have been working then.

One Christmas when Dad was out of work, he sent to Shahan's store in Arden and got a bag of candy. That candy was our only holiday treat. Sitting around in the rosy warmth of the burnside stove, snow flakes turning our world Christmasy, sorting through that candy was just the greatest! We appreciated everything so much! We never thought to look for sleigh tracks, nor did we wonder how reindeer fly.

In that day and time you learned early that it's much more rewarding to work and plan for something than to have a fairy godmother wave it out of the air or an elf bring it in a sleigh. You lived a life that promoted the very kind of hard work and integrity that made this country great, and Christmas was a part of that lifestyle.

When you grow older and find something nice under the tree, you know who made it all possible and you know who the giver really was.

AUTHOR: *Claris Mitchell McDaniel, daughter of Monzell and Daisy Moats Mitchell, grew up near Philippi, in Barbour County.*

200-001-ST-WV-002-1998

Author with her sister and two brothers (l-r): Claris Mitchell McDaniel, Russell Mitchell, Minnie Mitchell Reed, and Ralph Mitchell, circa 1974.

The Story of a Tunnelton Landmark

n 1830, what was to become Tunnelton, West Virginia was unbroken forest. Encircled by maternal mountains, the deer, bear, and fox played their Disney games, oblivious to the fact that, in Baltimore, a steam engine made a thirteen-mile round trip "running at speeds up to *eighteen* miles an hour and pushing a car carrying *twenty-three* passengers . . ." (*The History of the B&O*, Jacobs, 1989). Those deer and foxes didn't know it, but their days were numbered. In four years, that steam engine had become a train and was running to Harpers Ferry. By 1851 it was in Cumberland, and in 1852 it chugged into Tunnelton. Only Tunnelton wasn't anything yet, it was simply a place where one of the eleven tunnels on the Baltimore & Ohio line was built. But our tunnel WAS the longest

and most amazing. Stretching 4,100 feet, our tunnel at that time was the longest tunnel in the United States. Hand dug, too: no machines had violated its pristine naturalness.

It's a good thing the railroad got here when it did so that, when the Civil War began nine years later, it was there to be pillaged and guarded and raided and to become a subject of great historical significance. The North and the South both lusted after our tunnel to the point of licentiousness. For were the tunnel to be closed or blown up, it would have been months before it could be reopened. Consider that, in 1863, when the Northern general Rosencrans retreated from the Battle of Chickamauga (in Georgia) and called Washington for help, the B&O carried 20,000 men and supplies from DC through Tunnelton to Grafton and north to Benwood, south of Wheeling. From Benwood they reached the Ohio River and traveled on to Rosencrans—a procedure taking just eleven days. The Blitzkrieg of its time.

The Tunnelton depot, built in 1913 and shown here in April, 1996, before renovation. The tile roof was restored in 1997, and in 1998 the interior will be redone.

It took years for the B&O to recover from the ravages of the Civil War years. Once back on its feet, it turned to building a series of depots—one of which the Tunnelton Historical Society is starting to restore. The society is not really sure just why Tunnelton and not other towns was gifted with a brick, not a frame, building, AND a tiled roof, when so many other depots had to make do with inferior materials. The Tunnelton depot's wide, low outline follows a pagoda form, probably influenced by the Richardson Romanesque architectural style. The depot's interior, too, shows an architectural elegance not found in the depots of surrounding towns. Our dowager depot imparted to entraining and departing passengers that they were not in some little coal backwater but in a thriving, enterprising community—it had finally become Tunnelton in 1897. Four passenger trains a day stopped here, and while ours was not of the magnitude of Grafton's, it was a little jewel of a depot, reflecting the miniature possibilities of Tunnelton itself.

Iris Jennings, 1990.

The coming and going of "the train" gave a bustling atmosphere to Tunnelton, and its station beamed on fondly as the citizenry came out to view who got on "the train" and who got off. It was the social hub of the town, especially on Sunday evenings when fellas and their girls could walk up to view the train travelers, meet friends, see and be seen. A date of perfect propriety.

If the B&O was baptized in the blood of the Civil War, the Tunnelton depot could only look on with fright and alarm as once more in 1918 and again in 1941 uniformed men stepped onto the train—some for the last time. Anyone who lived in Tunnelton during the 1940s feels a clutch in the stomach remembering the goodbyes of noble young innocents who had formerly ridden the train to a basketball game in Newburg or Terra Alta, then grimly bound for Nice, France or for the island of Tarawa in the south Pacific.

After World War II, the railroad and depot and the value of the tunnel declined. In the 1970s, the depot was closed. But now, in the late 1990s, there's increasing activity at the depot. The Tunnelton Historical Society has received National Register of Historic Places status for the building. Come back in a year or two and check out our restored depot with its newly created museum, and you'll be really impressed. Perhaps you can give us some information about the depot, or add a memory or two of your own to preserve for future generations.

AUTHOR: Iris Jennings. Ms. Jennings is a retired English teacher—six years at Tunnelton and Fellowsville high schools and thirty-four years at West Virginia University —and is a life-long resident of Tunnelton, West Virginia. She is a 1997 West Virginia History Hero, honored for her work in bringing to light some of Tunnelton's important heritage.

301-001-ST-WV-002-1998

Chapter 9: Mountaineer Country

A Gunner's Nightmare

There we were over the target area of Ludwigshaven, Germany, and I began to lose consciousness. This mission, one of thirty-five, was to be one that I would never forget . . .

There were thousands like me in 1944—nineteen-year-olds fighting battles far from home. My Air Force experience began in February of that year, when I left my home in Reedsville, West Virginia, and entered basic training at Kessler Field, Mississippi. Because of the urgent need to push the Allied offensive forward, training was quick and efficient, and continued during service. Gunnery training was given at Nellis Air Force Base, at Las Vegas, Nevada. My first view of a B-17 bomber plane caused feelings of fright and anxiety. I had never seen such a large plane. We were taken up on an orientation flight by a former fighter pilot who was not very well trained to fly a B-17 and a co-pilot who was on his first B-17 flight. At one point, the pilot tried a gradual descent dive, and I saw the red-line at a dangerous 310 mph—maximum speed for a safe flight. Force of gravity made it very difficult to get up from a sitting position. The pilot was luckily able to correct the problem, then leveled out and went over the Sierra Nevada mountains. This was where Clark Gable's wife, Carole Lombard, had been lost in a plane crash, and we were told to look for any possible remnants of her plane. After several hours our plane landed.

On another orientation flight, we were trained to fire guns while in flight. The target plane was towing a colored sleeve, and our bullets had certain colors to identify hits. We also had air-to-ground shooting practice from about 500 feet up.

Our next training location was Dyersburg, Tennessee, where we were instructed for overseas action. We were given more orientation in gunnery training with various targets, flying in formation that simulated overseas flying raids. On one occasion, a Bell Cobra fighter making a pursuit curve, as a fighter would do to attack a bomber, collided with one of the B-17s in formation. Several members of the bomber crew and the fighter pilot were killed.

Later, we were assigned to individual crews and flew with them for some time. Each crew had nine members: a pilot, co-pilot, navigator, bombardier-nose gunner, engineer, bottom-turret gunner, waist gunner, tail gunner, and radio man.

In December, 1944, after about ten months' total training time, we were sent overseas. A tour of duty consisted of the completion of thirty-five combat missions. My bomber group, the 100th, was a part of the Eighth Air Force based in Diss, England. Its nickname was the Bloody 100th, because it suffered heavy losses. There were forty such groups in the Eighth, and each group had forty-eight planes, mainly bombers and some fighter planes.

I was assigned to the position of ball-turret gunner. This is the most dangerous position on the plane because of its exposure to enemy fire. I was able to wear only a parachute harness because there was not enough room in the turret for a parachute. We wore shirts and trousers under heated suits. Our outerwear was fleece-lined. After descending into the turret, I would close the door back into the plane. As I sat in my tight, solid metal seat, my movement was very restricted and I felt like a sardine. The enclosed metal and plexiglass turret was only large enough for the seat, the gunner, and two fifty-caliber guns equipped with a Sperry computer sight. The turret could rotate by hydraulic electric power that I could control, as long as it didn't malfunction. I thus had a 360° span of vision and about 90° vision downwards. I was able to see the bombs dropping and, if not obscured by the smoke that sometimes rose 10,000 feet into the sky, I could see the targets as they were being hit.

Our planes flew about five miles up, but many were still victims of flak. The 88-mm anti-aircraft guns were fired from the ground, and the flak ammunition would explode at a certain height, creating a cloud of shrapnel. Our plane was very lucky to escape these attacks.

As the plane rises in flight, the air thins. As instructed, we put on our oxygen masks at 10,000 feet. We were told to constantly squeeze the mask to break up the ice formation caused inside by the condensation in our breath. As we flew, I was to watch for enemy fighters approaching and to observe the underside of the plane to see if any damage occurred from flak. On one occasion, there was a leak of fuel that I saw. The tanks were self-sealing, but if that failed, an explosion was possible. A spark could cause fire to break out. If this happened, the entire crew had to bail

Frank W. Volk in gunner's uniform in 1945, at age twenty, then of Reedsville, West Virginia.

out. Sometimes when this happened, some crew members could not get out in time because of the speed with which the fire spread.

Around my tenth bombing raid, in January, 1945, my plane was at an altitude of 26,000 feet as we approached the railroad yards at Ludwigshaven, when I suddenly found myself confronted with a mortal enemy: freezing up of my oxygen mask. In the excitement of performing my duties of watching for fighter planes and observing the underside of the plane, I suddenly discovered that my oxygen mask had built up too much ice to break up. With oxygen cut off, I became dizzy and disoriented. It was like being under water and needing to get to the surface. I was barely able to radio the waist gunner through the intercom for a spare mask. Time was of the essence because of the altitude. As he searched for a mask, I finally put the turret into position so the lid could be opened. He found a mask and gave it to me. I had difficulty putting it on, and couldn't find the breathing hole. The waist gunner helped me and finally I was able to adjust the replacement mask and resume my normal breathing. Had I completely passed out, I would have had to be mechanically removed by others, and that may have been too late. If I had fallen against the hand control in the turret, this would have completely prevented my extraction. Without oxygen, I would have suffocated.

While I was engrossed in my problem, the bombers in the group had steadily weaved their way to the target, an important oil installation. The bomber struck accurately, and the target became a mass of fire and smoke. Flak burst all around us, but our mission was soon accomplished. Because of the intense experience of being on a bombing mission, I didn't realize how close I had come to death until we were flying homeward to our base in England.

Other missions had other threats. The last of my thirty-five missions as a member of a bomber crew on a B-17, in April, 1945, was also very memorable and just as frightening. Over Touen, France, near Bordeaux, we had a near miss with another B-17 in our group. Bombing raids required tight formation for protection from fighter planes. Another plane had a new crew on board, and they became too excited. Their flying was very erratic and our planes came exceedingly close to a collision—the wings of both planes were within nearly twenty feet of each other. We knew that if we came any closer, it would be the end of our flight. Perspiration poured from our bodies as we anticipated a collision. Quickly our pilot strongly advised them by radio to move off and they did as he said.

Because of similar experiences in the air and in face-to-face combat on the ground, many, many young men became mature adults very quickly during World War II. Many never returned home from the war. The war experience caused many to have ongoing anxiety problems. There were times when I was asleep that I felt as though I were twenty feet up in the air. Some veterans never did overcome their nerve problems.

This was a harrowing experience, and I will never forget it. I am certain that everyone who was on a mission has a story to tell. To this day, I remain amazed by the sense of duty and bravery shown by those young men so that good could triumph over evil.

AUTHOR: *Jessie E. Volk wrote this true experience as told to her by her husband, Frank W. Volk. Mr. Volk was awarded the US Air Force Air Medal for "exceptionally meritorious achievement," commending his performance in the military. See index for additional work by Ms. Volk.*

302-001-ST-WV-002-1998

Challenges in a New Country

arrett Anthony Volk was born on July 1, 1997, in Charleston, West Virginia. I wondered if he would ever know the story of his great-grandfather, Antonio.

Antonio De Prospero was born in Italy in 1889. He and his father, Domenico De

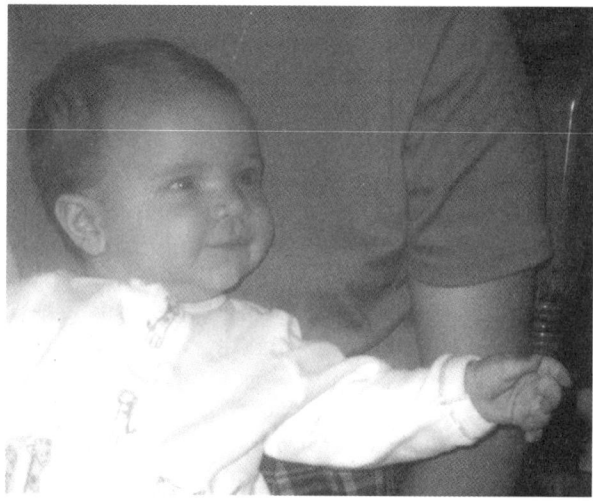

Garrett Anthony Volk.

Prospero, mayor of the Italian town of Bagnatura, came to America in 1903. They worked together in the coal mines in Harding,

Chapter 9: Mountaineer Country

Antonio De Prospero, 1917.

West Virginia, near Elkins. In 1913, Antonio went back to Italy and married Angiolina Mastrogiuseppe, and he returned with her to America in the following year to find work.

Antonio served in the US Army during World War I. After the war, he was employed in a general store in Harding, and lived in Harding with his wife and their first daughter, Natalie. Being a bright, aggressive person, Antonio soon learned the skills necessary to operate a store, and in 1920, he and his two brothers took a five-year lease on a grocery store in Bretz, West Virginia, in Preston County. The store was called De Prospero Bros.

Their beginnings were difficult because they were strangers in the area. Most people had very little money because wages were so low. Much merchandise was sold on credit, but people were honest and paid a little each payday. Antonio and Angiolina, Antonio's brother Agostino and his wife Anna, and third brother Venanzio, whose wife was in Italy, worked very hard. The women cooked, cleaned, did laundry, and worked in the garden, and they stocked shelves at night. The store had a bakery with a stone oven in an adjoining building, and the oven was heated at 3:00 AM. By the time the bread was baked and cooled, individual grocery orders taken the previous day were packed in boxes. Delivery was made by horse and wagon. Few people had automobiles. Meat was available from calves purchased from local farmers, and the brothers raised pigs and chickens. Fresh produce was also purchased from local people, and other groceries were brought in by rail, then picked up with a small truck. Other items sold included shoes, boots, mine tools, and dinner buckets.

When the De Prospero Bros. lease expired in 1925, Antonio returned to Italy with his wife and four children. He purchased property there, but it was difficult to make a living. In 1928 he returned to America. He bought into a partnership in Mona Supply Co. in Granville, West Virginia, and in 1929 he became the sole owner. In 1932 the Great Depression struck. Antonio provided many free groceries for poor families. In 1939, Arkwright Coal Company purchased the store from him. Antonio had also been selling beer as a wholesaler, and he continued this business under the name Mona Supply Co. in a building he had purchased in Morgantown. As a distributor, he employed two of his three daughters, his two sons, and two sons-in-law.

Having lived a successful life and raised a family with all five children settled in their own businesses, Antonio died on May 2, 1970.

AUTHOR: Jessie E. Volk, youngest daughter of Antonio De Prospero. See index for additional work by Ms. Volk.

303-001-ST-WV-002-1998

Ida De Carlo and son David De Carlo in front of Bretz, West Virginia building where the De Prospero Bros. grocery store operated from 1920 to 1925. Ida was the second daughter of Antonio De Prospero. Photograph taken October, 1996.

A Club with a History

In 1919, the United States was recuperating from World War I. Women did not yet have the right to vote, nor could they serve on juries. Women who worked earned only a portion of what men earned. Children were working in sweat shops, practically as slave labor. "Civil rights" would not become a catch phrase for another four decades. From this climate emerged an organization dedicated to promoting equity for all, particularly for women in the workplace.

Today that organization, Business and Professional Women / USA (BPW), has over 70,000 members in more than 2,000 local organizations in every congressional district in the country. Members are women and men of every age, race, religion, political party, and socio-economic background. As one of the original backers of the child labor laws, and among the first of the women's organizations to endorse the Equal Rights Amendment in 1937, BPW has been a leader in passing much of the nation's landmark civil and women's rights legislation.

Mary Susan Dadisman, right, with Morgantown mayor Charlene Marshall. Ms. Marshall joined the Morgantown Business and Professional Women's group for the festivities of National Business Women's Week, in October, 1996.

In West Virginia, BPW was founded in 1921; Morgantown had a chapter in that very first year. The club's first state president, Virginia Foulk, reflected on a half-century's accomplishments in 1969, writing, "So much done, so much more to do!" As a member and past president of the Morgantown BPW group, I recognize and appreciate all the chapter has done through the years and continues to do. It provides a much-needed support and networking environment for women in business at a time when woman- and minority-owned businesses are on the rise. Finding strength in their association with each other, the members of BPW place a high priority on offering resources back to their communities, in accordance with the original aims and purposes set forth by the National Federation of Business and Professional Women's Clubs.

Aims and Purposes

To elevate the standards for women in business and the professions;

To unite women across the country to work for legislation advantageous to women who work and for legislation for the social and economic advancement of all;

To increase opportunities and facilities for job training;

To promote more and improved vocational guidance and education for leisure;

To help women advance themselves;

To standardize wages;

To improve living and working conditions; and

To bring about a spirit of cooperation among business and professional women.

As part of its commitment to helping women advance themselves, Morgantown BPW recently reached out to local teenage girls through its "Choices: Women Helping Girls with Choices" program, under the leadership of Robin Morris, committee chair. Fourteen girls, ages twelve to fifteen, gathered overnight in Bruceton Mills, West Virginia in February, 1998, with BPW Choices committee members, to learn about the implications of career choice: the real after-tax incomes that can be expected in various careers, and the real costs of college, housing, and other adulthood expenses. At the end of the weekend, many of the girls expressed surprise at what it will take to support themselves as adults. The follow-up question, "What did you learn that you did not know before?" drew responses like "how to balance a checkbook" and "planning out your money," along with "how expensive life is going to be" and "the financial problems about being an adult." Several asked for future workshops on skills like self defense, parenting, and cooking.

Beyond service, if you ask most members, certainly those in the Morgantown club, what BPW has meant to them, it has meant support, friendship, understanding, and

CHAPTER 9: MOUNTAINEER COUNTRY

Three teenage participants in Morgantown BPW's Choices program enjoy a pre-breakfast stroll in Bruceton Mills, West Virginia, February, 1998.

The Beauty of It All

In 1990, I was laid off from a glass factory after working for them for sixteen years. It seemed so unfair at the time; the only things I felt I knew were that job, raising three children, and doing what mothers are supposed to do. I went into a deep depression. Oh, yes, there were jobs out there for only four dollars and twenty-five cents an hour. Give me a break! Being out of work in these later years, with the children raised and gone, I was wondering how to cope. I tried to apply for schooling but found the waiting list as long as my arm. Besides, here I was, almost "over the hill," and it is "school days" again? I was older, more dense than ever, hoping something might sink in. I hadn't even taken the time to "stop and smell the roses" all these years because I'd been on a merry-go-round.

With the help of family and friends, I decided to try my hand at writing children's stories. My friend loaned me a typewriter. Ha! I had not touched one in over thirty years. I also discovered that, having worked all my life, I had forgotten the mechanics of the English language. Spelling, punctuation, and grammar were all gone. But I tried

personal growth and development. Carla Uphold was BPW West Virginia state president for 1988–89. BPW has provided her with new friends and contacts, and through her role as president, has given her confidence as a public speaker. Evelyn Howdershelt, 1998–99 state president, says that her involvement in the organization has allowed her to make a difference in the lives of many women through legislative issues and her leadership roles. She has enjoyed the opportunity to network nationwide, elevating the standards of women in business and their professions. Evelyn's sister, Debbie Billings, the 1997–98 chapter president, has found a new pride in herself as a woman, a person, and an achiever as a result of her participation in BPW's Individual Development Program. Another Morgantown club member, Rebecca Bills, has become acquainted with more women in the community, and has enjoyed contributing to the advancement of women and girls. Sharon Weimer says that being part of such a diverse group of high energy women dedicated to proactively engaging in issues of concern for women and families provides advocacy, networking, and "new beginnings" for many members.

The history of women's rights and civil rights has been turbulent. It is exciting to be part of a dynamic group of women whose aims and purposes have remained true since 1919, and who have played such a significant part in furthering equity for all.

A bee collecting pollen while dancing from flower to flower.

learning as I went, and it was good therapy for me. I decided I would write about children and critters, the things I knew about, and one incident especially came to mind.

Back in 1988, my son Ronald wanted to purchase a skunk with his graduation money. We made an agreement. He could buy it, but he had to build a cage and take care of the skunk. I wanted no part. All I could envision were claws and teeth. Much to my surprise,

Author: Mary Susan Dadisman has worked at the Morgantown Public Library since 1964, and currently works there as a library assistant. A BPW member since 1971, Ms. Dadisman served in 1978–79 and 1987–88 as president of the Morgantown club; she has also been active in committees through much of her membership, and is currently a state committee chair.

304-001-ST-WV-002-1998

Two hummingbirds, tiny, delicate, and alluring, in a rose of Sharon tree in the Bunners' front yard.

however, "Peppy" and I became friends, and he soon had me wrapped around his fat little toe.

After a year or so, my son fell in love, got married, and had to leave the state to get work. I got custody of Peppy. By then, other skunks had come along, some injured and in need of nursing, and I raised and enjoyed them too. As time went by, my skunks became my therapy and I noticed more and more the beauty that surrounds me in nature, right here in my own back yard. For the first time, I began to "smell the roses" all around me.

Simply looking out the kitchen window, the beauty was evident: watching birds soaring, squirrels happily playing, and bees collecting pollen while dancing from flower to flower . . . the young deer romping through the grass, without a care in the world . . . the swift hummingbird, tiny, delicate and alluring, stopping only long enough to learn which flower has the better nectar. We should all be so busy! Hummingbirds flock especially to the "rose of Sharon" tree in droves, right in the front yard. I photographed these birds.

At night I noticed the tranquil sounds of tree frogs, crickets, owls, and something coming through the thicket: a deer, a fox, or whatever the darkness would bring. I love watching the seasons change, particularly in autumn when the colors transform to vivid reds and golds. What splendor we have here in wild, wonderful, by God, West Virginia. I learned to appreciate life.

Now, after twenty years on my own, I am happily married to a wonderful, God-fearing man. Ed and I have seven wonderful children, with four grandchildren. Yes, we still have a skunk, too. His name is Coco, and he is as broad as he is long. We do take time to "smell the roses." I guess what I learned is to remember, when you're down, to look up through those billowing clouds and think of God's creations.

There is a song, "How Great Thou Art," that constantly lifts my spirits. If you are down, listen to the words. Matthew wrote in chapter 6, verse 22 and verses 28–33, that we should "consider the lilies of the field." But we are worth much more. That's the beauty of it all!

AUTHOR: Sandra Bunner. Sandra has three children, all graduates of the former Flemington High School. Originally from Philadelphia, Sandra has lived in West Virginia for thirty-seven years and loves the state.

305-001-ST-WV-002-1998

Changing Times for Osage and Morgantown

I was born September 17, 1933, in Osage, in Monongalia County, West Virginia, and have lived in the area all my life. My mother is Christine Jenkins Jennings Cranford, and my father was Charles Jennings. When I was in the second grade—I had three sisters and a brother and my mother was pregnant at the time—my father was killed at the Osage #3 mine, right down over the hill from our house. My mother later remarried, to Ollie Cranford, and they had a child. When that child was four years old and I was in college in Bluefield, my stepfather was also killed, in the mines that had their entrance on Arkwright Road.

The end of large-scale coal mining operations in the Scotts Run area of northern West Virginia and the construction of Interstate 79 through Osage in the early 1970s have changed the area drastically, but I have many happy memories of my childhood and teenage years.

Our house, #40—there were no street names— had four rooms. Basically, that was what most of the houses were like in the area where we lived. You just had to be neat and compact, because there wasn't that much

Chapter 9: Mountaineer Country

space. We made do with what we had. I helped to cut the wood and carry the coal and, in winter, if the water froze, to carry more water.

For an African American family, Osage was a great place to live in the thirties and forties because, although the schools everywhere were still segregated, the community of Osage itself was essentially integrated. I went for one semester in first grade to the one-room school in Pursglove, while the Floyd B. Cox Elementary School was being built. These schools were for African Americans. But we and our friends, black and white, might walk together to and from school, and would separate just to go to our own individual schools. Aside from that, everybody in the community did things together. We would borrow things from one house to another, and if there was ever a death in the community, we all supported each other. Going to school was the only thing we didn't do together. I guess it was just a way of life with us, and we didn't even imagine it could be different. One of my sisters went to Pennsylvania to live with relatives and went to school there. She told us that blacks and whites went to school together, and that was something we were just not familiar with.

There was a theater in Osage at the time, and several restaurants, and jewelry stores. It was a thriving community then, and the coal mines were the main source of income for the area. It was a good place to raise a family and I'm sure that most people who lived in that area have fond memories of growing up there.

For fun in the summer we would sometimes go to the elementary school playground. I remember that Esther Brown, when she was playground leader, always had some fun activity for us to do. We would also get to go to movies in Osage on weekends, to see a cowboy movie or something.

There was a small church not too far from our house, where we went to Sunday school. I remember getting a Sunday school card each week, with a colorful scene from the Bible on one side and a short story or Bible verse on the other. A fun time for us was the Sunday school picnic. The superintendent of the Sunday school would get someone in the area with a truck. We would pack a lunch and load up the truck, with our food in a suitcase or a basket. I remember telling someone recently about having the Sunday school picnic out at Cooper's Rock. At that time, Cooper's Rock seemed so far, I'd have sworn it was a day's drive away! I can also remember going to a swimming hole some place when someone was going to get baptized. My mother didn't have a car, so getting in a car or a truck to go to that swimming hole and watch someone being baptized was exciting.

Of course, Christmas was always exciting, too. These days, when we try to figure out when and where we are going to put up our Christmas tree, I think back to childhood—of course, with our smaller house, we always put the tree up on Christmas Eve, and it stayed up for just one week. I always thought everyone did that. And then we'd always put our names around the tree so Santa Claus would know who we were and where to put our gifts. I can't imagine how my mother kept anything secret from us, in that house!

Very few people had telephones in those days. One of the first families that I can remember having a telephone lived about a five-minute walk away. We would go there and knock on the door and ask to use the phone, and I thought that was a big deal. Over time, some people who lived closer to us got phones, and today I can't even imagine giving out my neighbor's telephone number, but as youngsters that's what we did. Our neighbors would just call us to the phone. I can remember when my family got our first telephone, and I'm surprised I can't remember the number now. Of course, it was a party line, and you had to be careful what you said because anyone could be listening. You knew that your ring was two short, or one long, one short, whatever. And these days, if you hang the receiver up improperly, it eventually gets disconnected, but I can remember when that wasn't true and, if you didn't hang up properly, no one on the line could use their phone—but they could hear everything that went on in your house! They'd have to send someone down to tell you to hang up your phone.

Back then, no matter where you lived in Monongalia County, as an African American, you went to Monongalia High School in Westover. There's a plaque on the building that states when it was built and that it was built for African Americans. Eleanor Roosevelt came for the dedication.

The high school had seventh through twelfth grades, and we mainly had reading, writing, and arithmetic. We had excellent teachers at Monongalia High, some from all over West Virginia—my home economics teacher, Dorcas Carter, for example, graduated from West Virginia State College, in Institute—and some recruited from other states. Dorcas Carter really sparked enthusiasm in me for sewing. To this day, I still like to cook and bake bread, and I'm sorry I didn't pursue sewing more.

Monongalia High School also had an outstanding drum and bugle corps. The band director, Charlie Johnson, was actually the

maintenance supervisor, and he directed the band on his own. When the Monongalia High School Drum and Bugle Corps was in parades in downtown Morgantown, everyone wanted to see them.

We had basketball and football teams, and there are photos of our football team before I went to school there as state champs, competing on the national level. I also know of one basketball team that was state champs and went to national competition. We had some great athletes.

I took my first big trip when I was in the ninth grade, in about 1947. Aunt Rhoda, my mom's oldest sister, took me to Cincinnati. She thought I deserved a trip because my mother's mother, Mary Elizabeth Keller Jenkins Flowers, was ill, and I had been helping a little with her. So I was allowed to take a week out of school to go to Cincinnati, and that was exciting. Aunt Rhoda took me to the zoo and to the large stores downtown. I think this was the first time I was able to go into a large restaurant and order, and I remember thinking how great it would be if I could do this any day that I wanted. Going out to breakfast was too much! Aunt Rhoda died about two years ago. A lot of people here, both races, knew her and referred to her affectionately as Aunt Rhoda.

While I was in high school, I always thought I had to have a job and have my own money. My first job was a babysitting job on Prospect Street, in Morgantown. The house isn't there any longer. For another job I had, I would ride the school bus to Morgantown High School five nights a week and walk up to a fraternity house and help serve dinner. I made ten dollars a week doing that, and I thought I was rich. As soon as I got paid I probably went downtown and bought a skirt.

Once I started working, I always had a couple of jobs. One day I was walking down the street, and a lady approached me—I talked to everybody and some people think I smile too much—and she said, you have the most pleasant look on your face. She asked me, do you work? I told her I had a part-time job, babysitting, and she told me to go to Morgantown Florist and talk with them. So I went and spoke with John Batlas' father, and they hired me—not out front but in back, making background baskets for funeral arrangements, one of my first jobs. I was in ninth or tenth grade. It always amazed me that that lady, Jean Andy, one of their employees, sent me to talk with them. The Batlases were kind to me. One thing that always sticks out in my mind is, when it was time for lunch, someone would say, Charlene, Mrs. Batlas wants you to come upstairs for lunch. I thought that was awful nice for them to do that, but I guess they realized there was nowhere else that I was able to go—Morgantown wasn't quite as integrated as Osage was at that time!

There seemed to be plenty of part-time jobs to earn a little extra money. Families looking for students to work for them after school would call the high school office and talk to the secretaries, Bernadine Moore and Willa Beauford. A lot of youngsters acquired after-school jobs that way. Miss Beauford gave me a phone number once to call, and the family that I went to interview with was the Wade family, Rebecca and Georgia Wade, two sisters. I spent a number of years doing housework and cooking for them after school.

I was a cheerleader in high school, and I also participated in many clubs, but one of my most enjoyable activities was when I was elected Miss Monongalia, in 1952. The African American high schools throughout the state each had a "Miss," almost equivalent to a high school homecoming queen, but chosen during the basketball season. The year that I was Miss Monongalia our basketball team was runner-up in the region, so I was able to travel to the state basketball tournament at West Virginia State College. The other "Misses" from around the state were there, and there were activities for us, and we had nice banners to wear. That was a highlight of my time in high school.

I graduated high school in 1952. As a graduation gift, the Wade sisters, for whom I had been working for several years, treated me to a shopping trip in Pittsburgh. Miss Beauford, one of the school secretaries, accompanied me on that trip. That was an outstanding thing that the Wade family did for me. I was also honored at graduation to receive the Most All-Around Senior medal for participation in the most activities. When I think back now about all the activities I've been involved in as an adult, I wonder if maybe some of the things you do as a younger person are an indication of what you will do later.

Monongalia High School closed in 1954, and later reopened as Westover Junior High, an integrated school. Many students who graduated from Monongalia High went on to higher education, and have achieved good things throughout the United States and possibly in foreign countries. There's an alumni association, and every two years we have a high school reunion. Classes were so small that we don't have a reunion based on the year that you graduated, but rather for anyone who attended, so people of all ages who graduated high school up through May, 1954 come to the reunions.

CHAPTER 9: MOUNTAINEER COUNTRY

Some of the author's first- and second-grade classmates at the Floyd B. Cox Elementary School in Osage, West Virginia, 1938 or 1939. Standing (l-r): Alma Messenberg, John Boyd, Evelyn Younger, Ernestine Woods, Wesley Morton, and Leroy Messenberg. Seated: an unidentified girl, with Charlene Jennings, the author, on the right.

The Osage of today is very different from what I remember, and most of us have moved on to Morgantown and other places. My mother lived in Osage until 1969 or 1970, when they started construction of Interstate 79, and then she left the area for a while. The house that I grew up in had to be torn down to make way for the interstate. After some years, my mother moved back, and she lives here in Morgantown now. Before the interstate, Osage was incorporated, but so many people had to move that it seems like eventually there was hardly anyone there to have a city. It's sad what has happened because that was a really booming little town.

I often visit Osage for special occasions. I was there in the spring of 1997 for the opening and dedication of the Osage Coal Camp Museum. The following fall, the Scotts Run Settlement House in Osage gave a class on breadmaking, and invited me to show them how to do bread. We had an interesting day. I think we made forty-some loaves, and they sold it through the Settlement House. I know that I still have friends there. In the last couple of years it's better than it was before, and I hope they'll be able to do something in Osage that will draw attention to the area, so that the few businesses that are there will thrive again.

I ran for Morgantown City Council in 1991. The students at West Virginia University played an active part, along with many others, in my candidacy. I even had a student as a campaign manager. At that time, the student body president was Sam Sutton, and I was also helped by Sam's good friend Chip Slaven; Sam went on to then-Governor Caperton's office, and Chip became an aide for US Senator Bob Wise. I still maintain my connection with them.

I stay in contact with many other students who've gone on, for example, Steve Robinson, from Virginia, now graduated and in Tennessee. Many times I say I'm going to quit getting attached to students, but every time I say that, I'm already attached to someone else. Kevin Berry, a student who works out of the WVU president's office with the Parents' Club, is a friend of mine. I used to threaten to call his parents if I thought he wasn't doing something right.

With the help of my student friends and many others, I became mayor of Morgantown in July, 1991. Many people have come forward to support me, and I have been so pleased and so appreciative of what everyone has done and the way that they have shown their kindness for me as mayor. Some people thought that Morgantown wouldn't be able to accept an African American mayor, but that's one of the things that I'm proud of about Morgantown.

AUTHOR: Charlene Marshall and her husband Rogers Leon Marshall have three children: daughter Gwen Marshall, a graduate of West Virginia University, lives in Star City, West Virginia; elder son Roger Marshall, Jr., is retired from the Air Force, and lives in Riverside, California; and younger son Larry Marshall, a graduate of San Diego State, lives in San Diego, California. All three graduated from Morgantown High School. Charlene and Rogers have four grandchildren as well.

Editors' Note: Scotts Run coal, prized for its use in the production of steam power, came into great demand during World War I. As in coalfields throughout West Virginia, the importation of workers to Scotts Run produced a racially and ethnically diverse population; most came from southern and eastern Europe, with native whites and blacks making up about forty percent of the population. Osage, the center of activity in Scotts Run, boomed. By the late 1920s, though, production in the region began to decline. The Scotts Run Settlement House, part of the nationwide Settlement House movement, was established in 1922 to provide assistance to local mining families. It continues to serve as a focal point for the community that remains in Scotts Run following steady depopulation since the Depression and the loss of land for construction of Interstate 79 in the early 1970s. (Reference: Lewis, Ronald L. "Scotts Run: An Introduction." West Virginia History 53 (1994): 1-5.)

306-001-ST-WV-002-1998

No Greater Love

My brother Joseph turned sixteen April 25, 1996. To celebrate, my family plotted a humiliating cowboy theme party complete with ten-gallon hats, paper vests, and all the Garth Brooks albums a person could stand. My daddy showed up in a pair of bib overalls, sporting a straw hat, chewing a corncob pipe, and walking lopsided from the weight of a little brown jug he had tucked beneath his arm. I couldn't have been more proud of him for playing the role we all relished, even if it was at his own expense. At that moment, he wasn't too shy or too busy to revel in our foolishness. Our joy was contagious, and he welcomed the laughter openly.

William M. Compton, April 25, 1996.

My daddy's name is William, but most everyone calls him Billy for short. Just turned sixty-three, and he has skin the color of chestnuts and a voice that rings deep in your ear, hinting of laughter but touched with sadness, too. I was his first-born of a second marriage and he has reminded me of his epic romance with my mother each month for every one of my twenty-four years. I am always overcome by his sensitivity and by his ready recollection of the wistful past.

It has taken us much of my lifetime to know one another. I remember him as a younger man, but barely. He spent much of that youth in the coalfields. Yet I am not sorry for the lost moments we might have shared. Despite our distance during the days of my childhood, it was then that I learned from him about responsibility and about the ties that bind us to this land. And within me there are the images of his youthful presence, stark and certain. I recall waking early on Sundays to the smell of his silver-dollar pancakes, and I remember the medicinal calm of his cherry cigar smoke being blown into my aching ears. I see dirt racetracks, blackberry wine, yellow dozers, and the initials of my family members carved into an ancient oak tree in the forest where we hunted for persimmons and for ginseng. In particular, I remember the butterflies as they filled the late August sky with iridescent shades of orange just a hue darker than the westward sun. And I remember shooting stars and moonlight sonatas.

My daddy has taught me much, though I know he'd never admit it. Even now, if he is reading this, my daddy will believe it to be about some imaginary father. In fact, he'll likely look up and, with a coy smile, tell me that I certainly have a talent for B.S. But the beauty of being a daughter is that it matters not if your father is too humble to accept your compliments—it matters only that you can give them. And I am blessed, because I can. Because of my father, I strive always to find the best in others. I laugh often, and I try to leave the world a bit better than when I found it. Most important, I can recite the story of the little Dutch boy who kept his finger in the dike and I can recognize that the only true unhappiness is in not knowing what we want and killing ourselves to get it.

In my family, we don't say how we feel as often as we should. But if we did, and if he would listen, I would say to him, "Daddy, in this lifetime, there are few constants. You are a constant. As far as I'm concerned, there can be no greater compliment, just as there can be no greater love."

AUTHOR: Amy Compton Shaffer. Mrs. Shaffer is married to Jeremy L. Shaffer, and resides in Cheat Lake. She works as business prospects manager for the West Virginia High Technology Consortium Foundation, and is a full-time third-year law student.

Summer in a Washtub

In 1980, my younger sister Rachel and I wanted our parents to buy a swimming pool. We were both waterbabies; neither of us can remember a time when we couldn't swim. We paddled and splashed our way through years of swimming lessons at West Virginia University, enthusiastically learning to hold our breath underwater and to perform exotic, graceless strokes, such as the dolphin. (I have never heard of this since, prompting me to wonder if the instructor did not devise it simply for her own amusement, and our torture.) In elementary school, as Rachel and I graduated from pollywogs to sharks, we yearned for a pool in our backyard to hone our skills.

Every year my parents planted a garden. Scores of plants—tomato, zucchini, beans, peas, cucumbers, and an occasional smattering of broccoli or asparagus, as well as herbs—flourished on a plot perfectly suited for an inground swimming pool, complete with waterslide and diving board. A swimming pool, my sister and I proffered, would relieve our parents of all that gardening work—the weeding, planting, picking, and canning. Their knees and backs would thank us, and just think of all the free time! In addition, they'd never again have to invent strategies for shooing from the yard deer and bunnies intent on reaping a premature harvest. A logical argument, we were convinced. We even offered to dig the hole. Mom and Dad, however, simply were obstinate.

To placate us, my father, as usual, used his imagination. His inventions are well known throughout the neighborhood and the family. Neighbors still talk about the yellow broom handle he duct-taped to the rear of our bicycles to help us learn to ride. Rachel and I pedaled like mad down the gravel, oil-covered road as Dad jogged behind us, holding us up by the broom handle. Dad is a very tall man, and stooping to hold the back of a pink Huffy strained his back. The broom handle allowed him to follow and protect us while standing upright. It wasn't pretty, perhaps, but it worked. His plan for individual swimming pools was not particularly grand, but Rachel and I extracted plenty of splash from the situation.

In my parents' basement was an old ringer washing machine. Rachel and I kept pretty clear of it since the day Rachel ran her fingers through the ringer. We'd slapped the machine's red metal release bar before any damage was done, but after that the sound and the thought were enough to scare us away. That summer the machine still saw use, and the rinse cycle utilized large, metal washtubs. My family had two of them. Filled with cool water on a humid summer day, those tubs were just as refreshing as an inground pool, if not as spacious. We couldn't do laps, but we could practice holding our breath. We jumped and played in the water, and if the water level got too low, Mom refilled the tubs for us. She also provided tall glasses of lemonade and liberal doses of sunscreen. The tubs kept us content, and we used them every summer until we were simply too big. By that time, we weren't interested in hanging around the house much anyway. If Rachel and I went to a pool it was a public one, where we could socialize with our friends and try to ignore each other, as most preteen sisters do.

I often wonder what my childhood would have been like if I hadn't grown up on Hickory Hill.

Rachel and Amy enjoy the good life on their back porch, circa 1980.

I had cousins and friends who grew up in treeless yards. Their front porches were not covered by the annual meandering, fragrant morning glories, or abuzz with the sound of bees and birds visiting flowers and building nests. They didn't spend their days catching fat salamanders by the tail and rounding up big, rusty coffee cans full of locust shells, cocoons, and miscellaneous other woodland treasures. Cable television wormed its way into their homes years before it reached the Hill, keeping them indoors while Rachel and I played outside—at least until Mom's shrill, two-finger whistle called us back home for dinner. And I can say for certain that I don't know anyone else who "swam" in a metal washtub—a true pleasure on a humid summer day.

AUTHOR: *Amy Stevenson. Amy lives in Latrobe, Pennsylvania, but grew up in Morgantown. Her parents are Paul and Susan Stevenson.*

308-001-ST-WV-002-1998

William D. Smith and Dick Rittenhouse

In 1892 or '93, William D. Smith, a young man from Greene County, Pennsylvania, came to Mannington, West Virginia in search of work. Within a few years he had a hundred horse teams working for him. He was a large man of colorful speech, well liked and respected. His horse barn was between Water Street and the railroad tracks.

Richard Stanford "Dick" Rittenhouse standing in front of the First Exchange Bank in Mannington, West Virginia, circa 1935 (photo courtesy of Ron Rittenhouse).

Dick Rittenhouse was born a slave in Harrison County, then Virginia. When he was small, his family moved to the Teaverbaugh section of Marion County. Dick became an excellent handler of horses, and in the early 1890s began driving for Bill Smith.

Through many years of working together, they became fast friends. Their most difficult job was to haul the large boilers that provided power for oil and natural gas well drilling and other tasks. The boilers were the heaviest items that had to be hauled, and the boiler wagons were stronger, with larger wheels and wider tires. Bill and Dick spent a great deal of time together at this task, and eventually made it the center of a "friendship pact": Whoever died first, the other would haul his casket on a boiler wagon with six black horses for Dick's funeral, or six white horses for Bill's.

It happened that Bill died first, in his late 40s. So Dick hauled his casket on a boiler wagon with six of their best white horses. Mannington had its own Board of Education at that time, and the Mannington High School principal must have felt that Bill's death held historical importance for the town, as he let school out for a few minutes as the funeral passed. Reverend Prichard told me many years later that he stood on the corner as they passed, and tears streamed down Dick's cheeks on the way to the Mannington Cemetery.

This happened in 1915. Bill's granddaughter was Charlotte Koon, who was a community leader throughout her life. She donated photographs of Bill and Dick to the West Augusta Historical Society Museum, and they hang side by side in our Pioneer Room, preserving some of Mannington's colorful past.

AUTHOR: Bill Efaw. Mr. Efaw is past president of the West Augusta Historical Society. He adds to his story, "Dick Rittenhouse was the first colored person I ever saw. I was a small child of about seven. Dick sat on the bank corner, and I walked out to the curb over and over. After a couple trips, Dick must have known I was curious, so he called me over and gave me a penny."

309-001-ST-WV-002-1998

FIRE! FIRE! FIRE!

In the early 1940s, when I was about seven years old, our Preston County community had a forest fire that started when a Plainview School neighbor's burning trash spread to broomsage and then on to the woods behind our school.

I, along with my two sisters Betty and Shirley and and my brother Tom, had to walk a dirt road between home and school each day. I don't remember just how long the fire

Chapter 9: Mountaineer Country

lasted—days, possibly weeks—and it was smoky and smelly and very frightening to pass as near to the fire as we did. Even though the fire was not dangerously close to us, its effects were close enough for me and I was always glad to get home or to school.

Our father, Brandum Kennedy, and older brothers would take shovels and walk to help fight the fire in the evenings and sometimes late into the nights. This was after my father had worked eight or more hours at Kelly Creek Mine. After Mother, Etta Walls Kennedy, put us three sisters to bed (we all slept in one bed at that time), she would sit by the window in our very small bedroom and watch in the direction of the fire. Oh, the questions we must have asked her. We could see the worry on her face, even though she tried to hide it. Having her there helped us to fall asleep. At night time the sky was red from the fire. This spooky sky was the most frightening to me. Mother never went to bed until her "men" came home.

One day shortly after the fire started, our teacher, Mrs. Blanche Reppert from Arthurdale, decided she should act to save the wood-structured one-room schoolhouse. I'm sure it was difficult for her to teach a dozen or so worried kids who were looking out the windows. She sent a few older boys, my brother Tom was one, outside to burn off one side of the grass on the school lot. This way, if the fire came close, we would be safe inside the school. The boys were well instructed and the deed was

Plainview School, Preston County, 1980.

accomplished without any trouble. The Plainview School and its "nervous Nellies" were safe if the fire changed direction. Fortunately, the wind kept it going away from the school. No homes were burned either.

1980 picture of "home" for the Kennedy family of nine.

Our schoolyard usually had scrubby grass, and the following spring the burned-off side of the yard produced the nicest grass. Mrs. Reppert said we should burn the other side in the fall.

Even to this day, this grandmother's nostrils will quickly flare and a panic washes over me at the slightest hint of burning forest or wood—just like it did over fifty years ago.

Author: Patricia (Kennedy) Newhouse, a 1953 graduate of University High School in Morgantown, West Virginia, resides in Wooster, Ohio, with her husband, Russ. She is a retired executive secretary from Rubbermaid Inc. See index for additional work by Ms. Newhouse.

310-001-ST-WV-002-1998

My Autograph Book

uring my junior high and early high school days in Monongalia County, West Virginia, at Cassville School, Riverside School, and then University High, autograph books were quite the rage. I received mine from Santa, played by Mother and Daddy (Brandum and Etta Kennedy), of course. This is a very dear part of my West Virginia memories. Come walk with me down memory lane in the late 1940s and early 1950s as this well-worn and faded book speaks to us:

> *I love you little, I love you big.*
> *I love you like a pig.*

Patricia and Russell Newhouse, 1991.

When you get married
   and have twins,
Don't come to my house
   for safety pins.

The higher the mountain,
   the cooler the breeze.
The younger the couple,
   the tighter they squeeze.

It tickles me
   and makes me laugh
To think you want
   my autograph.

When the angels pull open the curtains
   and pin them with a star
I'm thinking of you, darling,
   and wondering where you are.

Snow on the mountain top and sun can't melt it.
I love you and I can't help it.

U R 2 sweet 2 B forgotten.

When you get old and cannot see,
Put on your spectacles and think of me.

When you get married and live across the lake
Send me a piece of your wedding cake.

Roses on my shoulders, slippers on my feet
I'm Patty's darling, don't you think I'm sweet?

Patty had a little dog, she fed her on tin cans.
When the little puppies came, they came in Ford sedans.

Inspiration won't come. Can't write, too dumb.
No ink, bum pen. That's all, Amen.

I love you on the hill top, I love you on the level.
If I had you in my arms, I'd squeeze you like the devil.

Way out in the ocean carved on a rock
Are these three words, forget me not.

Here's my wish for you:
   I wish you health. I wish you wealth.
   I wish you all you wish yourself.

T is for toffee. T is for tea.
But the best T in my language is loyalty.

Remember well and bear in mind
An old cow's tail hangs down behind.
Though it be long and full of burrs
She's proud of it because it's hers.

It's fun to go to school
   to learn to read and write.
It's fun to hold your boyfriend's hand
   out in the pale moonlight.
It's fun to be with friends
   who know your secrets, too.
But the most fun I can think of
   is the fun I have with you.

Sure as a vine grows around a stump
You are my darling sugar lump.

A page from Patricia Newhouse's autograph book.

Roll my pants above my knees.
I'll go see Patty when I please.

Some kiss beneath the lilacs.
Some kiss beneath the rose.
But the proper place for you to kiss
Is just beneath the nose.

Because you have many a friend
   and many a lover,
I'll save space and write this
   on the cover. (And it was!)

CHAPTER 9: MOUNTAINEER COUNTRY

Now it's time to come back to reality and 1998. Memory lane is closed for a spell.

AUTHOR: *Patricia (Kennedy) Newhouse. See index for additional work by Ms. Newhouse.*

Editors' Note: School children across the country enjoyed autograph books for many decades, beginning some time before the turn of the century. Girls participated in the custom perhaps more than boys, although boys did sometimes join in the fun. Teachers, friends, and family were coerced into adding to the books. Rhymes and sayings like those above were popular; many such rhymes were widely known, and appear in autograph books from all over. In addition, students sometimes affixed colorful stickers of flowers or animals alongside their entries. In some places, the books were used each school year, while in other places they were used only on graduation from elementary and high school. The books were typically bound in leather or in imitation leather, and some had pages in many pastel colors. A student might save the front pages for best friends, and when handed a book to sign, would first look at the other poems there to avoid being repetitive.

311-001-ST-WV-002-1998

"Ol' Pancakes"

In the summer of 1946, when I was five, I lived with my parents on my mother's old home place near Cuzzart, West Virginia, in Preston county. My cousin Naomi Moon Williams was staying with us at the time. One morning she awakened me to come downstairs, as there was something for me to see. Knowing that it was July and we were out of buckwheat flour, I made the comment "Nuthin' but ol' pancakes," as I thoroughly disliked pancakes made from wheat flour. Anyway, I dressed and made my way downstairs to my mother's and father's bedroom, where I saw my new sister, Linda Lou Nedrow Hermanson, for the first time. At the time, being five years old, I don't remember her birth making much impression on me. Of course, now I love her dearly. But the lasting impression to me was eating those wheat flour pancakes that I hated so much! I still remember my sister as "Ol' Pancakes."

AUTHOR: *James E. Nedrow lives in Shinnston, West Virginia. He is married with one daughter, and has worked for AT&T / Lucent Technologies for thirty-three years. His hobbies are genealogy, collecting straight razors, gunsmithing, and hunting.*

312-001-ST-WV-002-1998

Glimpses of 1924

My maternal grandmother was Ray Pefley Hutchinson. She passed away on August 18, 1967. The following story is part of a manuscript that she wrote years ago. The characters in the story were her family: her husband, Brooks Swearingen Hutchinson; his parents, Clyde Effington Hutchinson and Lyda Watkins Hutchinson; and his seven brothers and three sisters-in-law.

The story is a look back in time to 1924, before the Depression, when my great-grandfather Clyde—an influential coal baron—and great-grandmother Lyda embarked on a trip around the world. The family anxiously awaited each postcard, every bit of news, and most of all Clyde and Lyda's return.

The family lived at Sonnencroft, a twenty-eight-room Fairmont, West Virginia landmark of red tile and stucco that echoed with the sounds of grandchildren playing and family gatherings. The name means, appropriately, "home of many sons." In the summer, however, they often traveled to the mountains in Maryland. This story gives us a glimpse into their summer 1924 retreat there, as well.

Sonnencroft, the Fairmont, West Virginia home of the Hutchinson family, 1920.

January, 1924 comes with Harold and Margaret, Brooks and myself in New York with Mother and Father, rushing around doing last minute shopping before they sail on their voyage around the world. Then we stand one midnight on a pier, weeping and waving as the Cunard's great *Laconia* slowly glides out to sea. We watch her lights grow dim and then fade in the darkness. "How far is around the world?"

My own little-girl question echoes in my ear, and I tremble to answer it.

Then letters, first from Panama, then Los Angeles. We all long to charter a plane and fly out there and stop them before they start on the Pacific, but sail they do. There are stormy nights at home, and everyone's heart echoes the prayers lisped by the grandchildren to "Please, dear God, keep Mamman and Papaw safe and bring them home soon."

Letters arrive from Japan about the awful earthquake that happened just before they reached there; from Hong Kong, Shanghai, Singapore, Rangoon. How wonderful to even glimpse so many fairy-tale places. There's such a funny picture of Father and an Indian fakir: Father with a sickly grin on his face, his hair standing upright, and a great python around his neck! When we tease him about it afterwards, he always declares he was not the least bit afraid, and that the wind made his hair look that way, but we always have our doubts!

Then come pictures of them on camels in Egypt

Clyde Effington Hutchinson with Indian fakir and python, 1924.

at the pyramids. Then Greece, then Rome, then Paris, and finally we again find ourselves in New York. This time it is June, and the ship comes sailing in with bands playing and flags flying. Eagerly, we scan the decks and locate Mother and Father. The gangplank is lowered, tears and kisses, and again the family is complete.

We spend a gay week in New York, seeing all the theaters and shopping, and then finally return home again to West Virginia. Mother and Father left with two trunks—they return with eight. We give them just the first evening to rest, and then, the next day, we open the baggage.

Such excitement, wonder, and joy! Gifts from every country for everybody. Mother's bedroom turns into an Oriental bazaar, with four of everything for the girls. Gorgeous ceremonial bridal robes from Japan, shading from hyacinth blue to softest gray, shine with heavy gold embroidery; Mother's is black, lined in red, with a red obi. She brings out houri coats of heavenly blue from Kobe. "Ray, this one with the cherry blossoms and the doves on it is yours," "Bonnie, take this one with the lotus flowers," and so on.

From Japan come strings of pearls and square-cut crystals, tiny bright-flowered kimonos for the children, and Japanese dolls. And there's so much more! Strings of turquoise-matrix and antique amber from Shanghai. Gorgeous Mandarin coats from Hong Kong, and carved ivory combs. Strings of pink carnelian from Bombay. Lace from the Philippines, and a native costume. Velvet bags embroidered with gold peacocks from Agra. Batiks from Java. Silver toe-rings, silver anklets, and huge earrings from India, and a native robe. Interesting embroidered bags and donkey beads from Greece. From Egypt, tent work, silver scarves, scarabs, and a sheik's robe of pale blue silk shot with silver. Scarves from Florence, and marvelous beaded bags from Paris. For the boys, carved ivory cigarette holders from China, amber cigarettes from Egypt, heavy silk robes from Japan, bill folders of carved leather from India.

We feel such excitement and thrill at each new gift, and at the tales of far-off lands and peoples. One tale is of Father walking sedately down the steps of a temple in India with a cow, not daring to drive it away because they are considered sacred there. He says he heard so much of reincarnation there, that this must have been the reincarnation of old Beauty, our old cow who died, from the way she followed him!

Then Mother tells of the poor woman who died on the ship and had to be left in India, while her husband was left to complete the trip alone; of the time she almost missed the train in Agra for lingering at the Taj Mahal too long; of the awful heat and how they hung wet sheets at the windows of the compartment to cool off the air. She tells also about the burying towers in India, where the vultures sit, and of how cold it was in China, especially in the temples, where they had to remove their shoes. We listen, but cannot settle down for long, itching to stroll around the room and gloat over our possessions.

During the remainder of that most gorgeous month of June, we simply revel in all being together again, and bask in the sun-

CHAPTER 9: MOUNTAINEER COUNTRY

Lyda Watkins Hutchinson, back from round-the-world trip, with daughters-in-law (l-r) Bonnie Bonsell Wood Hutchinson, Ray Pefley Hutchinson (author of this piece, and maternal grandmother of Sylvia Elaine Parker), and Margaret Owens Hutchinson, wearing souvenirs, June, 1924.

shine of Sonnencroft's garden. The children romp and race all day over the whole estate, and resemble young Indians. We never know where to look for them—in the fish ponds, or the stables, where Polly, the Irish setter, has again presented us with a large litter of adorable but worthless coal-black puppies.

Incessant splashing comes from the swimming pool each afternoon, as some of the boys decide it is just the right hour for a dip. Loud yells are heard frequently from some of the girls who join them. The terraces are beautifully ablaze with color: heavenly blues of delphinium mingling with the gorgeous shade of pink of the Oriental poppies. Everywhere is beauty.

We gather early evenings by the weeping willow tree that hangs over the lily pond on the lowest terrace. The air is heavy with the perfume of roses. The golden days slowly melt into the silver evenings. Jimmy, flat on his back by the rim of the pool, gazes dreamily at the clouds. Paul holds one of the children on his knee. Robert smokes and hums a tune. Everyone is contented, restful, happy. At the dinner hour, Henry, the butler, appears with trays for each one of cold chicken, raspberry ice, delicious rolls, and tall glasses of iced tea.

"Oh Mother, how did you know we all wanted to stay right here this marvelous evening and enjoy the sunset?" Katherine exclaims. Mother smiles and we all enjoy watching the clouds draw their gray chiffon over the crimson sun as it sinks behind the hills. The fireflies dart everywhere and the children begin chasing them. The dark descends slowly, almost lovingly, over this beautiful garden where we are all so contented. Someone hums "Carry Me Back to Old Virginia," and we all join in.

Finally one evening, Father becomes restless and walks around the pool, where the stars are now reflected—he is never still for very long at a time. He remarks at last that he thinks we should all prepare to go to Deer Park, in the mountains of Maryland, before the weather gets too hot. We have spent several summers there in the cottage Father purchased for his grandchildren. The mountain air is most beneficial for them. His sons spent every summer in that vicinity when they were small.

Without much discussion, we find ourselves in a few days on our way to the cottage. "Cottage" it was called, but it was really a rambling house of about thirty rooms. It had to be large to accommodate the family, which grew apace every year. Our summer neighbors always wanted to know who had had the latest baby. My first child, Elaine, had been added to the list over these recent years, and Katherine had added two more as well. Such happy hours those children had together—so many happy ones, the childish quarrels and fusses didn't count.

Rainy days were difficult, though. Shut in, seven or eight children can create more noise than all the animals in a zoo. We were almost wild with the confusion, until Mother suggested in her mild way that we girls go up to her bedroom and let the children have the downstairs. This we always did after that, to the happy solution of the problem.

A woman once said to me, "It surely is not true that you four daughters-in-law can live for months in the same house together, with your mother-in-law, and never quarrel?" But that is exactly what we did. No one ever seemed to want to quarrel around Mother. There might be arguments or discussions, but never hard words nor hurt feelings. Her influence permeated the atmosphere of the whole house. Sometimes one of the girls might get tired of the others, and then she

Hutchinson family summer retreat in Deer Park, Maryland.

had her own room in which to retreat and enjoy her solitude. But by the time for the next meal, everyone would be together again.

And such meals they were! Made for men: gigantic roasts surrounded by squadrons of potatoes, great bowls of gravy, several species of vegetables, salads, hot bread, and coffee, three times a day. The luncheons were dinners and the dinners banquets. Mother had raised her family before calories and vitamins and cod liver oil were heard of, and she never thought of a balanced meal.

The dining table was always set for fourteen or sixteen at least. The children had their own dining room where their nurses looked after them. Usually, there were several guests, as the boys felt perfectly free to ask anyone who happened to be with them. There was always room for more.

We saw little of the boys during the day, except as they passed and repassed the house on the golf links that completely surrounded it. But in they would troop at luncheon, and all conversation would stop, except, "Did you see that drive I made on number nine?" or "I made a three on the fourteenth hole." We girls had a standing joke about them having hoof and mouth disease. In fact, there were many family jokes, the mere mention of which would send everyone into gales of laughter. One joke we had about Bonnie was that all the things passed at the table finally surrounded her plate, for she never bothered to pass anything on, unless requested. We teased her about her southern accent, too, which everyone copied at times, but she always remained calm as the summer sea.

After a leisurely luncheon, some of us would play a rubber or two of bridge on the wide porch, the green velvet golf course brocaded with beautiful trees, spreading in all directions, and the blue haze hanging over the mountains all around us. Then, the afternoons stretched before us. Nothing to worry about except, perhaps, the mail or the latest magazine or novel not arriving on time. Gorgeous, languorous, carefree days.

In the evenings we always had a log fire, for the mountain air was chilly. Sometimes the children popped corn or toasted marshmallows. At other times, we all played games with them or worked puzzles or had charades.

The golfers, even after their strenuous day, were always ready for bridge, so we usually had two tables. Mother was the most enthusiastic and tireless player of all. Once she and three of the boys played all night. She never lost the spirit of youth.

Some evenings, after the children were in bed, we told ghost stories. My room was supposed to be haunted, and many a time I shivered as I turned out the light. One night, after several particularly gruesome tales, I was slowly making my way upstairs, wishing the others would hurry and come too,

Hutchinson brothers (top to bottom): Brooks Swearingen (maternal grandfather of Sylvia Elaine Parker), Bernard Lee, Frank Ehlen, Harold Herbert, Paul Mason, Robert Jay, and James Jeremiah (brother Claude Effington not pictured), at Deer Park, Maryland summer retreat, August, 1925.

when something white fluttered in front of me, while someone grabbed me and groaned, "I want my golden arm!" Everyone was horrified at the scream I gave, which wakened

Chapter 9: Mountaineer Country

the servants on the third floor. Harold had thrown a white Spanish shawl over the stair rail, and Robert had grabbed me! They collapsed on the stairs and laughed until they were weak!

Breakfast time was always funny. First and last bell signaled the beginning and end of breakfast, and Mother held us to the rule. The night before, we always declared with much emphasis that we would not get up for breakfast but would diet; in that climate, though, ravenous appetites are chronic, so that the last bell always brought a great rush of the queerest assortment of dressing gowns. The girls usually arose early enough to indulge their vanity by appearing in golf costumes, but the boys would rush in, attired in pajamas and robes, demanding "just a cup of coffee," but managing to eat everything in sight. Robert, always the comedian, would sometimes appear as a Chinaman, with Mother's mandarin coat and her sewing basket for a hat, jabbering in sing-song Chinese, much to the delight of the children. Once he appeared all bent over, attired in a raccoon coat with a pillow stuffed under it on his back, and announced in snarling accents that he was the Hunchback of Notre Dame!

Katherine kept the house decorated with flowers, and sometimes I went with her. We would stroll through the woods and gather huge purple thistles and yellow black-eyed Susans. She could find more ferns and ground pine and prettier flowers than anyone else. A drive in the country with her meant constantly stopping to gather goldenrod or wild asters. She knew everyone in the village, too: the grocer, the postmaster, and the neighbors. One of the latter she christened "Blacky Daw," and he became one of our standard laugh-producers. He was a very large man, with a bristly black mustache, and seemed exceedingly shy. He would look longingly at our house, but if any one of us appeared, he would rush past in a great hurry, scuttling across the golf course toward the railroad station, for all the world like a frightened crow.

The children, the sons' sons and daughters, are growing up. They seem to have this same love of family. Though only cousins, they are as close to each other as most brothers and sisters. In retrospect, I can only hope that my own three little girls, when they marry, will acquire just such a family. I could wish for nothing better for them.

Granddaughter's Note: How nostalgic all this becomes in light of my mother and father's recent travels. For their forty-fifth wedding anniversary, in November, 1997, Daddy took Mother on the Cunard's Queen Elizabeth II, *setting sail for London, England. They were joined by close family friends, and had the time of their lives. Mother particularly relished life aboard ship—shopping and sunning and dancing 'til midnight every night! They even renewed their wedding vows, with the ship's captain officiating.*

AUTHOR: *Ray Pefley Hutchinson, submitted by her granddaughter, Sylvia Elaine Parker of Morgantown, West Virginia. Mrs. Hutchinson, born in Idaho in 1897, met Brooks Swearingen Hutchinson while on a trip to Morgantown from Mount Vernon Seminary, a finishing school in Washington, DC. They were married at St. Michael's Episcopal Cathedral in Boise, Idaho in September, 1917. Mrs. Hutchinson, an only child, deeply appreciated the love and kinship she felt in the Hutchinson family.*

313-001-ST-WV-002-1998

A Front Porch in Halleck

ary Brown bought twenty acres on the Halleck Road south of Morgantown in 1965. He was eighteen and too young to hold title to property, so he bought it in his dad's name; his friends were spending their money on cars. Gary drove down the sloping driveway to old Mr. Richardson, who sat legless on the front porch, and said, I heard you're selling your place. Mr. Richardson, who'd lost his legs to sugar, said Yes, but if you're thinking of paying anything less than thirty-five hundred dollars for it, you can turn your truck around and drive back out of here. Gary bought the place with no dickering, and that's how he sold it to us.

The Repperts' one-and-a-half-story log house, updated with clapboard according to the fashion, probably some time before 1900. The porch was a sunny place to sit of a morning.

Evan and I saw Gary's ad some time in January, '98, and took a walk around the property a few days later. We wouldn't have looked a second time at the place if a neighbor hadn't stopped us as we were leaving. The springs were good, the buildings sat well off the road, and twenty acres felt about right, but the house was too far gone. Gary had moved to Morgantown in the middle of some major repairs four or five years before and left nature to finish them. He'd torn the front porch off but stopped short of replacing it, and a family of starlings had nested in one of the gaps it left. The white clapboard paint had thinned to gray where it hadn't come off entirely, leaving the wood to rot. The septic tank had fallen in on itself and filled with mud. We talked a while in the driveway with neighbor Bob and, just when we were heading back to town, he said, It's log, you know. That changed it all for us.

Sylvanus Reppert and family on their well-tended Halleck farmstead, early 1900s. The roof had been raised to a full two stories. A tree that no longer stands shaded the front porch in the afternoons.

Sylvanus and Mary A. (Smith) Reppert, on the side porch of their lifelong creation, some time before 1918.

As far as we can tell, Gary Brown never had a real good look at the log house under the weathered clapboard. Henry and Repher Richardson probably never saw it, and Elijah Summers, who sold Richardsons the place in 1949, most likely never saw it either. Mary (Smith) Reppert, whose estate sold the house to Elijah, might have been able to picture her log house when she died around 1920, but even she hadn't seen it for well over twenty years, and maybe closer to forty.

Mary's husband Sylvanus Reppert built the original one-and-a-half-story log house when he got back from the Civil War. He built the house higher on the hill from where it sits now, but it's said that he and Mary got tired of hauling their water uphill, so they eventually gave up their view and took their house, log by log, down near the spring.

Sylvanus and Mary took pride in their home. Like a lot of people before the turn of the century, they neatened up their rough log house with clapboard. They added a distinctive square front porch, and an extra room on the back. When they laid tongue-and-groove poplar on the walls inside, probably some time well before 1900, the logs were covered completely.

As the years went by the Repperts farmed the land, building a barn and other outbuildings, clearing pasture, and constructing fences. They had some children—I don't know how many—and found the need for more space. At some point they raised the roof from one and a half to two stories. They added a large dining room and kitchen with ten-foot ceilings and brick fireplaces to the back of the house, and a cozy porch on the side of that. They saved up for a carved oak staircase to their spacious new upstairs, and a fine mantelpiece for the dining room. Their rough log house and land became an elegant farmstead.

Sylvanus died about 1918 and was laid out in the dining room. Mary was not far behind, and when her estate was settled in 1921, Elijah and Emma Summers acquired the property. They farmed the land, too: They kept a hundred chickens and sold the eggs to buy food, and the sale of lambs paid the taxes. They tended an orchard and built a milk house around the spring, on a cut-stone foundation, to store the dairy from their cows.

Their daughter Gayle grew up and married a Reppert, so when she and two of her sons moved back to the farm for a time in the

CHAPTER 9: MOUNTAINEER COUNTRY

'40s, there were Repperts living there again. Bob Reppert, Gayle (Summers) Reppert's son and Sylvanus Reppert's great-grandson, was in his teens at that time, and is now retired and lives a ways down the Halleck Road. He told me much of this history of the house. He misses the front porch.

The farm changed hands two more times before we got it. The Richardsons spent almost two decades there, and Gary Brown spent three. Gary left because he had to, and he was sorry to let the place go. I think all the people who've lived there loved it.

Rather than repaint, we're ripping the clapboard down entirely to show off Sylvanus's logs. We chased the birds out, and soon we'll replace the septic system. One of these days we'll have Bob Reppert over to sit a while on our square front porch.

The original logs are exposed for the first time in a hundred years, spring, 1998. This house is badly in need of a front porch!

AUTHOR: *Pam Kasey is thirty-six. Her Irish and German ancestors migrated at various periods through Appalachia to Kentucky and to Indiana, where she was born. She and her fiancé, Evan Hansen, plan to spend a good long time in Halleck, West Virginia.*

314-001-ST-WV-002-1998

Nature's Clemency

Spirit that lurks each form within
Beckons to spirit of its kin;
Self-kindled every atom glows,
And hints the future which it owes.
—from Emerson, "Nature"

Grace is a funny thing. I never considered the meaning of the word until I needed some . . .

I've always tried to leave anywhere I've ever been. I have liked one place for certain reasons, another for others, but have never liked a place so fully and so heartily as I do West Virginia. I have never been to a place with so many lessons to learn, free from all the frills. I never realized how much I loved West Virginia until the last time I tried to leave.

My family is originally from the Huntington area and Lincoln County, West Virginia. That is, after generations of Dahls, Kesslers, Joneses, Johnsons, Lucases, etc. migrated from Wales, England, Poland, and, I think, Germany, to West Virginia a few generations back. I've lived in and around Huntington for short periods several times in my life.

I returned to the Huntington area from New York City in March, 1995 to try to work out a five-year relationship. It ended instead, and I was soon on my way back out, headed somewhere with interesting work in nature photography and graphics. Oh, I considered many places—Brooklyn, New York again; San Antonio, Texas; New Mexico to study Flamenco dancing—I even thought about Paris, France. It crossed my mind to recapture the French that I had learned over four years in school. I was finding now that I was barely able to recall how to say "Fermez la fenêtre" ("close the window"). This bothered me. It bothered me to lose something.

Family stuff and the end of my relationship kept me in Huntington for two years, longer than I had intended. I just couldn't decide where to go. I researched different things about all of those places about which I dreamed. I looked in their city phone books for listings of photographers, publishing companies, and restaurants. I wanted to know where I would sample food . . . where I would work

Julia Lucas, October, 1996, on the Gauley River, West Virginia. Photo taken by Tony Alterman, a photographer, musician, philosopher friend of Julia's from Brooklyn, New York.

Deckers Creek, at the Pioneer Rocks area running along Route 7, during the March 22, 1998 Adopt-a-Highway trash pick-up.

when I got to where I was going. I wanted to leave West Virginia. I couldn't make a living here. No one wanted nature photos, and every little piece of me inside was shattering. It felt like the Snow Queen's mirror splintering all over again. That childhood book read through me again and again.

I set out for one last drive around West Virginia in April, 1997, combining business with contemplation. By the end of that trip, I would have some answers, a destination, or at least a place in Fayetteville, some new scenery where I could photograph and think about where to move some more.

I passed through Morgantown on that trip. I had some business to tend to in that town. I had never really been there—I had only stopped at the Westover exit a few times on my way to New York; Berkeley Springs, West Virginia; Pennsylvania; somewhere else. There's an Exxon off that exit.

I got into Morgantown late on a Friday night, stayed at a motel close to the exit, and the next morning took some landscape photos and went downtown to sell books and calendars for someone. I did my business, then walked down High Street. The weather was rain. It was a warm rain, though.

My trip took me in a wide circle through the state. Some time between being in Morgantown and arriving back in Huntington a few days later, I saw nature's grace and the possibility of finding peace in West Virginia. I saw my reflection in a herd of deer's eyes at Blackwater Falls State Park. The spring snowfall and the silence on that Sunday cleansed my spirit and rejuvenated my soul! I knew I had to stay in West Virginia.

I finished my trip after continuing around West Virginia for a couple more days until I looped back around to Huntington. I decided not to get a place in Fayetteville. Instead, upon my arrival back in Huntington, I went to the library to look at the Morgantown phone book. I looked up the photographers, publishing companies, and restaurants. I wanted to see where I would eat and work when I moved to Morgantown.

Grace is defined in many different ways: charm of expression, decency, goodwill, mercy, thanks, elegance with appropriate dignity. I find that most of the definitions of grace are applicable to my experience in West Virginia. Through grace, I've been able to get through many difficult times—those times anticipated that made me originally think I needed to leave West Virginia. I'm glad I didn't leave, though, for I find grace here in each day.

AUTHOR: Julia Lucas. Julia moved to Morgantown, West Virginia on June 11, 1997. She does layout and graphic design for Populore Publishing Company. She also has her own greeting card company using her nature photographs. The Friends of Deckers Creek organization and how to help clean up that stream, a main tributary to the Monongahela, are persistently on her mind. She is working on her first garden, and loves the Cafe of India and Mountain People's Kitchen restaurants! Julia was born in Parkersburg, West Virginia.

315-001-ST-WV-002-1998

Chapter 9: Mountaineer Country

Growing Up Around Here

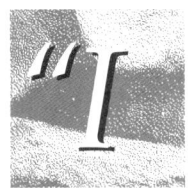"I bet it's a great place for kids to play," an out-of-state friend and city dweller said with a smile as she heard me describe my new backroads home in Monongalia County a few years back. Indeed.

My husband, Ken St. Louis, and I live about six miles west of Morgantown. So often I look around our farm and imagine the great times my four brothers, two sisters, and I could have had growing up around here. Not to say we didn't have fun where we were! Between school and chores, we specialized in making our own fun. Out in California, our suburban home and backyard, the park down the street, and community centers offered terrific playgrounds. Little League, scout activities, crafts classes, skateboarding, street football, and the like filled our '50s and '60s free time.

Our farm is a great playground for these kids enjoying this old out-of-use cattle rack.

What we loved *most*, though, involved creatures (usually dogs and lizards), water (puddles and drains), hideouts (the carport roof), and treasures (often found in the street). On a lucky day, all could be found quite close to home. However, to ensure a successful adventure featuring these favorites, we had to head for the yet-to-be-developed foothills—a fifteen-minute uphill bike ride away—or wait for a family trip to somewhere less built-up.

Our West Virginia farm, with its rolling pastures, wooded groves, and barn and other outbuildings, would have been perfect.

Creatures

Just imagine what we seven could've done here!—with such enticing countryside at our doorstep, twenty-four hours a day. For starters, there are so many interesting animals that would've entertained us. I've met plenty of them since moving here in 1993: I remember not too long ago walking through the nearby hayfields and spotting something dark brown and smallish. Closer up I saw a beautiful bright yellow and brown pattern. I'd never seen such a turtle. Another day I was awed—and startled—to discover a very long black snake skin in our woodshed. I chuckle thinking of what we children might've done with that.

Other animals we might have caught, tracked, and/or watched include newborn calves, woodchucks, furry caterpillars and tent caterpillars, barn kittens, raccoons, wild turkey, and deer. There's no question that we would've found lightning bugs and those green stick-like insects (praying mantises) irresistibly fascinating. And looking up, there might have been Canada geese, bats, maybe an owl, hummingbirds, and those pesky carpenter bees. A trip to the pond might have meant seeing a snapping turtle or two, darting fish, and bullfrogs or pollywogs, depending on the season.

Water

How we seven were drawn to water! This might've had something to do with our proximity (less than an hour) to the Pacific, love of the rare rains, or learning to swim practically before we could walk. Mostly, though, I think it had to do with a simple belief that where there was water, fun was close by.

Here on our farm, the possibilities for water fun are endless: fishing, wading, toy boats, real boats, and standing outside—head back, mouth open—during the worst of a downpour. And, of course, there's digging and diverting. My brothers and sisters and I used to construct some very elaborate water-moving and -damming systems using straws, popsicle sticks, clay, string, and whatever else we could find or talk Mom out of. Plenty of room for that on the farm here, and after a good spring rain, plenty of running and standing water.

Our farm has two long hoses, too, perfect for filling water balloons from opposing sides. What great water balloon fights we might've had, not having to worry about throwing them over a fence and into a neighbor's yard or against a house or passerby. Plus, as children we never really had quite enough space, or just the right ground (soft) for slip-'n-sliding. On the land here we could've created an ideal run. Getting a running start

and then sliding a long, long way on wet slimy mud could have been so much fun.

Other days we might have been drawn to the creek, the pond, or the waterfall down the road to search for water life, to skip stones, or to just marvel at cascading water, a cool breeze, or the allure of still, damp, secret places.

Hideouts

Needless to say, finding a place to hide out in the country is a lot easier than finding a place amidst small fenced-in neighborhood yards. As children playing street games, we sometimes hid while playing games like "hide and seek," "kick the can," and ditch so-and-so. But sometimes we used to hide and hang out just to be away from

The neighbor boys'—grown now—hideout in the woods behind our house.

our parents—no good reason other than wanting to be an elusive, mysterious, fun-seeking band. Other times we did it to get away from each other, to enjoy a little individual or gender privacy out in a clubhouse ("no girls allowed") or playhouse ("no boys allowed"). Sometimes a subgroup just wanted to play superior for a while ("no little kids allowed" or "no big kids allowed").

What we could've built and hung out in, here in our wooded West Virginia mountains! Forts, tree houses, and lookouts, I'm sure. We might have even found some caves or at least an interesting rock overhang. Plus, there'd have been a barn with all its nooks and crannies, hatches, bales of hay, and dark corners. Ideal for lying low, but also for those times we wanted to scare another or pull a prank.

Other outbuildings would have been possibilities, too: the tractor garage, the woodshed, and miscellaneous sheds and shelters. Or we could've used spring and summer growth to hide in—climbing up a tree covered with leaves or getting pleasantly "lost" among the tall blades of grass and ironweed.

Treasures

It was hard to say exactly what a treasure was, but the seven of us sure knew when we found one. Often, but not always, it fit in a pocket. Sometimes treasures were devoured, for example, some candy someone left in the car's glove compartment; sometimes they came out of nowhere.

Here in our West Virginia countryside, both natural and man-made treasures are abundant. Surely, our wild berries and ramps would've qualified. A first-appearing vegetable in the garden might count, 'cause it involved discovery. Same with an early-blooming crocus or daffodil. A bird, wasp, or mouse nest, too. Looks of satisfaction, wonder, and awe would've certainly crossed our faces, chancing upon one of these.

As children, we often brought junk home to show the others. For us, discovering lost items such as coins or pocketknives meant a smug look from the lucky one, and listening to "finders keepers, losers weepers" for way too long. Out here in the expansive countryside, we probably would not have found too many treasures that had fallen out of pockets or purses—not enough foot traffic. On the other hand, here we have room for "things forgotten" and "things misplaced," be it in a barn or basement, under the porch, or in a field. My brothers and sisters and I would've spent hours rummaging around. We might've wandered to the barn and found a box of brass hardware, a cider press, a rusty rabbit hutch, or an old feed sack. (Next thing you'd know, our tree house would have had a fancy door knocker, fresh juice, a small caged critter, and a faded flag!)

Or, we might've gone out to the stream bed after a heavy rain. With sticks in hand, we would've dug away at the earth looking for things of interest that had washed down from the turn-of-the-century household

Chapter 9: Mountaineer Country

The author—wet, dirty, and happy at age three.

dump up the hill. On a good day we might've found a discarded miner's head lamp, a fancy amber bottle, canning jars, or stoneware and ironware shards. Wandering back to the house, a few of us might have been a bit contemplative for a minute or two, wondering who else had walked this land and who else might walk it in years to come . . .

Today this land is home to creatures, water, hideouts, treasures, and me. And although I didn't live here as a child, with my brothers and sisters, I feel fortunate to be here now. I enjoy the present moments as they pass, sometimes perhaps seeing this land as a child might—as a prime spot for simple, homemade fun.

Author: Rae Jean Sielen.

316-001-ST-WV-002-1998

Appendix I

The Project

"What a great idea! I'm so glad you're doing this!"

This is a sentiment we've heard over and over as we've spread the word about this project. Anyone with a story to share about West Virginia was invited to participate in *Our Mountain State Heritage: West Virginia Stories of the People*. Our brochure, distributed across the state, sought true, original stories that celebrate or honor significant West Virginia experiences or places; memories of growing up in the state; native West Virginians, living or not, as well as people who have moved to the state; and individual, community, or state traditions or accomplishments. Many people were delighted at the opportunity to ensure that their story wasn't lost by having it included in this book.

For this project and its other activities, Populore Publishing Company is a cooperative preservation publisher: we and a group of authors, all with a common goal—in this case, "preserving West Virginia heritage"—work together to create a book. It is much like the members of a family or community self-publishing a history, except that the individuals are freed from the hassles of self-publishing.

Populore's role begins with a call for manuscripts. As project organizer, we provide guidelines to potential authors, help with writing when requested, and gather the finished manuscripts. As editors, we ensure clarity and consistency of style throughout a collection, while respecting each author's unique contribution and voice; and, while we do not formally verify or research the stories submitted, we allow our general knowledge and common sense to guide us in seeking clarification or additional details. We invite special members of the community to contribute the foreword and the introductory narrative. We pull together the materials that tie it all together, such as the preface, introduction, and index. Then, as designers, we place the finished stories and their accompanying photographs in a pleasing layout that is inviting to read or to just browse. Finally, as publishers, we oversee printing and binding in attractive volumes, and distribute the books.

The result is more than a simple compilation of stories. Each book is a resource, with authors' and editors' notes clarifying practices or concepts that may be unfamiliar to readers, and a comprehensive index of the names, places, and topics that appear in the stories. Appendices offer tips and resources for family history and personal story preservation. And each book's foreword, introductory narrative, and invited cover photograph make it unique.

Appendix II

APPENDIX II

Ideas and Resources

We hear many reasons for preserving a piece of personal history. "I just had to get the stories about Grandma's childhood down while she's still around." "We always tell about Uncle Jimmy's ornery mule at reunions—that story shouldn't be lost." "I want my grandkids to know what it was like when I was little." Maybe you have other reasons. If you'd like to try your hand at preserving a story, here are some hints and resources to help with your narrative.

Your reasons for preserving stories may help you decide what stories would be appropriate.

• Do your older relatives have valuable experiences to pass down? Sitting with a grandparent or a great-aunt or -uncle and writing down their reminiscences is meaningful and fun. Although you may have heard some of their stories many times, you might be surprised at what you've never heard because you've never asked. Do you know what your grandfather's first job was? Have you ever heard about how your grandmother learned to dance? Not only will this be entertaining for you, but they'll most likely appreciate your sincere interest.

• Are there favorite old stories in your family that have been told and retold, and shouldn't be lost? Already polished, these familiar gems can be some of the easiest to record. Catching lightning bugs in Aunt Violet's back yard . . . the time the family milk cow got into the neighbors' house . . . the night Mary was born. Have someone in your family tell the story for you, or write it down in your own words.

• Would you like to put your own memories down as a gift for the next generation? Choosing stories from one's own life is sometimes the easiest—the right story may be obvious to you—or sometimes takes some thought and encouragement. If you're looking for narrative ideas, read on.

Where should you start? Try sharing your desire with a family member. Often a parent, sibling, child, or other close relative is enthusiastic about the idea of having a story preserved. If you need inspiration, family members can easily think of good potential subjects, or fill in useful details about specific people, places, and events. A family dinner or reunion can be an especially good place to get stories and encouragement. In our experience, relatives are often as excited about a story project as the authors themselves!

Use this book as a resource, too. Flip through and find a few narratives that appeal to you, or stories that make you think, "I could write something like that." Someone else's memories of holidays or of the old farm will remind you of meaningful times and places in your own life. Maybe you'd like to write your own perspective on childhood fun . . . fox hunting . . . homemade ice cream. Or just react to a title that gets you thinking: "The Weekly Cleansing Ritual," "An Embarrassing Moment," or "Mother's Visits."

For more ideas, turn to pages 180 and 181 and work on the family history form. Reaching up into your family tree is sure to remind

Our Mountain State Heritage

you of people and stories you haven't thought of for years. There may be a special family member who deserves a tribute, or you might gain some interesting perspective on your ancestors as a group.

Remember, there's no need to do it all at once—choose an easy writing project for your first one. Even the shortest narratives in this book tell us a great deal about the authors and their lives.

Finally, we think one of the best things you can do is to encourage the children in your family to try one of the projects suggested above. By interviewing an older friend of family member, they strengthen their relationships, increase their understanding and appreciation of others, and improve their communication skills; by putting their own experiences on paper, they become better observers and writers.

Readers who want to know more about West Virginia history or genealogy can visit the state's Cultural Center, in the State Capitol Complex in Charleston. The Archives and History Section is the state's genealogical research center, and contains printed and microfilmed collections of family, local, and state genealogy and history materials.

The Mining Your History Foundation sends its members a quarterly newsletter of informative articles and updates on genealogical and historical topics related to West Virginia. For membership information, write to: Mining Your History Foundation, Archives and History, The Cultural Center, 1900 Kanawha Boulevard East, Charleston, WV 25305-0300; or call (304)558-2779.

For specific local history and genealogy information, visit your local community or college library for a list of West Virginia's historical and genealogical societies. Some of these societies have their own libraries, and can put you in contact with helpful people. Or if you have access to the world wide web, the West Virginia GenWeb Project at http://www.rootsweb.com/~wvgenweb/ has links to each West Virginia county, as well as to sites where you can research specific surnames, the military, and other family history–related topics.

Populore Publishing Company offers its 220-page *Put It In Writing Guide For Populore Narratives* to spur your story-gathering efforts. Also, we collect stories on a continuous basis for our *Populore Narratives: Stories of the People* books (the "Heritage Series"), and at various times may be collecting stories for a special project book such as *Our Mountain State Heritage: West Virginia Stories of the People*. For information on the *Guide*, the Heritage Series, and other projects, or to visit our office, write to us at Populore Publishing Company, 3009 Grand Central Station Drive, Morgantown, WV 26505; or call (304)296-7867, e-mail stories@populore.com, or visit our web site at www.populore.com.

Readers interested in gaining or improving writing skills can contact West Virginia Writers, Inc. Members receive a quarterly newsletter listing upcoming events, workshops, and conferences. Articles contain hints, opportunities, and more for the aspiring and professional writer. Write to: West Virginia Writers, Inc., PO Box 5205, Charleston, WV 25361.

And the Association of Personal Historians is a national organization of individuals and businesses that help people preserve their personal histories, using methods that range from editing and publishing to ghostwriting, videotaping, and multi-media preservation on CD-ROM. For information, see their web site at www.PersonalHistorians.org.

Appendix III

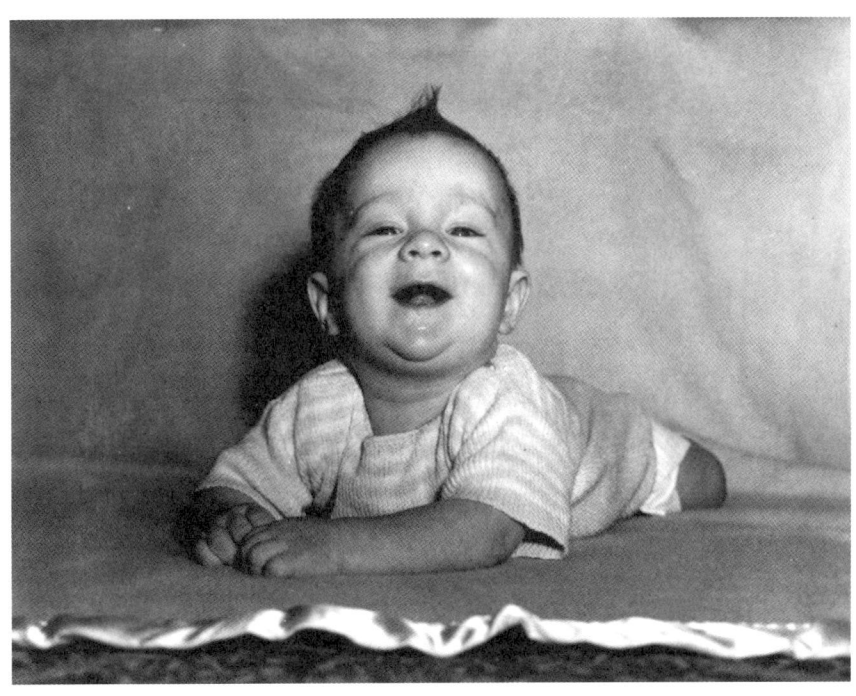

Our Mountain State Heritage

Our Great-Grandchildren: *Our Grandchildren:*   *Our Children:*

*Some of my family's history is preserved in this book.
See pages(s): _____*

APPENDIX III

Who's Who

My Name

- My Father
  - My Grandfather
    - My Great-Grandfather
    - My Great-Grandmother
  - My Grandmother
    - My Great-Grandfather
    - My Great-Grandmother
- My Mother
  - My Grandfather
    - My Great-Grandfather
    - My Great-Grandmother
  - My Grandmother
    - My Great-Grandfather
    - My Great-Grandmother

Tips

Fill in as much information as you can. A little is better than none at all.

Beneath each name list the dates and locations of the person's birth and death.

Use women's maiden names.

Modify this form to accommodate siblings, step-children and step-parents.

Spouse

- Spouse's Father
  - Spouse's Grandfather
    - Spouse's Great-Grandfather
    - Spouse's Great-Grandmother
  - Spouse's Grandmother
    - Spouse's Great-Grandfather
    - Spouse's Great-Grandmother
- Spouse's Mother
  - Spouse's Grandfather
    - Spouse's Great-Grandfather
    - Spouse's Great-Grandmother
  - Spouse's Grandmother
    - Spouse's Great-Grandfather
    - Spouse's Great-Grandmother

Index

Populore's mission is preservation, and our index is designed to make the treasures preserved in these pages accessible.

People can be found under their last names, with married women cross-referenced under maiden names when available, and with namesakes distinguished by the designation (son) or (father) when possible. *Places* that our authors chose to feature appear in the category "Places," while the many towns, schools, churches, and businesses that received mention in the narratives are each indexed under their individual names, and often further identified here by location. *Topics* are gathered under primary categories like foods, holidays, occupations, music, and industry.

Look up people and places you've known, but glance through the topics listed, too. They may lead you to a story you'd overlooked, or give you another perspective on life in West Virginia as seen through the eyes of people who've chosen to preserve a piece of it.

A

Acord
  Andreas Lawrance 107
  Ben Henderson 107
  Betty Jo 107
  John (father) 107
  John "Old Jack" (son) 107
  Mary Eva Ann Allen 107
  Mary Helen 107
  Myrna Catherine 107
  Myrtle Lilly Hager 102, 107–108
  Nancy Allen 107
  Nancy Carol 107
  Nancy Harper 107
  Rachel Combs 107
  Robert 102, 107–108
  Robert Edward 107
  Robert Lee 107
  Stallie Elizabeth 107
  Sylvia Ann. *See* Bragg
  Virginia Lee 107
Acords Branch (WV) 107
Acuff
  Roy. *See* Music: Musicians
Adamston Flat Glass Company (Adamston, WV) 134
Admiration. *See* Emotions

Adventurousness. *See* Characteristics
Afflictions
  Alzheimer's Disease 65
  Asthma 69
  Blindness 58
  Broken bones 119
  Gunshot wound 55
  Measles 58
  Pinkeye 83
  Small pox 31–33
  Speech impediment 75
  Stroke 65, 69, 87
Air Force. *See* Military: US Air Force
Airport. *See* Places
Alkire
  Hattie <u>45</u>
Allen
  Agnes 107
  Alma 35
  Ann 107
  Eleanor 35
  Elizabeth Lafferity 107
  Eloise. *See* Sibold
  Elwyn 99
  Henley 107
  John "Crap" 107
  John R. 107

Allen (cont.)
  Juliet Ann Blankenship 107
  Mary Eva Ann. *See* Acord
  Mary Lewis 107
  Nancy. *See* Acord
  Nancy Daniels 107
  William (father) 107
  William (son) 107
Alpine Theatre (Marlinton, WV) 120
Alsace (France) 68
Alsace-Lorraine (France) 30
Altenheim Home for the Aged (Wheeling, WV) 33
Alzheimer's Disease. *See* Afflictions
Ambition. *See* Characteristics
Amusement. *See* Emotions
Ancestors. *See* Family
Anchor Hocking Glass Company (Harrison County, WV) 138
Anderson
  Leon 66
  Velva Iris Boyles 97
Andy
  Jean 152
Anger. *See* Emotions

Animals and insects
  Bears 92
  Bees 102–103, *148*
  Catfish 126
  Chicks (by mail) 33–34
  Cows <u>102–103</u>
  Coyotes 62
  Farm animals 93
  Foxes 39
  Hummingbirds *151*
  Mules 105
  Prairie dogs 62
  Raccoons <u>40–41</u>
  Skunks 105, 149–150
  Snakes 35
  Wild turkeys <u>118</u>
  Wildlife 149–150, 167–169
Anniversary. *See* Life events
Apartments. *See* Places
Appreciation. *See* Emotions
Architectural styles
  Greek Revival 125–126
  Richardson Romanesque 144
Arden (WV) 143
Arkwright Coal Company (WV) 147
Arlington Public School (Arlington, VA) 133

Page number in bold indicates "Author" • Page number in italics indicates "Photo" • Page number underlined indicates "Featured"

Armentrout
  Betty Lou 83
  Charles 83
  Jacqueline 83
  Willa 83
Army. See Military: US Army
Arriving. See Immigrants; West Virginia: Newcomer
Arthur
  Luella Conner 53
Arthurdale (WV) 157
Ash
  Oral 133
  Stan 81–82
Ashland (KY) 59, 75, 81
Assessor. See Occupations
Atha
  Charlotte Stilwell 137
Atlantic & Pacific Tea Company (A&P) (Marlinton, WV) 120
Aunt. See Family
Austin
  Mary. See Webb
Autograph books. See Customs
Automobile. See Transportation
Automobile repair. See Occupations; Skills
Autumn. See Seasons
Awards. See also Community; Military; School
  For bridge restoration 28
  Harmar Silver Wreath 33
  Outstanding Elementary Teacher of America 108–109
Awe. See Emotions

B

Bagnatura (Italy) 146
Bailey
  Annie Belcher 101
  Chole. See Cook
  Floy Blanch. See Decker
  James 101
  Margaret Stinnett 101
  Richard 101
Bailey Lake and Dam (WV) 100
Bainbridge
  Helen Rosella (Martin) 70–71, 74
  Margie Fay. See Sheets
  Richard 70–71, 72–74, 74
  Robert 70–71
Baking. See Skills
Ball
  Pat 88–89
Balloons 'N Tunes 35
Baltimore and Ohio Railroad (B&O) 87, 136, 143–144
Banker. See Occupations
Baptism. See Life events
Barbour County (WV) 19–24, 119, 142, 142–143
Barger
  Pauline 83

Barger (cont.)
  Philip 83
  Robert 83
  William 83
Barn Elementary School (Camp Creek, WV) 102
Barnhart
  Betty 57–58
Bartlett
  Barbara. See Wagoner
  G. Thomas 137
Baseball. See Sports
Basham
  Juanita Austin 108–109
Basketball. See Sports
Batlas
  John 152
Battles
  Battle of Blair Mountain (WV) 107, 126
  Battle of Chickamauga 144
  Battle of the Bulge 65
Baughman
  Juanita 83
Beamer
  Julian Seigle 106
Bears. See Animals and insects
Beauford
  Willa 152
Beckley (WV) 72, 109, 135
Beckley Junior High School (Beckley, WV) 109
Beer distributor. See Occupations
Bees. See Animals and insects
Belcher
  Annie. See Bailey
Belington (WV) 19–24, 121
Belles. See Extension Homemakers
Bellsville (WV) 42
Bender
  Arla 23
  Brenda Kay 19–24
  Cheryl Lynn. See Ware
  Darryl Keith 19–24
  Herbert Ellis 19–24
  Herbert "Henry" Loren 19–24
  Jesse 22
  Kevin Lyle 19–24
  Lillie 22
  Marlene Edith Streets 19–24
  Paulette Barbara "Barbie." See Miller
  Roger Wayne 19–24
  Sandy 23
  Stuart Allen 19–24
Bennett
  Judith Drumpus 138
  Nellie (Sallie Swecker) 86
Benwood (WV) 144
Berea (WV) 45–46
Bergdoll
  Ella 116–117
  Patsy Harper 117
  Thomas Jefferson 117

Bergdoll (cont.)
  Virginia. See Whitesell
Bermuda 106
Berries. See Foods
Berry
  Kevin 153
Bias
  Clothilde Gaujot 68
  Sarah. See Hager
Bible 138, 150
  Reading. See Customs
Bicycling. See Recreation
Bielecki
  Mary 44
Big Harts Creek (Logan County, WV) 58
Big Wheeling Creek (WV) 35
Billings
  Buddy 97
  Burette 97
  Buster 97
  Colena 97
  Debbie 149
  Delta 97
  Ellen 97
  Flora 97
  Oma 97
  Raymond 97
  Roberta 97
  Velva Iris. See Boyles
Bills
  Rebecca 149
Birch River (WV) 87
Birth. See Life events
Birthday. See Celebrations; Life events
Bistany
  Roberta Coberly 137
Black walnuts. See Foods
Blackberries. See Foods
Blackwater Falls State Park (WV) 166
Bland
  Archie 65–66
  Marian Kay 66
  Ned 66
  Ruby Lynch 66
  Vivian 66
  William 65–66
Blankenship
  Juliet Ann. See Allen
Blawnox (PA) 119
Blessing
  Annia 56
Blindness. See Afflictions
Bluefield (WV) 150
Boker
  Becky Louise 41
Bonaparte
  Napoleon 68
Bonds
  Virginia 109
Bonnell's Repair Shop (Berea, WV) 46
Boone County (WV) 107

Booth
  Ashley 54
  Mildred Dawson 54
Bossart
  Gail Means Pope 135–136
Bowman
  Mary Keller 107
Bowman's Boardinghouse (West Liberty, PA) 32
Boyd
  Betty Beatrice Chedester 29–30, 34–35
  Earl Robert 30, 34, 34–35
  Earl Woodrow 30
  John 152
Boylen
  Janet. See Ward
Boyles
  Velva Iris Billings 97
Brady
  Guy P. 127
Bragg
  Albert 101
  Barbara 100
  Barbara Ann Short 102
  Carol 100
  Cody Shawn 102, 108
  Danford Earl (father) 100–102, 106–108
  Danford Earl (grandson) 102, 108
  Danford Earl (son) 101, 102, 108
  Danice Lilly 101, 102, 108
  Debra Ann. See Cagg
  Dennis 100
  Fredrick 100
  Hubert 100
  James 100
  Jimmy 100
  Judith 100
  Kelli Harbour 102
  Kimberly 100
  Lloyd F. (Hager) 100
  Patsy 100
  Rita Irene Elkins 100
  Sylvia Ann Acord 101, 102, 106–108
  Taylor Ann 102, 108
Bravery. See Characteristics
Braxton County (WV) 87, 93
Bread. See Foods
Bretz (WV) 146–147
Brewster
  Agnes 83
Bridges. See History; Places
Bridgeville (PA) 89
Brooks
  Elaender "Nellie" Cook 101–102
  Margaret "Peggy." See Cook
  Richard 101
  William 101
Brooks (WV) 104
Brother. See Family

INDEX

Broward Center for the Performing Arts (Ft. Lauderdale, FL) 106
Brown
  Esther 151
  Gary 163
  James 101
  James H. "Harley" 101
  John 126
  Mary "Millie" Vance 101
  Nancy C. Toler 101
  Virginia "Jensy." See Elkins
Buchanan (VA) 77
Buckner
  Jennie Mae Jones 63
Bunker Hill School (CO) 61–62
Bunner
  Ed 150
  Ronald 149
  Sandra **149–150**
Burke
  Brenda **59–60**
  Katheryne K. See Taylor
  Michael 60
  Nathan D. 60
Burke's Hallmark (Summersville, WV) 60
Burning Creek (WV) 69
Burroughs
  Betty Facemire 87–88
  Emery 87–88
  Ernest 87
  Margaret. See Stapleton
  Okey 87
  Ruby 87
Bus. See Transportation
Business and Professional Women (BPW). See Clubs and organizations
Business person. See Occupations
Businesses. See Names of individual businesses
Butler School (Pettry / Hilltop, WV) 108
Butter and sugar sandwiches. See Foods
Byrd
  Robert C. 61

C

C&S Restaurant (Richwood, WV) 92
Cabell County (WV) 54, 75–76
Cabin Creek Junction (WV) 76
Cabins. See Places
Caboose Museum (Hurricane, WV) 89
Cagg
  Debra Ann Bragg 102
  Helen Cleone Stewart 102
  Tonya Renee 102
Calhoun County (WV) 42, 58
Camaraderie. See Emotions
Camp Joy (Berea, WV) 46
Camp Pickett (VA) 99

Campbell
  Kathryn **65**, **74–75**
  Polly 108
Campbell Creek (WV) 65, 121
Campbelltown (WV) 121
Camping. See Recreation
Canaan Valley (WV) 137
Cannelton (WV) 72–74
Canning. See Skills
Caperton
  Gaston 153
Carneal
  Adrian Francis 46
  Darrell Dewain 46
  Linda Louise 46
  Mary Genieve Sutton *45–46*
  Paul Edwin 46
Carpenters Fork (WV) 87
Carr China Pottery (Grafton, WV) 136
Carroll
  Chet 35
  Esther 44
  Glenna G. **97**
Carter
  Dorcas 151
Case
  Barbara *83*
  Cecila *83*
Cassville Hollow (WV) 93
Cassville School (WV) 157
Cavins
  Betty Jane 28
Cedar Grove Personal Care Facility (Parkersburg, WV) 44
Celebrations. See also Festivals; Holidays; Life events
  Birthday 35, *136*, 154
  Homecoming Picnic (Berea, WV) 46
  Maypole 116–117
  Parades 57
  Wheeling Suspension Bridge Sesquicentennial 27–28
Cemeteries. See Places
Central Land Company 52
Central Methodist Church (Charleston, WV) 53
Centuries
  19th. See Life
  20th. See Life
Chaffin
  Mary Jane. See Estep
Chaperones. See Customs
Characteristics
  Adventurous 167–169
  Ambitious 146–147
  Brave 75–76, 145–146
  Civic-minded 61, 68, 153
  Clean 53
  Committed 165–166
  Common sense 34–35
  Compassionate 65, 135
  Competitive 33
  Constant 75–76, 154

Characteristics (cont.)
  Courageous 40–41
  Creative 81–82, 116
  Deceptive 81–82
  Dedicated 108–109
  Determined 27–28, 108–109, 149–150
  Dutiful 145–146
  Empowering 108–109
  Enthusiastic 88–89, 155
  Entrepreneurial 146–147
  Formal 69
  Fun 139
  Generous 30, 39–40, 44, 54, 77, 87–88, 108–109, 159–163
  Hard-working 29–30, 42, 55, 68–70, 87–88, 93, 146–147, 156
  Helpful 92–93, 139, 156–157
  Heroic 139–140
  Hospitable 162
  Humble 135–136
  Imaginative 28–29, 60, 134
  Impulsive 81–82
  Independent 54, 146–147
  Infamous 73
  Ingenious 89–91
  Innocent 74
  Introspective 135–136
  Inventive 155
  Kind 30, 65, 77, 139
  Lawless 73
  Lovestruck 81–82
  Loving 44, 159–163
  Loyal 138, 156
  Mischievous 34, 134–135
  Patient 77
  Playful 104–105
  Proper 31–33
  Proud 106–108, 135–136, 163–165
  Prudish 44
  Quarrelsome 55, 134–135
  Religious 45, 69, 91, 138
  Resourceful 28–29, 39–40, 46, 63–64, 82–85, 115–116, 116, 142–143, 167–169
  Respected 61
  Respectful 52
  Satisfied 82–85
  Self-sufficient 46–47, 93
  Self-taught 89–91
  Sensitive 154
  Short-tempered 55
  Sly 64
  Spirited 102–103
  Strict 31–33, 44
  Strong 75–76, 77, 93
  Studious 31–33
  Talented 84, 89–91
  Thankful 142–143
  Thrifty 82–85, 115–116, 116
  Wise 54
Charles Town (WV) 125–126, 139

Charles Town Presbyterian Church (WV) 129
Charleston (WV) 51, 52, 53, 55, 59, 63, 64, 65, 66–67, 72–74, 102, 146
  Capitol building *62–63*, 67
Cheat Lake (WV) 154
Chedester
  Betty Beatrice. See Boyd
  Ola Lindley *34–35*
  William 34
Chernault
  Pam 85
Cherry River (WV) 121
Chert Mountain Orchard (WV) 118
Chesapeake and Ohio Railway (C&O) 72, 75–76
Chestnuts. See Foods
Chewing tobacco. See Customs
Chicken feet. See Foods
Chiefton (WV) 134–135
Childers
  Alton 133
  Mary Jane Porter 103
Childhood 167–169
Children. See Family
Chores. See Customs
Chow Chow. See Foods
Christmas. See Holidays
Church. See also History; Places
  Attending 43, 53, 91, 98, 118, 129, 139, 141
  Hymns. See Music
  Sunday school 29, 118, 120, 129, 151
Cincinnati (OH) 152
Cinderella Cafe (Williamson, WV) 65
Circleville (OH) 60
Civic-mindedness. See Characteristics
Civil engineer. See Occupations
Civil War. See Wars
Civilian Conservation Corps (CCC) 121
Clarksburg (WV) 139
Clay
  Mary. See Stewart
  Mitchell 101
  Phoebee Belcher 101
Clay County (KY) 108
Clay County (WV) 87–88
Clay County High School (WV) 88
Claysville (PA) 29, 34
Cleanliness. See Characteristics
Clere
  Slim. See Music: Musicians
Clevenger
  James *83*
Clothing
  Four-buckled arctics *85*
  From feed sacks 29, 55
  Hand-me-downs 115–116, 116

Page number in bold indicates "Author" • Page number in italics indicates "Photo" • Page number underlined indicates "Featured"

Clothing (cont.)
  Homemade 84, 115
  Sneakers 51
  Snow boots 97
Clubs and organizations. *See also* College; School
  4-H 41, 114, 139
    Philosophy 44–45
  Boy Scouts of America 137
  Business and Professional Women (BPW) 140
    Aims and Purposes 148–149
    History 148–149
  Daughters of the American Revolution 136
  Extension Homemakers. *See* Extension Homemakers
  Farm Women's Club 41
  Friends of Deckers Creek 166
  Friends of the Krenn School 133
  Friends of Wheeling 27–28
  Girls of '54 136–137
  Golden Age Club 88
  Homemakers Club 41
  Lions Club 57
  National Trust for Historic Preservation 27–28
  Senior Citizens 43
  United Methodist Women (St. Albans, WV) 77
  Victorian Wheeling Society, Ltd. 27–28
  West Virginia State Association of Letter Carriers 77
  Women's Christian Temperance Union 31
  YMCA 41
  YWCA 54
Coach. *See* Occupations
Coakley
  Andrew 83, 91
  Gerald 83
  Nellie 83
  Ruby 83
Coal. *See also* Industry
  Stove 120
  Transporting 66
Coal camp 135. *See also* Life: Coal camp
Coal mine owner. *See* Occupations
Coal mining. *See* Occupations
Coal Valley (WV) 72–74
Coalton
  Leslie 83
Cobbler. *See* Foods
Cochrans, The. *See* Music: Groups
Cogar
  Amy 83
  Eulajean 83
  Herman 83
  Philip 83
Coiner
  Brenda. *See* Burke

Coiner (cont.)
  Faye Coyner. *See* Estes
College
  Clubs
    Bryant Literary Society 31–33
    Irving Literary Society 31–33
Columbus (OH) 106
Combat. *See* Military
Combs
  Rachel. *See* Acord
Commitment. *See* Characteristics
Common sense. *See* Characteristics
Community. *See also* Service
  Awards 84
  Neighbors 30, 40–41, 45–46
  Reunions 136–137
  Sense of 45–46, 59–60, 82–85, 151
  Support 66
  Working together 27–28, 45–46, 52, 84, 93, 114–115, 133, 143–144, 156–157
Compassion. *See* Characteristics
Competitiveness. *See* Characteristics
Compton
  Amy. *See* Shaffer
  Joseph 154
  William "Billy" 154
Concord College (Athens, WV) 108–109
Confusion. *See* Emotions
Conner
  Bernard 83
  Dan 83
  Hubert 53
  Ida Page 53
  James 83
  Luella. *See* Arthur
  Patty 83
Constancy. *See* Characteristics
Contentment. *See* Emotions
Cook
  Chole Bailey 101
  Elaender "Nellie." *See* Brooks
  John (father) 101–102
  John (son) 101
  Kemper 107
  Margaret "Peggy" Brooks 101–102
  Serrilda. *See* Elkins
  Thomas 101–102
  Thomas Green "Doby" 101–102
  William "Doby" 101–102
Coolidge
  Calvin 118
Cooper
  Clarinda. *See* Price
  Elizabeth Smith 107
  Mary Arabess "Arispa" Price 107

Cooper (cont.)
  William 107
Coopers Rock State Forest (Preston County, WV) 151
Cornflakes. *See* Foods
Cornstalk fiddle. *See* Music
Cottage cheese. *See* Foods
Cottageville (WV) 39
Coughlin
  Flora Jane 103–104
  Hazel Mae. *See* Franklin
  James Neal 104
  John Alvin 103–104
  Mary Emma. *See* Hutsenpillar
  Michael L. (Mike) 103–104
  Michael Lake 104
  Opal Lorena. *See* Robertson
  Sara Vena. *See* Walthall
  William Clark 104
Country. *See* Life: Rural
Courage. *See* Characteristics
Court house. *See* History; Places
Cows. *See* Animals and insects
Coyner
  Faye. *See* Estes
Cranberry Glades (WV) 81–82, 92–93
Cranford
  Christine Jenkins Jennings 150
  Ollie 150
Crawford
  Audrey George 33
Creativity. *See* Characteristics
Crocheting. *See* Skills
Crolley
  Aleva Lynn 127
  Dennis 127
  Mary Jo Crouse 127
Cross Lanes (WV) 102
Crouse
  Daisy Marie. *See* Fox
  Darrell Walter 127
  Dorothy Michael **126–127**
  Mary Jo. *See* Crolley
  Robert William 127
Crowder
  Ronald 65
  Ruth Long 65
  William 65
Cumberland (MD) 143
Cumberledge
  Imogene 28
Cunningham
  Alice 62
  Annie. *See* Shimer
  Charles 62
  Clyde 86
  Lillian Miller **61–62**
  Marshall 62
  Sally 62
Cunningham School (Dot / Igeria, WV) 108
Currey
  Mary Jane. *See* Ford

Customs. *See also* Holidays
  Autograph books 157–159
  Bible reading 32, 113, 117
  Chaperones 23
  Chewing tobacco 75, 121
  Chores 20
  Decorating gravestones 46
  Flag raising 113, 117
  Flag salute 58
  Pledge of Allegiance 113
  School prayer 58, 113
  Separation of young men and women 31–33
  Shivaree 128
  Socials 85, 113
Cuzzart (WV) 159

D

Dadisman
  Mary Susan **148–149**
Daly
  Flora Mae 102
Daniels
  Nancy. *See* Allen
Daughter. *See* Family
Davidson
  Blevins 108
  Daniel 108
  Elizabeth Smith 108
  Ellen Roumania Potter 108
  John 108
  John Madison 108
  Margaret 108
  Samuel 108
  Silas 108
  Sylvia Belle. *See* Hager
  William 108
Davis
  Bertha. *See* Sutton
  Elizabeth **40–41**
  Gary 86
  Guy 86
  Jerry **40–41**
  Mildred Esther. *See* Meade
Davis Run (WV) 29
Davisville (WV) 88
Dawson
  James Jared 54
  Marian. *See* Ireland
  Mary Helen Lannen 54
  Robert Harold 54
Dawson (WV) 103–104
Day and Night Restaurant (Williamson, WV) 65
Death. *See* Life events
Decades. *See* Life
De Carlo
  David 146
  Ida 146
Deceptiveness. *See* Characteristics
Decker
  Billy D. **89–91**
  Clara Keefer 89
  Floy Blanch Bailey 90
  Frank 89–91

INDEX

Decker (cont.)
  Frank Levi 89
  Harry George 89–91
  Harry Joe 90
  Robert L. 90
Decker Brothers Garage (Sand Fork, WV) 89–91
Dedication. *See* Characteristics
Deer Park (MD) 161–163
Delegate. *See* Occupations
Delmore Brothers, The. *See* Music: Groups
Dent
  William H. 98
Dent (WV) 142
Depot. *See* Places
Depression. *See* Emotions
Depression, The. *See* Life
De Prospero
  Angiolina 146–147
  Anna 147
  Antonio 146–147
  Domenico 146
  Jessie E. *See* Volk
  Natalie "Nellie" 147
  Venanzio 147
De Prospero Bros. (Bretz, WV) 147
Determination. *See* Characteristics
Detour (MD) 127
Detroit (MI) 81
Dialect. *See* West Virginia
Dickens
  Jimmy. *See* Music: Musicians
  Margie Fay. *See* Sheets
Dickson
  Charlotte Mason 98
Diller
  Dwight 56
Dillon
  Aileen 83
Disappointment. *See* Emotions
Disasters
  Fires 156–157
  Flood 61, 121
    Hughes River (WV) 46
    Scotts Run (WV) 139–140
Discrimination 63–64, 120
Disease. *See* Afflictions
Diss (England) 145
Doddridge County (WV) 28, 133
Dogs. *See* Pets
Dot (WV) 108
Douglas
  Ora 86
  Wilson. *See* Music: Musicians
Draft. *See* Military
Dried fruit. *See* Foods
Droop Mountain (WV) 121
Drumpus
  Andrew 139
  Carole Lee. *See* Flowers
  Edna 139
  Judith. *See* Bennett
  Lois Jean. *See* Neff

Drumpus (cont.)
  Myra Lou. *See* Sienkiewicz
Dudley
  Margaret "Maggie" Lewis **55**
Dugan
  Howard 143
  Nala Shaw 143
Dunbar (WV) 52, 55, 65, 75
Duncan
  Troy 86
Dunfee
  M.L. 52
Dunn
  Christina Rose 104
  Christy Ann 104
  James Mortin 104
  Kelly Sue Johnson 104
  Morton 104
  Vena Rose Walthall 104
DuPont (Belle, WV) 72
Durbin (WV) 120
Duty. *See* Characteristics
Duvall
  Ada Catherine "Betty" McDonald 35
  Alan Norwood 35
  Diana "Dee" Lynn **35**
  Harry Norwood 35
  Scot 35
Dye
  Rooland 43
Dyersburg (TN) 145

E

Eastern Gas and Fuel (WV) 100
Economic conditions
  Boom town
    Mannington, WV 156
    Montgomery, WV 72–74
    Osage, WV 151, 153
  Business failure 136–137
  Decline 72–74
    Osage, WV 153
  Hard times 136–137
  Prosperity 72–74, 159–163
Eddy
  Gladys L. Snyder Shackelford **136**
Efaw
  Bill **156**
Eisenhower
  Dwight D. 137
El Segundo (CA) 34
Elden
  Ted **66–67**
Eleanor (WV) 63
Elizabeth (WV) 43
Elkem Metals (Alloy, WV) 72
Elkins
  Corby Stewart 100–102
  Denny Wirt 100–102
  George 101
  Rita Irene. *See* Bragg
  Serrilda Cook 101–102
  Virginia "Jensy" Brown 101
Elkins (WV) 116

Elkins High School (WV) 119
Ellamore (WV) 22
Ellet
  Charles 27–28
Ellison Ridge (WV) 108
Elm Grove (WV) 35
Embroidering. *See* Skills
Emotions
  Admiration 89–91
  Amusement 64
  Anger 55
  Appreciation 44–45, 66–67, 77, 134–135, 139, 155
  Awe 125–126
  Camaraderie 39, 88–89
  Confusion 74
  Contentment 35, 59
  Depression 149
  Disappointment 85–86
  Excitement 39, 66–67, 88–89, 109
  Fear 55, 139–140, 145–146, 156–157
  Friendship 59–60, 60, 63–64, 139, 156, 157–159
  Fun 28–29, 34–35, 63–64, 66–67, 88–89, 92–93, 167–169
  Gratitude 29–30, 30, 47, 89–91
  Grief 156
  Happiness 28–29, 34–35, 59–60
  Indecision 165–166
  Joy 97, 154
  Loss 29–30, 34–35, 59–60, 65, 72–74, 136–137, 149
  Love 29–30, 30, 34–35, 44–45, 59–60, 65, 74–75, 81–82, 98–100, 138, 139, 154
  Nostalgia 59–60, 61–62, 113–114, 116–117, 141, 155
  Pain 30, 87–88
  Pride 27–28, 45–46, 56–57, 89–91, 98–100, 113–114
  Reflection 92–93
  Sadness 149
  Satisfaction 31, 66–67, 138
  Security 138
  Tenderness 29–30
  Thrill 56–57, 88–89
  Wistfulness 167–169
  Wonder 149–150
Empowerment. *See* Characteristics
Eneix
  John Pearl 39
  Marietta Twyman 39
  Stella G. *See* Moore
Ensor
  Ada 86
  Ruth **85–86**
Enthusiasm. *See* Characteristics
Entrepreneurship. *See* Characteristics
Era. *See* Life
Escue
  Debbie 60

Estep
  A.J. 70
  John 68–70
  Mary Jane Chaffin 68–70
  P. Lester 70
  Wanda. *See* Meade
  William D. 70
Estes
  Faye Coyner Coiner 59
Ethnicity
  African-American 63–64, 150–153
  Cherokee Indian 105
  French 30, 68
  Irish 55
  Italian 146–147
Eureka Pipe Line Company (Sand Fork, WV) 89–90
Evans Ridge (WV) 39
Evans-Thomas
  Charleen *136–137*
Excitement. *See* Emotions
Extension Homemakers 56–57, 87
  Belles 29–30, 36, 41–42, 42–43, 45–46, 54, 56–57, 61–62, 85–86, 87, 87–88, 98, 98–100, 103–104, 108–109, 113–114, 114–115, 115–116, 116–117, 126–127, 127–129, 134, *142*
  Cabell County (WV) 54
  Clay County (WV) 87–88
  Doddridge County (WV) 133
  Fayette County (WV) *103–104*
  Grant County (WV) *113–114*, 114–115
  Greenbrier County (WV) 98
  Hardy County (WV) *116–117*
  Harrison County (WV) 134
  Jefferson County (WV) *127–129*
  Kanawha County (WV) 61–62
  Lewis County (WV) 87
  Marshall County (WV) 36
  Mason County (WV) 56–57
  Mineral County (WV) 118
  Monongalia County (WV) *142*
  Monroe County (WV) 98–100
  Morgan County (WV) *126–127*
  Ohio County (WV) 29–30
  Pendleton County (WV) *115–116*
  Raleigh County (WV) 109
  Ritchie County (WV) *45–46*
  Summers County (WV) *108–109*
  Upshur County (WV) 85–86
  Wirt County (WV) 42–43
  Wood County (WV) *41–42*, 44

F

Facemire
  Betty. *See* Burroughs

Page number in bold indicates "Author" • Page number in italics indicates "Photo" • Page number underlined indicates "Featured"

Fairfax (VA) 39
Fairmont State College (WV) 116
Family 19–24, 53, 59–60, 82–85, 103–104, 146–147, 155, 167–169. *See also* History; Stories
  Ancestors 68–70, 100, 100–102, 104–105, 106–108
  Aunt 44
  Brother 19–24, 65–66, 74, 90, 159
  Children 29–30, 34–35
  Daughter 154
  Father 39, 65, 70–71, 89–91, 118–121, 134–135, 141, 142–143, 154
  Father-in-law 77
  Grandfather 35, 75–76, 104–105
  Grandmother 35, 36, 74–75, 139
  Grandparents 22, 51, 68–70
  Great-grandfather 68
  Great-grandparents 159–163
  Husband 98–100
  In-laws 77, 159–163
  Mother 34–35, 44, 53, 59, 65, 70–71, 108–109, 118–121, 134–135, 136, 141
  Mother-in-law 41–42, 77
  Parents 19–24, 54, 102–103
  Roles 20
  Siblings 19–24, 28–29, 55, 102–103, 134–135, 167–169
  Sister 19–24, 74, 118–121
  Wife 98–100
Famous Sportswear Sales Company (Columbus, OH) 106
Farmers Home Administration 116
Farming. *See* Life; Occupations
Farms. *See* Places
Father. *See* Family
Father-in-law. *See* Family
Fayette Boiling Company (Fayette County, WV) 73
Fayette County (WV) 72–74, 103–104
Fear. *See* Emotions
Feelings. *See* Emotions
Fellowsville High School (WV) 144
Fenton Glass 65
Ferguson
  Tony 90
Ferrell
  Billie Fluharty 28–29
  Charles 29
  Judy. *See* Globokar
  Stanley 29
  Susan 81–82
Festivals
  Always a River Festival (Point Pleasant, WV) 56

Golden Delicious Apple Festival (Clay County, WV) 88
Great Annual Regatta Festival (Charleston, WV) 66–67
Pioneer Days (Pocahontas County, WV) 121
Sternwheel Regatta (Charleston, WV) 66–67
Valley Forge National Jamboree 137
West Virginia State Folk Festival (Glenville, WV) 43, 56–57, 87, 88
Feuds
  Hatfield and McCoy 61
Fiddle. *See* Music; Skills
Fires. *See* Disasters
First Baptist Church (Beckley, WV) 109
First Baptist Church (St. Albans, WV) 62
First Presbyterian Church (Williamson, WV) 68
Firsts. *See* Life events
Fishing. *See* Recreation
Fitzsimmons
  Juanita 30
Flag. *See* Customs
Flea market. *See* Places
Flemington High School (Taylor County, WV) 150
Floods. *See* Disasters
Floradell and Nellie. *See* Music: Groups
Florida Philharmonic Society (Ft. Lauderdale, FL) 106
Flowers
  Carole Lee Drumpus 139
  Mary Elizabeth Keller Jenkins 152
Floyd B. Cox Elementary School (Osage, WV) 151
Fluharty
  Billie. *See* Ferrell
  Creel 29
  Imogene. *See* Cumberledge
  J.S. "Bill" 28
  Lula Nichols 28–29
  Warren 28
Fluty
  Beverly B. 27–28
Foley
  Mary Louvenia. *See* Mills
Foods 33–34
  Berry preserves 71
  Black walnuts 84
  Blackberries 70–71
  Bread 77
  Butter and sugar sandwiches
  Chestnuts 85
  Chicken feet 33–34
  Chow Chow 70–71
  Cobbler 70–71
  Cornflakes 97
  Cottage cheese 93

Foods (cont.)
  Dried fruit 84
  Fried chicken 33–34
  Fudge 141
  Green tomato ketchup 33–34
  Huckleberries 85
  Ice cream 33–34, 69, 114–115, 126
  Lard 93
  Lemon crackers 36
  Milk and honey 97
  Mountain teaberries 142
  Pancakes 154, 159
  Persimmons 85, 142, 154
  Pickle beans 33–34
  Plums 34
  Popcorn 84, 141
  Preservation 93
  Pumpkin 39–40
  Raisin pie 43
  Raspberries 70–71
  Recipes
    Chow Chow 71
    Lemon crackers 36
    Pickle beans 33–34
    Raisin pie 43
    "Roas'eneers" 33–34
  Rolls 34
  Sausage 93
  Schmiercase 33–34
  Sowshead 93
  Wild greens 33–34
Foot. *See* Transportation
Football coach. *See* Occupations
Ford
  Mary Jane Currey 137
Formality. *See* Characteristics
Forren
  Effie 104
Fort Beeler (Marshall County, WV) 30
Fort Lauderdale (FL) 106
Fort McClellan (AL) 66
Fortney
  Lorain 31–33
Foulk
  Virginia 148
Four-H (4-H). *See* Clubs and organizations
Fox
  Daisy Marie Crouse 127
  Della 104
  Emmett 104
  Faye. *See* Madison
  Houston 104
  Imogene Waybright 105
  Jerry David 104–105
  John 104
  Oliver Quenton 104–105
  Steven 104–105
  William 104
Foxes. *See* Animals and insects
Francis
  Della Myrtle Mae. *See* Stewart
Franklin
  Hazel Mae Coughlin 104

Franklin (WV) 115–116
Fraternity Sportswear Sales Company (Columbus, OH) 106
Freed (WV) 42–43
French Creek (WV) 85
Fried chicken. *See* Foods
Friendship. *See* Emotions
Front porch. *See* Places
Fry (WV) 75
Fudge. *See* Foods
Fun. *See* Characteristics; Emotions

G

G.C. Murphy Store (Montgomery, WV) 73
Gainer
  Patric 87
Gallogly
  Ada 83
Gambrills (MD) 52
Games
  Board games 20
  Bowling machine 35
  Bridge 162
  Card games 20, 129
  Charades 162
  Checkers 20
  Cross question and silly answers 103
  Dead dog 51
  Dominos 20
  Drop the handkerchief 113
  Fox and geese 103, 113
  Hide and seek 20
  Make-believe 28
  Penny-ante poker 35
  Prisoner's base 113
  Ring around the rosy 113
  Rook 129
  Tag 113
Garden. *See* Places
Gardening. *See* Skills
Garland
  Todd 51
Garner Valley School (Dent, WV) 142
Garrett
  Helen Hall 87
Gas station manager. *See* Occupations
Gaujot
  Antoine 68
  Clothilde. *See* Bias
  Ellen "Nellie" McGuigan 68
  Ernest Rene Claude 68
  Julien E. 68
  Marguerite "Daisy" 68
Generations. *See* Family; Life
Generosity. *See* Characteristics
George
  Audrey. *See* Crawford
  Mary. *See* Simon
  Pete (Cecil Arnold) 33
  Ruth Gaynell Morgan 33–34

INDEX

George Washington University 52
George's Run (WV) 28–29
Getz
    Nettie Catherine. *See* Sites
Ghost. *See* Stories
Gillespie
    Betty Lou *83*
    Eileen *83*
    Harold *83*
    Vincent *83*
Gilmer County (WV) 56, 89–91
Ginseng, hunting. *See* Skills
Given
    Barbara *83*
    Betty *83*
    Dewey *83*
    Dorothy *83*
    Eunice *83*
    Goldie *83*
    Hanse *83*, 84
    Hercy *83*
    Herndon *83*
    Marjorie *83*
    Phyllis *83*
    Sammy *83*
    Susie *83*
Glass factory worker. *See* Occupations
Glensfork (WV) 107
Glenville (WV) 43, 56–57
Glenville State College (WV) 56–57, 60, 87
Globokar
    Judy Ferrell **28–29**
Goff
    Joan. *See* Rush
Good old days. *See* Stories: Nostalgia
Good Samaritan Hospital (Cincinnati, OH) 68
Goodykoontz
    Irene Hooper 68
    Lucinda K. 68
    Wells 61, <u>68</u>
    William 68
Gordon
    Estelle 87
Gould
    Lundie Jessie *86*
Grace
    John Joseph "Jack" 106
    Patty Kay Porter 103, ***105–106***
Graduation. *See* Life events
Grafton (WV) <u>136–137</u>, 144
Grafton High School (Grafton, WV) <u>136–137</u>
Grandfather. *See* Family
Grandmother. *See* Family
Grandparents. *See* Family
Grandview School (North Charleston, WV) 52
Grant County (WV) 113–114, 114–115, 118
Granville (WV) 147

Gratitude. *See* Emotions
Gray
    Elmer 33
    Roberta Kimmins <u>*31–33*</u>
Great Falls (MT) 100, 102
Great Kanawha River (WV) 72
Great-grandparents. *See* Family
Green Shoal (Lincoln County, WV) 58
Green tomato ketchup. *See* Foods
Greenbo Lake (KY) 81
Greenbrier County (VA) 107
Greenbrier County (WV) 58, 98, 103–104
Greenbrier River (WV) 120
Greencastle (WV) 39–40
Greene County (PA) 156
Greenup (KY) 81
Greenup County (KY) 81
Grief. *See* Emotions
Griffith
    Edith **42**, *43*
Grocer. *See* Occupations
Grocery store. *See* Places
Gross
    Harold *83*
    Howard *83*
    Irma Lou *83*
    Leonard *83*
    Marion *83*
    Mary Helen *83*
    Otto *83*
    Ted *83*
Gum
    George <u>88–89</u>
Guthrie
    Ada M. *142*
Guyandotte Valley (WV) 58

H

Haddad Riverfront Park (Charleston, WV) 66
Hagans (WV) 139
Hager
    Claibourne 107
    Enock Adam(son) 101
    Everet E. 101
    Johnny 58
    Lavina Adkins 101
    Lewis 107
    Martha 107
    Michael 107
    Myrtle Lilly. *See* Acord
    Phillip 107
    Rebecca Lovejoy 107
    Sarah Bias 107
    Sylvia Belle Davidson 107–108
    Watson Riley 107
Hale
    Elbert 42
    Myrtle 42
Haley
    Emma Mullins 58

Haley (cont.)
    James Edward "Blind Ed" <u>58–59</u>
    Milton 58
Halleck (WV) 163–165
Halloween. *See* Holidays
Hambrick
    Loretta *83*
Hampshire County (WV) 118
Hamrick
    Alma *83*
    Clinton *83*
    Elden *83*
    Gordon *83*
    Norma *83*
    Phyllis *83*
    Shelton *83*
    Verdun *83*
Handley (WV) 72
Handschumaker
    Elden *83*
    George *83*
    Robert *83*
Hanna
    Isabelle "Izzy" F. *See* Warren
Hansen
    Evan 163–165
Happiness. *See* Emotions
Harbour
    Kelli. *See* Bragg
Hard-working. *See* Characteristics
Hardin
    Sandy. *See* Bender
Harding (WV) 146–147
Hardway
    Dorr *83*
    Mable *83*
    Robert *83*
    Ruth *83*
Hardy County (WV) 116–117, 118
Harper
    Nancy. *See* Acord
    Patsy. *See* Bergdoll
Harpers Ferry (WV) 127, 137, 143
Harrison County (VA) 156
Harrison County (WV) 134, 134–135, 138
Hartford
    John C. 59
Hartman
    Alice Branson **115–116**
    Heidi Jon 116
    William "Bill" 116
    Woodrow Wilson 115–116
Hartman's Furniture (Franklin, WV) 116
Hastings (WV) 33–34
Hatcher (WV) 100–102
Hawvermale
    Alma Estella Michael 126
Hayes
    Sarah 108
Hazel Atlas Glass (Grafton, WV) 136

Heavner
    Clarence *86*
    Hallie *86*
    Laura *86*
    Lee *86*
    Tarsie *86*
Hefner
    Goff *86*
    Jud *86*
    Nellie *86*
Heim
    Anita 77
    Chelsea 77
    Colene <u>77</u>, **93**
    Diane 77
    Earl 77
    Jim <u>77</u>
    Joshua 77
Helpful. *See* Characteristics
Henderson
    Carl *83*
    Clarence *83*
    John *83*
    John L. 52
Hendrickson
    Mildred. *See* Steele
Henry
    Lillian 120
Hensley
    Belle 108
Heritage. *See* West Virginia
Hermanson
    Linda Lou Nedrow <u>159</u>
Heroic. *See* Characteristics
Hiawatha (WV) 97
Hickory Hill (Morgantown, WV) 155
Hicks
    Lawrence "Laury" A. 58
Highways. *See* Places
Hill
    James "Jim" Bernard 45, <u>*81–82*</u>
    Karolyn "Kay" Ann Young **44–45**, <u>*81–82*</u>
Hilltop (WV) 108
Hinkle
    Walter *83*
Hinton (WV) 92
Hissom
    Arden *83*
    B.R. *83*
    Dolly *83*
Historical and genealogical societies
    Clay County (KY) Historical and Genealogical Society 106
    Doddridge County Historical Society 133
    Grayson County (VA) Genealogical and Historical Society 101, 107
    Lincoln County (WV) Genealogical Society 101, 106

Page number in bold indicates "Author" • Page number in italics indicates "Photo" • Page number underlined indicates "Featured"

Historical and genealogical
    societies (cont.)
  Tunnelton (WV) Historical
    Society 143–144
  West Augusta (WV)
    Historical Society 156
  Wyoming County (WV)
    Genealogical Society 101,
    106
History. *See also* Military;
    School; Schoolhouse
  Bridge 27–28
  Church 98
  College 31–33
  Court house 126
  Family 19–24, 68, 68–70, 100–
    102, 104–105, 106–108,
    146–147
  House 52–53, 163–165
  Town 60–61, 72–74, 136–137,
    150–153
History heroes 27–28, 31–33, 60,
    65–66, 104–105, 143–144
Hobbies
  Collecting antiques 65
  Diary-keeping 54
  History of the presidency 68
  Reading 64, 121
  Stamp collecting 56
  Traveling 65
Hoboken (PA) 119
Hockensmith
  Ethel Pauline (Polly)
    Stonesifer 127–129
  Fannie Christine Melhorn
    Higgs 127, 128
  Margaret Ann 127, 129
  Mary Frances 127, 129
  Robert A. 127–129
  Samuel J. 128
Hofeldt
  Matthew 31
Holcolm
  Johnny 83
  Morg 83, 84
  Paul 83
Holcomb
  Mildred 83
Holidays
  Christmas 87–88, 97, 120,
    134, 141, 142–143, 151
    Carols. *See* Music
    Decorations 142–143
    Santa 121, 141, 143
    Tree 142–143
  Halloween
    Costumes 139
  May Day 116–117
  Memorial Day 46
Holmes
  Theo. *See* Stewart
Home. *See also* Places; West
    Virginia
  Feeling of 138
  Leaving 59–60, 61–62, 72–74,
    136–137, 146–147
  Returning 61–62

Home remedies
  Calomel 83
  Indian pipe 83
  Seiny tea 53
Homemaker. *See* Occupations
Honeymoon. *See* Life events
Hooper
  Irene. *See* Goodykoontz
Hoover
  Herbert 118
  Ollie Jackson 98
Horse and buggy. *See*
    Transportation
Horse-drawn wagon. *See*
    Transportation
Horse-team driver. *See*
    Occupations
Horseback. *See* Transportation
Horter
  Joe 30
Hospitality. *See* Characteristics
Housekeeping. *See* Skills
Houses. *See* History; Places
Howard
  Susanna. *See* Vance
Howdershelt
  Dana 140
  Evelyn 139–140, 149
Hoxter
  Brian 139
  Major 139
  Miranda 139
Hoy Chapel (Freed, WV) 43
Hughes River (WV) 39–40, 45
Humble. *See* Characteristics
Humor. *See* Stories
Hunting. *See* Recreation
Huntington
  Collis P. 52–53
Huntington (WV) 45, 52, 54, 59,
    60, 76, 81–82, 165–166
Huntington Hospital (WV) 66
Huntington Museum of Art
    (WV) 54
Hurricane (WV) 52–53, 59–60,
    76, 89
Hurricane High School (WV) 59
Husband. *See* Family
Husk
  Betty Ann Moore 88
  George 88–89
Hutchinson
  Bernard Lee 159–163
  Bonnie Bonsell Wood 159–
    163
  Brooks Swearingen 159–163
  Claude Effington 159–163
  Clyde Effington 159–163
  Frank Ehlen 159–163
  Harold Herbert 159–163
  James Jeremiah 159–163
  Lyda Watkins 159–163
  Margaret Owens 159–163
  Paul Mason 159–163
  Ray Pefley 159–163
  Robert Jay 159–163

Hutsenpillar
  Mary Emma Coughlin 104
Hymns. *See* Music
Hyre
  Amie 86
  Edwin 86

I

Ice cream. *See* Foods
Ice house. *See* Places
Igeria (WV) 108
Illnesses. *See* Afflictions
Imagination. *See* Characteristics
Immigrants 30, 146–147
Impulsive. *See* Characteristics
In-laws. *See* Family
Indecision. *See* Emotions
Independence. *See*
    Characteristics
Indianapolis (IN) 102
Industry
  Coal 60–61, 72–74, 150, 153
    Coal baron 159–163
    Coal tipple 88–89
    Decline 72–74, 150, 153
    Unionizing 126
  Natural gas 156
  Oil 156
  Railroad. *See also* Baltimore
    and Ohio Railroad
    (B&O); Norfolk and
    Western Railway;
    Norfolk Southern
    Railway
    Baltimore & Ohio Railroad
      (B&O) 143–144
    Chesapeake & Ohio
      Railway (C&O) 72–74,
      75–76
    Collis P. Huntington 52–
      53
    History 52
    Steam engine 88–89
Infamy. *See* Characteristics
Infantry. *See* Military
Ingenuity. *See* Characteristics
Innocence. *See* Characteristics
Insects. *See* Animals and insects
Institute (WV) 62–63, 63–64
Insurance agent. *See*
    Occupations
Internal Revenue Service. *See*
    Occupations
Introspection. *See*
    Characteristics
Inventiveness. *See*
    Characteristics
Inventory clerk. *See*
    Occupations
Ireland
  Marian Dawson 54
Island Creek Coal Company
    (WV) 100

J

Jackson
  Joy 51
Jackson County (WV) 39
Jacksonville (FL) 88
James
  Edward L. 63
  Helen R. 56
  Stella G. 63
  Sue 57–58
Jarvis
  Ada 83
  Carlene Amelia McCray 56
  Daisy 83
  Fred 83
  Joseph 53
  Lucy 83
  Luther 53
  Phyllis 53
  Rachel 53
  Regan 53
  Sarah 53
Javersak
  David 31–33
Jefferson County (WV) 125–126
Jenkins
  Christine. *See* Cranford
  Mary Elizabeth Keller. *See*
    Flowers
  Rhoda 152
Jennings
  Charlene. *See* Marshall
  Charles 150
  Christine Jenkins. *See*
    Cranford
  Iris 143–144
Jere (WV) 140
Jobs. *See* Occupations
Job's Temple (Glenville, WV) 57
Johnson
  Anita June 83
  Charlie 151
  Chester 83
  Edna 83
  Emma 83
  Frieda 83
  Kelly Sue. *See* Dunn
  Ona Lee 83
  Von 83
  Wilma 83
Johnson's Restaurant
    (Marlinton, WV) 120
Johnstown (PA) 54
Jones
  Charley 66–67
  Charlie 86
  Edgar Matthew (E.M.) 75–76
  Edith 86
  Fred 86
  George Hall 75–76
  Gertrude "Snooks" 63
  Ira 86
  Mary Ellen 66
  Minnie 86
  Nellie Hartley 36

INDEX

Jones (cont.)
    Nelson 66–67
    Virgil Carrington 101
Joppatowne (MD) 91
Joppatowne High School
    (Joppatowne, MD) 91
Joy. *See* Emotions
Justice of the peace. *See*
    Occupations

K

Kanawha City (Charleston, WV)
    51, 65
Kanawha County (WV) 45, 51,
    52, 53, 55, 57–58, 60, 61–62,
    62–63, 63–64, 64, 70–71,
    74–75
Kanawha County Public Library
    (WV) 63
Kanawha River (WV) 63, 65
Kanawha Valley (WV) 72–74
Kasey
    Pam 163–165
Keadle
    Mingo 61
    Newton Jasper "Doc" 61
    Virginia 61
Keefer
    Clara. *See* Decker
Keller
    Mary Elizabeth. *See* Flowers
Kellogg
    W.K. 97
Kelly Creek Mine 157
Kembridge (VA) 99
Kemp
    Emory L. 27–28
Kennedy
    Betty 156
    Brandum 157
    Conrad 136
    Elva L. 136
    Etta Walls 157
    Evelyn Teagarden **141**
    John F. 73
    Patricia. *See* Newhouse
    Shirley 156
    Tom 156
Kermit (WV) 68–70
Kessinger
    Clark. *See* Music: Musicians
Kessler Field (MS) 145
Keyser (WV) 54, 118
Keysville (MD) 127
Kimmins
    Roberta. *See* Gray
Kindness. *See* Characteristics
King
    Martin Luther 63
Kirk
    Brandon **58–59**
    Harriette James **62–63**, *63–64*
Knapp
    Louise 121
Knight
    Billy *83*

Knight (cont.)
    Evelyn *83*
    Gordon *83*
    Hazel *83*
    Orville *83*
    Ruby *83*
Knight Sisters, The. *See* Music:
    Groups
Kolsun
    Cynthia Phillips 121
Koon
    Charlotte 156
Kopperston (WV) 107
Kopperston Mountain (WV) 100
Korean War. *See* Wars
Krenn
    Adeline 133
    John 133
Krenn School (St. Clara,
    WV) 133

L

Lafferity
    Elizabeth. *See* Allen
Lakes. *See* Places
Lamm
    Barbara. *See* McAtee
Landmarks. *See* West Virginia
Language. *See also* West
    Virginia: Dialect
    Accent 105–106
    Slang 115–116
Lanham
    Dick *86*
    Roy *86*
Lannen
    Mary Helen. *See* Dawson
Lard. *See* Foods
Lashmeet (WV) 103, 106
Latrobe (PA) 155
Law
    Court cases 55
        Treason 126
    Legal age 81–82
Lawlessness. *See* Characteristics
Lawman. *See* Occupations
Lawrenceville (GA) 88
Lawson
    Anne. *See* Shaw
    Suzanne. *See* Miller
Lawyer. *See* Occupations
Layman
    Chauncy 139
    Nancy Rebecca Straight *139*
Layoff. *See* Life events
Leatherbark School (Smithville,
    WV) 43
Leatherman
    Ed A. 118
    Louise. *See* Malcolm
Leaving. *See* West Virginia
Lee
    Eleanor E. **56–57**
    Robert E. 126
Lemon crackers. *See* Foods
Lerona (WV) 108

Lessons. *See* Stories
Lester
    P. *See* Estep
Lewis
    Mary. *See* Allen
    N.J. 125–126
    Ronald L. 153
Lewis County (WV) 87
Lewisburg (WV) 98, 137
Libby Owens (Kanawha City,
    WV) 65
Life
    1800s, Late 163
    1900s, Early 31–33, 61, 68,
        89–91, 104–105, 146–147,
        156
    1910s 53
    1920s 28–29, 53, 61–62, 89–91,
        102–103, 159–163
    1930s 28–29, 30, 33–34, 39–40,
        62–63, 63–64, 64, 91, 97,
        116, 118–121, 141, 142–143,
        151–152
    1940s 30, 33–34, 41–42, 63–64,
        91, 100, 141, 145–146, 151–
        152, 156–157, 157–159
    1950s 19–24, 42, 136–137,
        157–159
    1960s 19–24, 70–71, 81–82
    1970s 19–24
    Boom town 72–74, 151, 156
    Coal camp 65, 97
    College town 63–64
    Depression, The 65, 97, 103–
        104, 115–116, 116, 118–121,
        127–129
    Farm 28–29, 29–30, 33–34,
        34–35, 35, 42–43, 55, 64, 65,
        69–70, 87–88, 91, 93, 99,
        102–103, 103–104, 104–105,
        114–115, 115–116, 126–127,
        129, 167–169
    Immigrant 30, 146–147
    Large family 19–24
    Rural 30, 46–47, 68–70
    Small town 42, 45–46, 59–60,
        60–61, 61, 68–70, 72–74
    Student 31–33
    Suburban 167–169
    Urban 40–41, 53, 66–67
Life events
    Anniversary 100
    Baptism 151
    Birth 159
    Birthday 35, 136, 154
    Death 156
    Firsts
        First car 104
        First job 42, 57–58, 152
        First recital 109
        First use of telephone 42,
            151
    Graduation
        High school 42
    Honeymoon 81–82, 128
    Layoff 149–150
    Life threatening experiences

Life events (cont.)
    Life threatening experiences
        (cont.)
        139–140, 145–146
    Loss of a friend 156
    Loss of family 30, 34–35, 58,
        65–66, 104, 150
    Marriage 77, 81–82, 98–100,
        128
    Moving 118–121, 165–166
    Quarantine 31–33
    Retirement 76
Lincoln
    Abraham 68
Lincoln County (WV) 101, 107
Lindley
    Ola. *See* Chedester
Linger
    Arlie *86*
    Gary *86*
    Mollie 86
Linwood (NJ) 57
Little Birch River (WV) 87
Little Bluestone (WV) 108
Logan (WV) 68
Logan County (WV) 58–59
Logger. *See* Occupations
Long
    Ruth. *See* Crowder
Longfellow
    Henry Wadsworth 59
Looman
    Patty. *See* Music: Musicians
Los Angeles (CA) 139
Loss. *See* Emotions
Loss of family or friend. *See* Life
    events
Louisville (KY) 65
Love. *See* Characteristics;
    Emotions
Lovejoy
    Rebecca. *See* Hager
Lowe
    Amanda. *See* Meade
    Ben A. 109
Lowery School 103
Loyalty. *See* Characteristics
Lucas
    Arno "Sam" **75–76**
    Julia ***165–166***
Ludwigshaven (Germany) 145–
    146
Lynch
    Ruby. *See* Bland
Lynch Chapel Community (WV)
    136
Lynco (WV) 102

M

Mabie (WV) 22
MacArthur (WV) 137
Machinist. *See* Occupations
MacKnight
    Sibyl 56
Madison
    Faye Fox *104*

Page number in bold indicates "Author" • **Page number in italics indicates "Photo"** • **Page number underlined indicates "Featured"**

Our Mountain State Heritage

Mail carrier. *See* Occupations
Malcolm
    Louise Leatherman Stickley **118**
Man (WV) 102
Mannington (WV) 156
Marcum
    Anna. *See* Meade
Marion County (WV) 56, 156
Marks
    Richard **52**
Marlinton (WV) 119–121
Marlinton Grade School (WV) 121
Marlinton Presbyterian Church (WV) 120
Marmet (WV) 74–75
Marriage. *See* Customs; Life events
Marshall
    Charlene 149, *150–153*
    Gwen 153
    Larry 153
    Roger 153
    Rogers Leon 153
    Thurgood 63
Marshall College. *See* Marshall University
Marshall County (WV) 29–30, 30, 34–35, 35, 36
Marshall University (Huntington, WV) 45, 52, 62, 81, 109
Martin
    Helen Rosella. *See* Bainbridge
Mason County (WV) 39, 56–57
Matheny
    Faye *83*
Matney
    Anna Mary Meade **68–70**
Matthews
    Bess *83*
    Bill *83*
    Charles *83*
    Frances *83*
    Louie *83*
    Virginia *83*
Mayor. *See* Occupations
McAtee
    Alice 134
    Barbara Lamm 134–135
    David 134
    Denise 134
    Eunice Rae 134
    Harry 134–135
    Janice 134
    Pamela 134
    Sharon 134
    Terry 134
McAvoy
    Roberta Withers *137*
McClancy
    Peggy 101
McClure
    Acie *83*
    Troy *83*

McCombs
    Alma Jean **36**
    Ivan W. 36
McCoy
    Green 58
McCubbin
    Lewis 82
McDaniel
    Claris Mitchell **142–143**
McDonald
    Ada Catherine "Betty." *See* Duvall
McDonough
    Mary. *See* Teagarden
McGuigan
    Ellen "Nellie." *See* Gaujot
McHenry (MD) 137
McMechen (WV) 36
McNew
    Gail Saugstad 44
McVeigh (KY) 65
Meade
    Amanda Lowe 70
    Anna Marcum *68–70*
    Anna Mary. *See* Matney
    James Alexander 70
    Jane Leander Rutherford 70
    John Dee 69
    Levisa Spaulding 70
    Lorenza Dow *68–70*
    Mildred Esther Davis 70
    Missouri Ann 70
    Ray C. 70
    Wanda Estep 70
    William Bingham (father) 70
    William Bingham (son) 70
    William Thomas 68–70
Meade-Matney
    Anna Mary. *See* Matney
Meathrell
    Calphurnia "Callie" Maxson 46
    Conza *46*
    Draxie 46
    John 46
    Julia 46
    Rupert 46
Media. *See* Publications; Radio
Memorial Day. *See* Holidays
Memories. *See* Life; Stories
Mercer County (WV) 97, 102–103, 105–106
Merritt's Creek (WV) 75
Messenberg
    Alma *152*
    Leroy *152*
Michael
    Alma Estella. *See* Michael
    Andrew Wilson 126
    Daisy Mae Stewart 126
    Harley Calvin 126
    James Andrew 126
    Laura May 126
    Lesta Francis 126
    Paul William 126
    William Elsworth 126

Military
    Combat 145–146
    Draft 41
    History 143–144
    Infantry 139
        Forty-fifth division 98–99
    Medals
        Congressional Medal of Honor 68
        US Air Force Air Medal 145–146
    US Air Force 100, 153
        Bombers 145–146
        Eighth Air Force 145–146
        Gunners 145–146
        Paratrooper 65
        Training 145–146
    US Army 19, 65–66, 147
    US Navy 106
    West Virginia Army National Guard 100
Milk and honey. *See* Foods
Mill Point (WV) 121
Miller
    Alice *83*
    Ernest *83*
    Ethel Shrover 116
    Floyd C. 116
    George *62, 83*
    Geraldine *83*
    Lillian. *See* Cunningham
    Owen *83*
    Paulette Barbara "Barbie" Bender *19–24*
    Roland *83*
    Suzanne Lawson *137*
Mills
    Charles Wesley 102–103
    Ellen. *See* Sneed
    Elmer 102
    Elsie 102–103
    Lawrence 102
    Mary Louvenia Foley 102–103
    Mary Magdalene "Maggie." *See* Porter
Mineral County (WV) 118
Mingo County (WV) 60–61, 61, 65–66, 68, 68–70
Mining. *See* Industry; Life; Occupations
Mining engineer. *See* Occupations
Minister. *See* Occupations
Minnehaha Springs (WV) 121
Mischief. *See* Characteristics
Mitchell
    Claris. *See* McDaniel
    Daisy Moats 143
    Monzell 142–143
    Rae 56
    Thelma 143
Moats
    Daisy. *See* Mitchell
Moffatt
    Ben *83*
    Golda *83*

Moffatt (cont.)
    Hazel *83*
    Howard *83*
    Leo *83*
    Loyd *83*
    Patty *83*
    Wellington *83*
Mona Supply Company (Granville and Morgantown, WV) 147
Money. *See* Economic conditions
Monongalia County (WV) 31, 56, 135–136, 136, 139–140, 141, 148–149, 150–153, 157–159, 163–165, 165–166, 167–169
Monongalia High School (Westover, WV) 151–152
Monroe County (WV) 98–100
Montgomery
    James C. 72
Montgomery (WV) 70–71, 72–74
Montgomery General Hospital (WV) 72
Montoya
    Lois 44–45
Moore
    Bernadine 152
    Betty Ann. *See* Husk
    Johnny Dale 88
    O.C. 88
    O.C. "Brownie" 88
    Stella 121
    Stella G. Eneix Nutter 39–40
Morehead (KY) 59
Morgan
    Mary Harr **134**
    Ruth Gaynell. *See* George
Morgan County (WV) 126–127
Morgantown (WV) 47, 93, 135, 147, 148–149, 150–153, 157, 163, 163–165, 165–166
Morgantown Florist (WV) 152
Morgantown High School (WV) 153
Morris
    Charles 61
    Lillian 61
    Susan 42
Morris Creek (Fayette County, WV) 73
Morrison School (Valley Grove, WV) 33
Morton
    Wesley *152*
Mother. *See* Family
Mother Maybelle and the Carter Family. *See* Music: Groups
Mother-in-law. *See* Family
Mound School (Dunbar, WV) 52
Mount Morris (PA) 139
Mount Olive (WV) 73
Mount Vernon Seminary (Washington, DC) 163
Mountain state. *See* West Virginia

INDEX

Mountaineer Hotel (Williamson, WV) 66
Movie theater. *See* Places
Movies. *See* Recreation
Moving. *See* Life events
Moyers
    Doris **41–42**
    Lewis L. 41
    Lewis V. 41
    Rhea L. 41–42
Mt. Trimble School (Morgan County, WV) 126
Mulberry Ridge (WV) 85–86
Mules. *See* Animals and insects; Transportation
Mullins
    Emma. *See* Haley
Munday (WV) 43
Murray
    Libby. *See* Newharth
Music
    Christmas carols 141
    Fiddle 58–59
    Folk 56
    Groups
        Cochrans, The 84
        Delmore Brothers, The 84
        Floradell and Nellie 84
        Knight Sisters, The 84
        Mother Maybelle and the Carter Family 84
        Reynolds Sisters, The 44
        Staton Brothers, The 84
        Three Bettys, The 84
        Three Shades of Blue, The 44
        Williams Family Singers, The 84
    Hymns 43, 121
    Instrumental 84
    Instruments
        Cornstalk fiddle 58
        Hammer dulcimer 56
        Player piano 119
        Pump organ 117
        Violin 109
    Musicians
        Buddy Starcher 84
        Clark Kessinger 59
        Curly Wellman 59
        Ernest Tubb 84
        Fiddlin' Cowan Powers 59
        Ford Williams 84
        Georgia Slim Rutland 59
        Hays Johnson 84
        James Edward "Blind Ed" Haley 58–59
        Jean Thomas 59
        Jesse Stuart 59
        Little Jimmy Dickens 84
        Molly O'Day 59
        Patty Looman 56
        Roy Acuff 84
        Slim Clere 59
        Wilson Douglas 59
    Piano lessons 54
    Recital 109

Music (cont.)
    Shape notes 57
    Singing 57–58, 75, 84
Musician. *See* Music; Occupations

N

Nashville (TN) 84
National Guard. *See* Military
National Historic Landmark. *See* Places
National Register of Historic Places. *See* Places
Natural gas. *See* Industry
Nature. *See also* Animals and insects; Recreation; West Virginia: Beauty
    Beauty 31, 39
    Cowpie 91
    Spring water 22, 84
    Weather 92–93, 116
    Wildlife 167–169
Navy. *See* Military: US Navy
Nedrow
    James E. **159**
    Linda Lou. *See* Hermanson
Neff
    Lois Jean Drumpus *139*
Nellis Air Force Base (Las Vegas, NV) 145
New Deal 97
New Era Living Heritage Museum (Mineral Wells, WV) 44
New Kensington (PA) 119
New Northern Hotel (Richwood, WV) 81–82
New Orleans (LA) 68
New York City (NY) 159, 165
Newbern (VA) 68
Newcomer. *See* West Virginia
Newharth
    Libby Murray *137*
Newhouse
    Patricia (Kennedy) **156–157**, *157–159*
    Russell 157, *158*
Newspapers. *See* Publications
Nicholas County (WV) 81–82, 88–89
Nichols
    Boyd 29
    Doris 29
Norfolk (VA) 106
Norfolk and Western Railway 61
Norfolk Southern Railway 61
North Bend (WV) 88–89
Nostalgia. *See* Emotions; Life; Stories
Nursing assistant. *See* Occupations
Nutter
    Polly. *See* Shepherd
    Stella G. Eneix. *See* Moore

O

Oakwood Baptist Church (Charleston, WV) 55
Occupations
    Assessor 61
    Automobile repair 89–91
    Banker 19
    Beer distributor 147
    Business person 106, 156
    Civil engineer 68
    Coal mine owner 154
    Coal mining 65, 100, 101, 103, 106, 146, 157
    Delegate 68
    Farming 55
    Farmworker 30
    Football coach 99
    Gas station manager 19
    Glass factory worker 149
    Grocer 146–147
    Homemaker 77
    Horse-team driver 104, 156
    Insurance agent 90
    Internal Revenue Service officer 42, 43
    Inventory clerk 42
    Justice of the peace 61
    Lawyer 68
    Logger 82
    Machinist 19
    Mail carrier 77
    Mayor (Morgantown, WV) 153
    Mining engineer 68
    Minister 19
    Musician 58–59
    Nursing assistant 19
    Oil pump station engineer 90
    Photography 165–166
    Police chief 69
    Postmaster 61
    Prohibition officer 61
    Railroad engineer 88–89
    Railroader 36
    Railway trackman 75–76
    Railyard worker 75–76, 88–89
    Realtor 77
    Road construction 118–121
    Screen printer 106
    Senator 68
    Sheriff 61
    Shoe repair 83
    Sternwheeler captain 66–67
    Stonemason 30
    Surveyor 126
    Teaching 33, 45, 57–58, 62, 99, 108–109, 116–117, 136
    Truck driver 19, 65
    Welder 19
    Writing 19, 149
Oceana (WV) 102, 106–108
O'Day
    Molly. *See* Music: Musicians
Ohio County (WV) 27–28, 29–30, 31, 34–35

Ohio River 144
Oil. *See* Industry
Oil pump station engineer. *See* Occupations
Old methods
    Bathing 53
    Building with logs 163
    Classroom 52
    Ice cream making 114–115
    Ice storage 114–115, 126
    Mattress making 126
    Pharmacy 36
    Refrigeration 114–115
    Shoe repair 85
    Threshing 126
Old Rough Run School 113
Oratory. *See* Skills
Orchards. *See* Places
Organ Cave (WV) 98
Organ, pump. *See* Music
Organizations. *See* Clubs and organizations
Ormond Beach (FL) 137
Osage (WV) 150–153
Osage Coal Camp Museum (Osage, WV) 153
Outhouses. *See* Places
Overstreet
    Paul 65
Owens
    Margaret. *See* Hutchinson
Oxley
    Leonard 52

P

Page
    Ida. *See* Conner
Pain. *See* Emotions
Pancakes. *See* Foods
Parades. *See* Festivals
Paramount and Pacific 100
Parents. *See* Family
Parker
    Sylvia Elaine 159–163
Parkersburg (WV) 42, 58, 166
Parkersburg High School (WV) 42
Parran School (Moorefield, WV) 116–117
Pasture. *See* Places
Patience. *See* Characteristics
Paugh
    Billy *83*
    Charles *83*
    Denzil *83*
    Elma *83*
    Joe *83*
    Junior *83*
    Martha Jean *83*
Payne
    Virgil *83*
Peerless Mills, Inc. (Parkersburg, WV) 42
Pefley
    Ray. *See* Hutchinson

Page number in bold indicates "Author" • Page number in italics indicates "Photo" • Page number underlined indicates "Featured"

Pendleton County (WV) 115–116
Perry
　Stella 86
Persimmons. See Foods
Personalities
　Carole Lombard 145
　Clark Gable 145
　Elizabeth Taylor 118
　Garth Brooks 154
　Glen Campbell 59
　Jackie Bouvier Kennedy 118
　Mickey Mouse 118
　Pearl S. Buck 121
　Shirley Temple 118
Petersburg (WV) 114
Pets
　Dogs 134
　Foxhounds 39
　Lambs 28
　Skunks 149–150
Pettry (WV) 108
Philadelphia (PA) 68
Philippi (WV) 119, 142–143
Philippi Grade School (Philippi, WV) 119
Philippi Methodist Church 119
Phillips
　Cynthia. See Kolsun
　Debra 34
　Patricia 34
　Rod Steele 121
　Ruth 33–34
　Sharon 34
Photography. See Occupations
Pickaway (WV) 99
Pickle beans. See Foods
Picnics. See Recreation
Pine Grove Cemetery (Berea, WV) 46
Pine Grove School (Charleston, WV) 64
Pine Grove School (Lerona, WV) 108
Pinnacle Creek (WV) 100
Pittston Coal Company (WV) 29
Places
　Airport 88
　Apartments 120
　Bridges 27–28
　Cabins 46–47
　Camp 35
　Cemeteries 46, 68
　Churches 57, 91, 98
　College 31–33
　Court house 125–126
　Creeks 63, 166
　Depots 143–144
　Farms 28–29, 29–30, 33–34, 34–35, 35, 55, 68–70, 82–85, 93, 97, 102–103, 128–129, 163–165, 167–169
　Flea market 139
　Four-county stone 118
　Front porch 51, 163–165
　Garages 90, 91
　Garden 55

Places (cont.)
　Grocery stores 120, 146–147, 146
　Grove, The (Institute, WV) 63
　Historic buildings 52–53, 125–126, 143–144
　Hollows 82–85, 93
　Home 138, 155
　Homeplace 30, 55
　Hotels 82
　Houses 52–53, 163–165
　Ice house 114–115
　Lakes 92
　Landmarks 27–28, 118, 125–126, 143–144, 159
　Movie theater 90
　National Civil Engineering Landmarks 27–28
　National Historic Landmarks 27–28
　National Register of Historic Places 133, 143–144
　Orchards 118, 129
　Outhouses 34, 62, 115–116
　Pasture 28, 91
　Restoration
　　Bridge 27–28
　　Depot 143–144
　　House 52–53
　　Log house 163–165
　　Schoolhouse 133
　Rivers and creeks
　　Deckers Creek (WV) 167
　　Hughes River (WV) 45
　　Kanawha River 66–67
　　Scotts Run 139–140
　Roads and highways 119–120, 121, 135–136
　　Interstate 64 72
　　Interstate 79 153
　　WV Route 39 121
　　WV Route 92 119
　　WV Route 99 100
　　WV Turnpike 72
　Schools. See School; Schoolhouse
　Skating rink 126
　Springs 22
　Suburbs 167–169
　Summer house 161–163
　Swimming pool 126
　Towns 45–46, 59–60, 60–61, 63–64, 65–66, 68–70, 72–74, 82–85, 118–121, 136–137, 150–153
　Tunnels 143–144
Plainview School (Preston County, WV) 156
Play. See Recreation
Player piano. See Music
Playfulness. See Characteristics
Pleasant Hill (WV) 108
Pledge of Allegiance. See Customs
Pocahontas County (WV) 119–121

Poetry 66–67, 125–126, 141, 157–159
Point Pleasant (WV) 56
Police chief. See Occupations
Poling
　Roy 86
Polino
　Sam G. 119
Popcorn. See Foods
Pope
　Gail Means. See Bossart
Porter
　Mary Jane. See Childers
　Mary Magdalene "Maggie" Mills 102–103, 105–106
　Patty Kay. See Grace
　Robert Jackson "Jack" 103, 105–106
　Thomas Michael 103
Post
　Clay 114
　Daniel 114
　Edna 113–114, 114–115
Postmaster. See Occupations
Potomac State College 116
Potter
　Ellen Roumania. See Davidson
Poulos
　George 91
Poverty. See Economic conditions
Powers
　Cowan. See Music: Musicians
Prelaz' Restaurant (Richwood, WV) 82
Preserving food. See Foods; Skills
Preston County (WV) 136, 143–144, 156–157, 159
Price
　Andrew 107
　Clarinda Cooper 107
　Jessica Dawn 60
　Mary Arabess "Arispa." See Cooper
　Sarah 107
　William 107
Prichard
　Mary 41
Pride. See Characteristics; Emotions; West Virginia
Princeton (WV) 103
Prohibition officer. See Occupations
Proper. See Characteristics
Prosperity. See Economic conditions
Proud. See Characteristics; Emotions; West Virginia
Prudential Florida Realty (Ft. Lauderdale, FL) 106
Prudishness. See Characteristics
Publications
　Bobbsey Twins, The 64
　Grit: America's Family Magazine 89

Publications (cont.)
　Hatfields and McCoys 101
　History of the B&O, The 143
　History of Wyoming County, The 107
　Mountain State Stories of the People 93
　Newspapers
　　Chessie News 76
　　Cincinnati Enquirer, The 73
　　Dominion Post, The (Morgantown, WV) 35
　　Mingo Republican 61
　　Times Leader, The (Martins Ferry, OH) 35
　Putnam Year Book 53
　Sears, Roebuck catalog 84, 127
　Webb Families of Virginias 101
　West Virginia History 153
Pulaski County (VA) 68
Pumpkin. See Foods
Pursglove (WV) 140, 151
Putnam County (WV) 52–53, 59–60

Q

Quarantine. See Life events
Quarrelsome. See Characteristics
Quillen
　Harold 104
Quilting. See Skills

R

Rader
　Stella 64
Radio
　WMON-AM (Montgomery, WV) 73
Railroad. See Occupations; Industry; Transportation
Railroad engineer. See Occupations
Railroader. See Occupations
Railyard worker. See Occupations
Rain. See Weather
Raisin pie. See Foods
Raleigh County (WV) 109
Ralph (PA) 135
Randolph
　Preston 45
Randolph County (WV) 116
Rankin
　Betty Lou 83
Rappold
　E.F. 53
Realtor. See Occupations
Recipes
　Chow Chow 70–71
　Grandma Jones' lemon crackers 36
　Raisin pie 43

Recreation. *See also* Festivals;
    Games; Hobbies; Sports;
    Toys; West Virginia
  Berry picking 70–71
  Bicycling 54, 119
  Board games 54
  Cake walks 142
  Camping 92–93
  Canoeing 92
  Card games 54
  Carnival 54
  Circus 54
  Cruise 100
  Dancing 54
  Exploring 167–169
  Fireworks 35
  Fishing 35, 92, 101, 119
  Games 167–169
  Hunting 101
    Fox 39
    Rabbit 75–76
  Movies 63, 129, 151
  Parties 103
  Picnics 35, 63, *114*, 151
  Play 167–169
  Putting on plays 84
  Radio shows 97
  Riverboat races 66–67
  Roller skating 63, 121
  Silent movies 90, 120
  Sledding 103
  Snorkeling 100
  Socials 85, 113, 142
  Stilting 54
  Swimming 54, 63–64, 155
  Television 20–21
  Travel 159–163
  Young People's Program
    (Upper Glade, WV) 84
Reed
  Joyce. *See* Royse
Reedsville (WV) 136, 145
Reflection. *See* Emotions
Religion. *See* Church
Religiousness. *See* Characteristics
Remedies. *See* Home remedies
Reppert
  Blanche 157
  Bob 165
  Gayle (Summers) 164
  Mary A. (Smith) *164–165*
  Sylvanus *164–165*
Resourcefulness. *See*
    Characteristics
Respect. *See* Characteristics
Restoration. *See* Places
Retirement. *See* Life events
Returning. *See* West Virginia
Revolutionary War. *See* Wars
Rexall Drug Store (Philippi,
    WV) 119
Reyburn-Steele
  Miriam 118–121
Reynolds
  Alberta 44
  Hannah C. 44

Reynolds (cont.)
  Kate 44
  Kim 85
  Lena Mae. *See* Young
Reynolds Sisters, The. *See*
    Music: Groups
Reynoldsville (WV) 138
Rich Mountain (WV) 22
Richard
  Arthelia Christina Shimer
    42–43
  Linza H. 43
Richardson
  Henry 163–165
  Repher 164
Richmond (VA) 52
Richwood (WV) 81–82, 88–89,
    92, 120
Ridgelawn Cemetery (Huntington, WV) 76
Rigsby
  Bill 91
  Gloragene "Jean" Williams
    82–85, 91
  Kim. *See* Reynolds
  Mike 85
  Pam. *See* Chernault
Riley
  James Whitcomb 59
Ripley (WV) 39
Ritchie County (WV) 41–42, 43,
    45–46
Rittenhouse
  Richard Stanford "Dick" 156
Riverside (CA) 88, 153
Riverside School (Monongalia
    County, WV) 157
Roads. *See* Places
Roane County (WV) 39–40,
    46–47
Roanoke (VA) 99
Roberts
  Linda 42
  Robert 52
  Virginia 52
Robertson
  Opal Lorena Coughlin 104
Robinson
  Angelia Sue 102
  Steve 153
Rodes
  David 109
  Shannon 109
  Wilma Lilly **108–109**
Roebling
  John 27–28
Roles
  Family 20
  Female 148–149
Ronceverte (WV) 98
Roosevelt
  Eleanor *62–63*, 151
  Franklin 118
  Theodore 31
Royse
  Donald 46–47
  Joyce Reed 46–47

Royse (cont.)
  Paige Elizabeth **46–47**
Rupert (WV) 104
Rural. *See* Life
Rush
  Joan Goff *137*
Rutherford
  Jane Leander. *See* Meade
Rutland
  Georgia Slim. *See* Music:
    Musicians

S

Sadness. *See* Emotions
Salem Presbyterian Church
    (Organ Cave, WV) 98
Sam G. Polino & Company
    (Elkins, WV) 119
San Antonio (TX) 100
San Diego (CA) 153
San Diego State University 153
Sand Fork (WV) 89–91
Sanders
  David 126
Satisfaction. *See* Emotions
Sausage. *See* Foods
Sayres
  Blanch Heavner *86*
Schmiercase. *See* Foods
School. *See also* Community:
    Working together;
    Customs; Occupations;
    Schoolhouse
  Activities 152
  Awards 33, 52, 152
  Bands 151
  Basketball 152
  Bell 64
  Classmates 121
  Clubs 52
  Curriculum 52, 142
  Discipline 102–103
  Field trips 62–63, 81–82
  Football 152
  Grades 20, 52
  High school queens 152
  Jobs, after school and
    summer 152
    Mowing 22
    Paper routes 22
    Waitressing 22
  Lunch 52, 85, 108, 139
  Music 57–58
  Old methods 52
  Readers 57
  Recess 113
  Reunions 136–137
  Spelling bees 57, 113
  Sports 152
  Summer vacation 35
  Textbooks 52
School prayer. *See* Customs
Schoolbus. *See* Transportation
Schoolhouse
  As community center 113–
    114, *133*

Schoolhouse (cont.)
  One-two room 57–58, 61–62,
    64, 85–86, 97, 103, 113, 116–
    117, 126–127, *133*, 142, 156
Scotts Run (Monongalia County,
    WV) 139–140, 150–151, 153
Scotts Run Settlement House
    (Osage, WV) 153
Screen printing. *See*
    Occupations
Searls
  Annie 59–60
Seasons
  Autumn 31
  Spring 33–34
  Summer 33–34, 51, 159–163
Seattle (WA) 121
Seckman
  Doris. *See* Nichols
Second Ward School (Dunbar,
    WV) 52
Security. *See* Emotions
Self-sufficiency. *See*
    Characteristics
Self-taught. *See* Characteristics
Senator. *See* Occupations
Sensitivity. *See* Characteristics
Service. *See also* Community
  Mentorship 88–89, 148–149
  Volunteerism 45, 106
  Scout leader 77
Sewing. *See* Skills
Sexton
  Agnes 83
Shaffer
  Amy Compton **154**
  Jeremy L. 154
Shahan's (Arden, WV) 143
Shamblin
  Jack F. 53
  Kay Smith 53
Shanklin
  Margaret Rodgers Boone 98
Shaw
  Anne Lawson *137*
Sheets
  Margie Fay Dickens 74
Shenandoah Junction (WV) 128
Shepherd
  Franklin D. 40
  Polly Nutter **39–40**
Sheriff. *See* Occupations
Shimer
  Annie Cunningham *42–43*
  Arthelia Christina. *See*
    Richard
  Okey *42–43*
Shirley (WV) 28–29
Shivaree. *See* Customs
Shoe repair. *See* Occupations;
    Old methods
Short
  Barbara Ann. *See* Bragg
Short temper. *See*
    Characteristics
Showers
  Cara 60

Page number in bold indicates "Author" • Page number in italics indicates "Photo" • Page number underlined indicates "Featured"

Shrover
  Ethel. *See* Miller
Siblings. *See* Family
Sibold
  Edwin *98–100*
  Eloise Allen **98–100**
Sielen
  Rae Jean *92–93*, **167–169**
Sienkiewicz
  Myra Lou Drumpus *139*
Sill
  John *83*
Simon
  Mary George *33*
Sissonville (WV) *52, 57–58*
Sister. *See* Family
Sites
  Jessie N. *114*
  Nettie Catherine Getz *114*
Skating rinks. *See* Places
Skills
  Automobile maintenance *54*
  Baking *36, 70–71, 77, 116, 153*
  Canning *29, 33, 71, 77*
  Crocheting *100, 142*
  Embroidering *54*
  Fiddling *58–59*
  Food preparation *33*
  Food preservation *93*
  Gardening *71*
  Housekeeping *54*
  Hunting ginseng *154*
  Oratory *31–33*
  Quilting *41–42*, *55, 116*
  Reading *54*
  Sewing *29, 54, 55, 84, 116, 151*
  Using/re-using items creatively *116*, *143*
  Writing *149–150*
Skunks. *See* Animals and insects; Pets
Slab Camp School *85–86*
Slab Fork (WV) *135*
Slaven
  Chip *153*
Sledding. *See* Recreation
Sleepy Creek (WV) *126*
Slyness. *See* Characteristics
Smith
  Buddy *119–120*
  Christopher *53*
  Eleanor *119–120*
  Elizabeth. *See* Cooper; Davidson
  Geoffrey *53*
  Helen *83*
  Linda *46–47*
  Marjorie *119–120*
  Mary A. *See* Reppert
  Mike *46–47*
  Nancy Peery **65–66**, *68*
  Ned *119–120*
  Oris *83*
  Rodney *53*
  Roy *83*
  Shirley *83*

Smith (cont.)
  Wallace Graham *68*
  William D. *156*
Sneed
  Ellen Mills *102*
Snyder
  Cecil *86*
  David G. *136*
  Gail Florence Watson *136*
  Gladys L. *See* Eddy
  Kris P. *56*
  Milton *86*
  Minor *86*
Soccer. *See* Sports
Social conditions
  Child labor *148*
  Civil rights *63*, *148*
  Ethnic diversity *153*
  Racial integration *151, 153*
  Segregation *63–64*, *120, 151, 152*
  Unequal pay *148*
  Women's right to vote *148*
Socials. *See* Customs; Recreation
Sonnencroft (Fairmont, WV) *159–163*
South Charleston (WV) *60*
South Hills (WV) *55*
Sowshead. *See* Foods
Spahr Lime and Stone Company (Thurmont, MD) *127*
Spaulding
  Levisa. *See* Meade
Spears
  Hamilton *101*
  Jerusha Spurlock *101*
  Lottie *101*
Spencer (WV) *46–47*
Spirited. *See* Characteristics
Sports. *See also* School
  Accidents
    Baseball *75*
  Baseball *113*
  Basketball *120, 139*
  Golf *162*
  Karate *139*
  Soccer *139*
  Track *139*
  Wrestling *139*
Springdale (PA) *119*
Springdale (WV) *103–104*, *104*
Springfield (MA) *74*
Springston
  Gerald *83*
Spurlock
  Jerusha. *See* Spears
St. Albans (WV) *62, 77, 104*
Stalnaker
  Mary Ellen *83*
St. Andrews United Methodist Church (St. Albans, WV) *77*
Stapleton
  Margaret Burroughs *88*
Star City (WV) *153*
Starcher
  Buddy. *See* Music: Musicians

Staton Brothers, The. *See* Music: Groups
St. Clara (WV) *133*
St. Clara Organized Community *133*
Steele
  Alfred Reyburn *118–121*
  Dorothy "Dotty" Jean *118–121*
  Mildred Hendrickson *118–121*
Stephenson
  B.H. "Hub" *88*
  Nellie Burroughs Moore **87–88**
Sternwheeler. *See* Transportation
Sternwheeler captain. *See* Occupations
Stevenson
  Amy *155*
  Paul *155*
  Rachel *155*
  Robert Louis *121*
  Susan *155*
Stewart
  Archie *30*
  Austin Rice *101*
  Charles P. *101*
  Corby. *See* Elkins
  Daisy Mae. *See* Michael
  Della Myrtle Mae Francis *101*
  Emily Webb *102*
  George P. *101*
  Juanita. *See* Fitzsimmons
  Mary Clay *101*
  Ralph *101–102*
  Theo Holmes *30*
Stickley
  James "Jimmie" R. *118*
  Louise Leatherman. *See* Malcolm
  Ray Arthur "Artie" *118*
Stilwell
  Charlotte. *See* Atha
Stinnett
  Margaret. *See* Bailey
St. James A.M.E. Church (Williamson, WV) *66*
St. Louis
  Ken *92–93*, *167*
St. Michael's Episcopal Cathedral (Boise, ID) *163*
Stone
  Myrtle Scraggs *74–75*
Stone & Thomas *116*
Stonemason. *See* Occupations
Stonesifer
  Ethel Pauline (Polly). *See* Hockensmith
  Mary *127*, *128*
Stores. *See* Names of individual stores
Stories. *See also* History
  Adventures *40–41, 75–76, 92–93*

Stories (cont.)
  Animal *134, 149–150*
  Childhood adventures *35, 39, 39–40, 46–47, 51, 55, 61–62, 63–64, 64, 88–89, 102–103, 118–121, 155, 167–169*
  Competition
    Hunt club *39*
    Riverboat race *66–67*
    Rolling pin–throwing *129*
  Family *19–24, 28–29, 29–30, 30, 51, 53, 55, 61–62, 68, 68–70, 74, 75–76, 89–91, 91, 97, 104–105, 114–115, 116, 118–121, 134–135, 142–143, 146–147, 159, 159–163*
  Ghost *75–76, 85–86, 162*
  Humor *19–24, 34–35, 40–41, 43, 59, 74, 81–82, 91, 102–103, 103–104, 104–105, 109, 115–116, 118*
  Lessons *30, 44–45, 46–47, 54, 55, 57–58, 77, 87–88, 118, 149–150, 165–166*
  Mystery *55*
  Nostalgia *35, 72–74, 74–75*
  Practical jokes *64*
  Suspense *40–41*
  Terror *139–140, 145–146*
  Tributes *34–35, 44–45, 58–59, 61, 65, 68, 74–75, 75–76, 82–85, 89–91, 108–109, 136, 141*
Stotler
  Lester Olie *126*
  Vietta Belle Michael *126*
Strader
  Susie *92*
Straight
  Nancy Rebecca. *See* Layman
Straub
  Evelyn C. *56*
Streets
  Harry *22*
  Helen *23*
  Marlene Edith. *See* Bender
  Rosa *22*
  Shirley *23*
  Sue *23*
Strength. *See* Characteristics
Strictness. *See* Characteristics
Stroke. *See* Afflictions
St. Simons Island (GA) *121*
Stuart
  Jesse. *See* Music: Musicians
Students. *See* Life; Life events; West Virginia University
Studiousness. *See* Characteristics
Suck Creek School (Little Bluestone, WV) *108*
Sugar Creek (WV) *119*
Sugar Creek School (Sissonville, WV) *52*
Sugar Grove (WV) *141*
Summer. *See* Seasons

Summers
  Elijah 164–165
  Emma 164
  Gayle. *See* Reppert
Summers Auto Parts
  (Morgantown, WV) 139
Summers County (WV) 104–105, 108–109
Summersville (WV) 60
Summit Lake (WV) 92
Surveyor. *See* Occupations
Sutton
  Bertha Davis 46
  Guy Toy 46
  Mary Genieve. *See* Carneal
  Sam 153
Swimming. *See* Recreation
Swimming pool. *See* Places

T

Talent. *See* Characteristics
Tamaqua (PA) 68
Taneytown (MD) 127
Taneytown High School
  (MD) 127
Tariff (WV) 39–40
Taylor
  Katheryne K. 60
Taylor County (WV) 136–137, 149–150
Teacher. *See* Occupations;
  School; Schoolhouse
Teaching. *See* Occupations
Teagarden
  Evelyn. *See* Kennedy
  Fred 141, *158–159*
  Mary McDonough 141
Teaverbaugh (WV) 156
Technological advances
  Aircraft 90
  Automobiles 89–91
  Cable television 116
  Electricity 89–91, 129
  Telephone 42, 151
  Wheeling steam tricycle 27
Television. *See* Recreation;
  Technological advances
Tenderness. *See* Emotions
Tennyson
  Lord Alfred 59
Terre Haute (IN) 106
Terrill
  Charles 30, 34
  Dorothy 30, 34
  Harold 30, 34
  Helen 30, 34
  Martha "Sue" 30, 34
  Norman 30, 34
  Phyllis 30, 34
  Roy 30, 34
  Russell Elmer (father) 29, 34
  Russell Elmer (son) 30, 34
Teter
  Jane 119
Thankfulness. *See*
  Characteristics

Thaxton
  Hazel 44
  Thelma 57–58
Thomas
  James Spurgeon 137
  Jean. *See* Music: Musicians
Thornhill
  Dixie Lee **134–135**
Three Bettys, The. *See* Music:
  Groups
Three Shades of Blue, The. *See*
  Music: Groups
Thrift. *See* Characteristics
Thrill. *See* Emotions
Toler
  Nancy C. *See* Brown
Touen (France) 145–146
Towns. *See* History; Life; Places;
  Names of individual
  towns
Toys
  Crayons 74
  Dollhouse 121
  Dolls 134
  Go-cart 28
  Rolling hoops 28
  Stick horses 134
  Stuffed animal 60
  Wagon 28
Trace Fork (Logan County,
  WV) 58
Trace Fork School (Sissonville,
  WV) 57–58
Trains. *See* Industry: Railroad
Traits. *See* Characteristics
Transportation. *See also*
  Technological advances;
  Vehicles
  Automobile 119–120, 135–136
  Bus 77
  Foot 85, 97
  Horse and buggy 136
  Horse-drawn wagon 33, 147, 156
  Horseback 33, 68, 136
  Mule 105
  Railroad 88–89, 143–144, 147
  School bus 62
  Sternwheelers 66–67
  Truck 147
  Wagon train 106
Triadelphia Grade School
  (WV) 33
Tributes. *See* Stories
Trinity Methodist Church
  (Glenville, WV) 57
Truck. *See* Transportation
Truck driving. *See* Occupations
Truman
  Harry S. 73, 137
Trumbo
  Martha Ella 58
Tubb
  Ernest. *See* Music: Musicians
Tug Valley (WV) 58, 60

Tug Valley Country Club
  (Williamson, WV) 66
Tunnelton (WV) 143–144
Tunnelton High School
  (WV) 144
Tuppers Creek (Kanawha
  County, WV) 45
Turner
  Ronald Ray 102
Twelve Pole Valley (WV) 58
Twin Ridge Orchard Company
  (Shenandoah Junction,
  WV) 128
Twins 60
Twyman
  Marietta. *See* Eneix
Tygart Valley River (WV) 136
Tyler County (WV) 28–29

U

Ulster (Ireland) 108
Uncle Tuck's Store (West Liberty,
  WV) 32
Union Carbide (Alloy, WV) 72
United Mine Workers of
  America 101, 107
University High School
  (Morgantown, WV) 157
University of Charleston
  (WV) 52
Uphold
  Carla 149
Upper Glade (WV) 82–85, 91
Upper Glade Methodist Church
  (WV) 83, 91
Upper Glade Presbyterian
  Church (WV) 91
Upshur County (WV) 85–86
Urban. *See* Life
US Air Force. *See* Military
US Army. *See* Military
US Army Corps of Engineers
  121
US Department of the Interior
  27–28
US Navy. *See* Military
US Steel 100

V

Vacation 92–93
Valley Grove (WV) 30, 33
Values. *See* Characteristics;
  Community; Family
Vance
  Abner 101
  Mary "Millie." *See* Brown
  Susanna Howard 101
Vanderlieke
  Diane. *See* Heim
Vandevender
  Cora 86
Vang Construction Company
  (Pittsburg, PA) 119
Van Meter
  Linda **60–61**, *61*

Vannin
  Mark 139
Vecillo and Grogan 100
Vehicles
  Automobile 89–91, 117, 119–120
Vessels
  Laconia 159
  Laura J. 67
  Queen Elizabeth II 163
  Snow Good Hope 107
  Virginia 67
Veterans. *See* Wars
Violin. *See* Music
Volk
  Frank W. 145–146
  Garrett Anthony *146*
  Jessie E. **145–146**, *146–147*

W

W.T. Grant Company 116
Waddle's Store (West Liberty,
  WV) 32
Wade
  Georgia 152
  Rebecca 152
Wagon train. *See* Transportation
Wagoner
  Barbara Bartlett *137*
Waller
  Betty **116**
Walls
  Etta. *See* Kennedy
Walnut Gap (WV) 107
Walthall
  James Willis 104
  Sara Vena Coughlin **103–104**
  Vena Rose. *See* Dunn
Wanamaker
  John 68
War of 1812. *See* Wars
Ward
  Janet Boylen *137*
Ware
  Cheryl Lynn Bender **19–24**
  Mark 23
Warren
  Carol **51**
  Isabelle "Izzy" F. Hanna 51
  J.T. "Scoop" 51
  Joseph T. 51
  Robert K. 51
Wars. *See also* Battles; Military
  1812 101
  Civil War 27, 107, 121, 136, 143–144, 164
  Korean 54
  Revolutionary War 101, 107, 108
  Veterans 46, 145–146
  World War I 65–66, 107, 144, 147, 153
  World War II 30, 65, 99, 100, 107, 136, 144, 145–146
Washington
  Charles 126

Page number in bold indicates "Author" • Page number in italics indicates "Photo" • Page number underlined indicates "Featured"

Our Mountain State Heritage

Washington (cont.)
  George 68, 121, 126
  Lawrence 126
  Samuel 126
Watkins
  Lyda. *See* Hutchinson
Watoga State Park (Pocahontas County, WV) 92–93
Watson
  Launa Shuttlesworth 136
  Thomas J. 136
Waugh
  Betty 121
Waybright
  Imogene. *See* Fox
Wayman's Ridge (WV) 36
Wayne
  Dennis *39*
  Mark Hampton *39*
Waynesburg College (PA) 35
Wealth. *See* Economic conditions
Weather
  Rain 92–93
Webb
  Alma *36*
  Austin 102
  Emily. *See* Stewart
  Giles 102
  Henry 102
  Jacob 101
  John *36*
  Mary Austin 101
Webster County (WV) 82–85, 89, *91*
Wedding. *See* Life events
Weimer
  Sharon 149
Welch (WV) 100
Welding. *See* Occupations
Wellman
  Curly. *See* Music: Musicians
West Alexander (PA) 31
West August Historical Society Museum (Mannington, WV) 156
West Liberty (WV) *31–33*
West Liberty Normal School (West Liberty, WV) *31–33*
West Union (WV) 28
West Virginia. *See also* Foods; History; Places
  Beauty *31*, 39, 85–86, 106, 118, 135–136, 149–150
  Dialect 120
  Heritage *27–28*, 52–53, 60–61, 72–74, 101, 125–126, 133, 163–165

West Virginia (cont.)
  Home *59–60*, *135–136*
  Landmarks
    Four-county stone 118
    Jefferson County Court House (Charles Town, WV) 125–126
    Sonnencroft (Fairmont, WV) 159–161
    Tunnelton Depot *143–144*
    Wheeling Suspension Bridge *27–28*
  Leaving *136–137*
  Lore 55
  Native 19–24, 28–29, 45–46, 55, 58–59, 59–60, 61–62, 62–63, 63–64, 82–85, 85–86, 87–88, 102–103, 103–104, 105–106, 106–108, 116–117, 126–127, 136, 136–137, 150–153
  Newcomer 30, 31, 68, 77
  Pride 82–85, 87, *136–137*
  Recreation 66–67
  Returning 62, 165–166
  Statehood 27
West Virginia Antiquities Commission 27–28
West Virginia Army National Guard. *See* Military
West Virginia Department of Highways 27–28
West Virginia Food Service Department 142
West Virginia High Technology Consortium Foundation 154
West Virginia Independence Hall (Wheeling, WV) 27–28
West Virginia Reform School for Boys (Grafton, WV) 136
West Virginia State College (Institute, WV) 63, 152
West Virginia State Road Commission 82
West Virginia Tech (Montgomery, WV) 72
West Virginia University 31, 136, 144
  Clubs
    Parents' Club 153
    Students 153
Westover Junior High School (WV) 152
Wetzel County (WV) 33–34
Wheeling (WV) *27–28*, *31*, 35

Wheeling Custom House (WV) 27–28
Wheeling Suspension Bridge (WV) *27–28*
White
  George 119
Whitesell
  Virginia Bergdoll 117
Wichita (KS) 77
Wife. *See* Family
Wild greens. *See* Foods
Wild turkeys. *See* Animals and insects
Wildcat (KY) 108
Wildlife. *See* Animals and insects; Nature
Williams
  Deral "Dubby" 82–85, 91
  Eva *82–85*, 91
  Flora Dell 82–85, 91
  Ford 82–85, 91
  Geraldine *83*
  Gloragene "Jean." *See* Rigsby
  Joe 88
  Joseph Mayse 83
  Lowell 82–85, 91
  Luther *82–85*, 88, 91
  Lyman 82–85, 91
  Naomi Moon 159
  Ralph 52–53, **88–89**
  Shirley Ann 82–85, *91*
Williams Family Singers, The. *See* Music: Groups
Williamson
  Benjamin R. 60
  Billie Bott *137*
  John B. 60
  Wallace J. 60
Williamson (WV) *60–61*, *61*, *65–66*, *68*
Williamson Cemetery (WV) 68
Williamstown (WV) 40–41
Willison
  James 133
Wilson
  Homer *140*
Wirt County (WV) 39–40
Wisdom. *See* Characteristics
Wise
  Bob 153
Wistfulness. *See* Emotions
Withers
  Roberta. *See* McAvoy
Women. *See* Roles
Wonder. *See* Emotions
Wood
  Bonnie Bonsell. *See* Hutchinson

Wood County (WV) 40–41, 42, 45, 81–82
Woodrow Wilson High School (Beckley, WV) 109
Woods
  Dora *83*
  Ernestine *152*
  Frankie *83*
  Georgia *83*
Wooster (OH) 136, 157
Wooten
  Danielle Elizabeth 102, 108
  Destiny Danice 102, 108
  George Fred 102, 108
  Travis Aaron 102, 108
Work. *See* Occupations
World War I. *See* Wars
World War II. *See* Wars
Wray (CO) 62
Wright
  Archie *83*
  Boy *83*
  Eva. *See* Williams
  Harold *83*
  Jennings *83*
  Leslie *83*
  Phyllis *83*
Writing. *See* Occupations; Skills
Wrongdoing
  Murder 73, 101, 126
  Shooting 55
  Spying 75–76
Wyoming County (WV) *100–102*, *106–108*
Wysong
  Bill 133
  Hazel Gallien **133**

Y

Yates Crossing (WV) 75–76
Yeager's Restaurant (Belington, WV) 22
York Colony (VA) 107
Young
  Elpha Rosetta *45*
  Karolyn "Kay" Ann. *See* Hill
  Lena Mae Reynolds *44*
Younger
  Evelyn *152*
Yuma County (CO) 61–62

Z

Zee Photo 27–28

Interested in More Populore Books?

Ask at your local bookstore... share this notice with them. Or, mail us the attached Action Form.

Celebrate your WV Heritage!

Great Gifts!

These anthologies are collections of stories and memories from people of West Virginia and beyond... in their own words. These fascinating collages of experiences and observations contain tributes, reflections on "the way it used to be," humorous anecdotes, historical accounts, and much more.

Our Mountain State Heritage: West Virginia Stories of the People, Book II. Pam Kasey & Rae Jean V. Sielen (Eds.), Foreword by WV Senator Robert C. Byrd, 1998. 200 pages; 108 narratives; exhaustive index (>4000 entries). ISBN 0-9652699-2-2, $18.00* (softcover), 8 1/4 x 11 3/4 inches.

Mountain State Stories of the People: Celebrating West Virginia, Book I. Amy A. Stevenson & Rae Jean V. Sielen (Eds.), Foreword by former WV governor Gaston Caperton, 1997. 204 pages; 207 narratives (43 from "young authors"); exhaustive index. ISBN 0-9652699-1-4, $18.00* (softcover), 8 1/4 x 11 3/4 inches.

Preserve important parts of your own personal history before they are lost forever — our Guide can help!

This illustrated manual walks you through the process of writing a personal narrative — from deciding what to write and getting started to choosing interesting details. Chapters include: Tributes; Life Events and Personal Anecdotes; Places; Treasures; and more. Appendices include: Writing Tips; Interview Questions and Worksheets; Notes on Genealogy; Selection of Photographs; and 150 Sample Narratives.

Put It In Writing Guide For Populore Narratives: Preserving Stories of the People. Melinda J. St. Louis, 1996. 232 pages; 8 chapters; 12 Appendices. ISBN 09652699-0-6, $16.00* (softcover), 8 1/2 x 11 inches.

Populore®

Preserving Stories of the People

Populore Publishing Company
P.O. Box 4382
Morgantown, WV 26504
304 - 296 - 7867
stories@populore.com
http://www.populore.com/

Action Form

I would like to order:

____ copies *Our Mountain State Heritage, Book II* ($18.00*)

____ copies *Mountain State Stories of the People, Book I* ($18.00*)

____ copies *Put It In Writing Guide* ($16.00*)

Please add **$2.50 per book** for shipping/handling. (WV residents add 6% sales tax on grand total — cost of book(s) plus S/H). Discounts available for orders of six or more books of the same title. Call for details. Please allow 1-2 weeks for book rate delivery. Checks payable to Populore.

____ I would like to preserve one of my stories in a Populore book. Please add me to Populore's mailing list.

My address and phone:

_____

_____

_____

_____

_____

Thanks for your interest!

*Prices subject to change. (7/98)

About the Editors

Pam Kasey is book editor for Populore Publishing Company. An enthusiastic letter writer—and receiver—from an early age, Pam has always been interested in the personal, day-to-day stories that people share with each other, both in conversation and in correspondence. She is a freelance writer and editor for nonprofit newsletters and, when not editing for Populore, writes about the agriculture and natural history of the Monongahela and Upper Ohio River valleys. Pam lives on a small farm south of Morgantown, West Virginia.

Rae Jean Sielen is president and co-founder of Populore Publishing Company. She was born and raised on the West Coast, but now lives in the Scotts Run area of Monongalia County in West Virginia with her husband Ken St. Louis. Rae Jean's fascination with language and languages led to a Bachelor of Arts degree in linguistics and a Master of Science degree in speech and hearing sciences. Her involvement with Populore is a natural result of this interest coupled with her business experience, love of words and graphics, and a delight in people's stories—the *real* stories of people from all walks of life and in their own language. Ken and Rae Jean developed the Populore approach to story preservation to offer everyday folks the opportunity to share in the joys of seeing their stories in print and knowing those stories won't be lost.

Our Mountain State Heritage

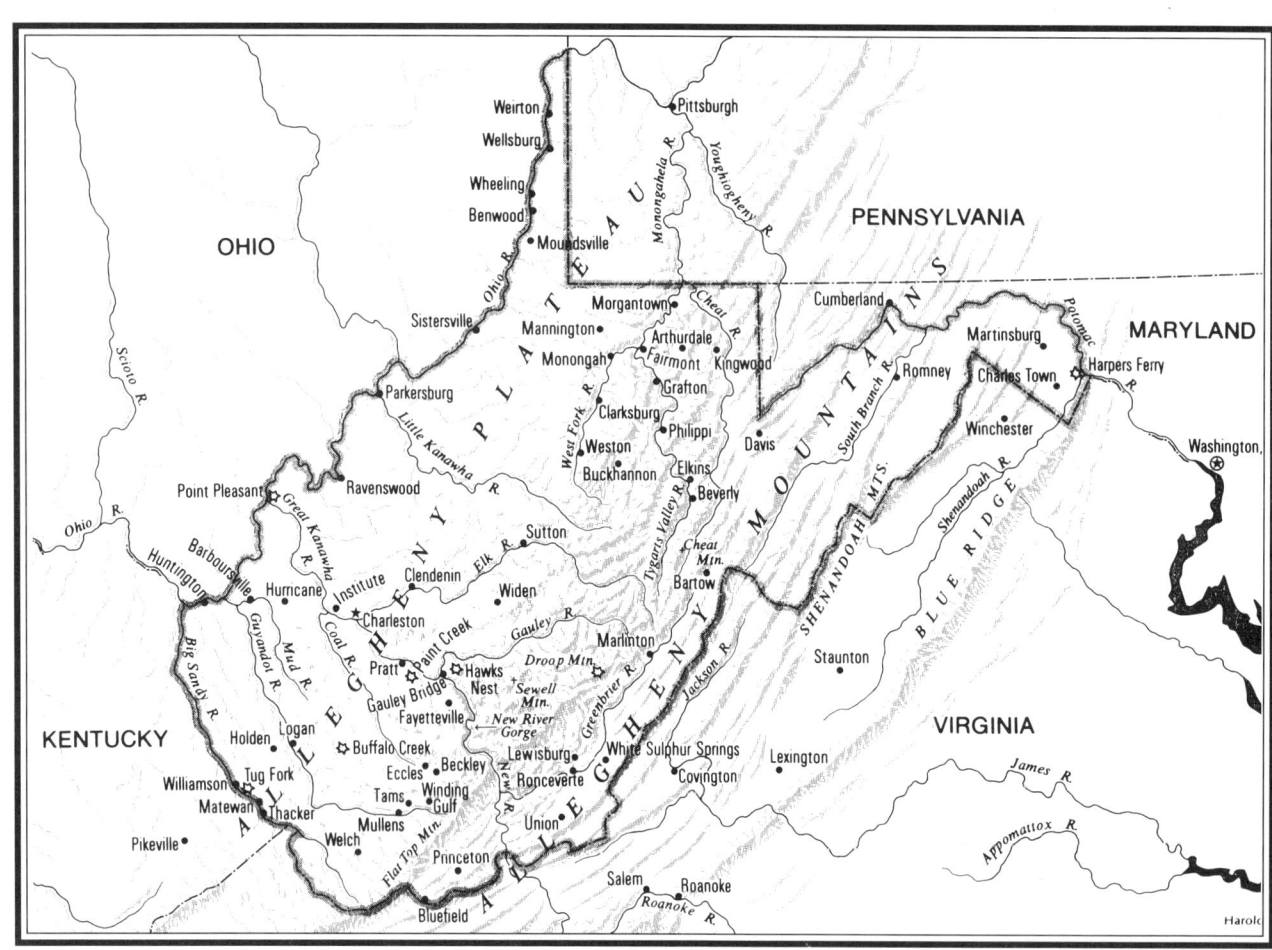